RENAISSANCE SINGAPORE?
Economy, Culture, and Politics

EDITED BY
KENNETH PAUL TAN

NUS PRESS
SINGAPORE

© 2007   NUS Press
National University of Singapore
AS3-01-02, 3 Arts Link
Singapore 117569

Fax: (65) 6774-0652
E-mail: nusbooks@nus.edu.sg
Website: http://www.nus.edu.sg/npu

ISBN   978-9971-69-377-0 (Paper)

National Library Board Singapore Cataloguing in Publication Data

Renaissance Singapore? : economy, culture, and politics / edited by
Kenneth Paul Tan. – Singapore : NUS Press, c2007.
p. cm.
Includes index.
ISBN-13 : 978-9971-69-377-0 (pbk.)

1. Public opinion – Singapore. 2. Singapore – Politics and
government – 1990– – Public opinion. 3. Singapore – Economic
conditions – Public opinion. 4. Singapore – Social conditions – Public
opinion. I. Tan, Kenneth Paul, 1972–

DS609
959.5705 -- dc22   SLS2007030063

Cover image is by Jason Wee, who is an artist and editor of softblow.com

Typeset by: SC (Sang Choy) International Pte Ltd
Printed by: Mainland Press Pte Ltd

Contents

Acknowledgements

The chapters in this multi-disciplinary book are written by passionate Singaporeans – public intellectuals from the various fields of academia, journalism, the arts, civil society, and politics – who care deeply about their country and where it seems to be going. As the book's editor, I have been very fortunate to work with and learn from them. I am also proud to be able to collect their insights and make them more widely known not only to a readership of similarly conscientious Singaporeans eager to gain new perspectives on their country's economy, culture, and politics, but to an international readership for whom Singapore has always been something of a political puzzle – Singapore is not a crudely authoritarian state, but neither does it fit neatly the familiar theories of liberalization and democratization. In these chapters are detailed accounts – including some very personal, painful, and colourful insights drawn from deep convictions – that present the reader with nuanced and prismatic explanations of how Singapore is or is not changing, for better or worse.

My students in the University Scholars Programme and Political Science Department at the National University of Singapore, without realizing it, helped to form some of the governing ideas in this book through lively class discussion and debate, proving to me time and again that student apathy in Singapore is a tired myth.

I am grateful to Tan Tai Yong for his crucial advice about getting this book published, to Kishore Mahbubani for being very supportive, and also to Lily Kong for her constant mentorship. Andy Mickey Choong provided efficient and cheerful research assistance. And I could always rely on Paul Kratoska and Cheong Yun Wan at NUS Press for wise and meticulous editorial advice. The Southeast Asian Conflict Studies Network and Lee Foundation provided funding for a public forum in 2003 out of which a few of these chapters emerged.

I dedicate this book to my wife Clara, parents Adeline and Philip, and godparents Bernice and Henry (who is no longer with us).

Contributors

CHNG NAI RUI is pursuing his Ph.D. at the London School of Economics and Political Science (UK) where he is researching the role of civil society in water regulation. He was a member of both The Working Committee and The Working Committee 2.

JANADAS DEVAN is a senior writer with *The Straits Times* (Singapore). He writes leaders for the newspaper as well as columns on international relations and language. In addition, he also does a weekly broadcast for Radio Singapore International. He divides his time between Singapore and the United States, where he lives.

COLIN GOH and his wife Woo Yen Yen founded Singapore's highly popular and award-winning satirical website, *TalkingCock.com*, and also produced and directed a movie based on it which has been screened in over 10 countries. They also co-authored the bestselling *Coxford Singlish Dictionary*, the first lexicon of Singaporean vernacular English, which the *Times of London* pronounced 'invaluable'. A law graduate from University College London (UK) and Columbia University (US), he practised international commercial litigation for several years before turning to multimedia production. He is a columnist for various publications, including *The Straits Times* (Singapore) and *8Days* (Singapore), and also writes and illustrates the comic strip 'Alien Talent' for *The New Paper* (Singapore). With their second film, *Singapore Dreaming*, Goh and Woo won the Montblanc New Screenwriters Award, the first Singaporeans to win a major international screenwriting prize.

SUZAINA KADIR is an assistant professor at the Lee Kuan Yew School of Public Policy (Singapore). She has a Ph.D. in political science from the University of Wisconsin-Madison (US). Her research interests and area specialization include religion and politics, with special focus on Muslim politics in Southeast Asia and South Asia; state-society relations and political development in Asia, with special focus on Southeast Asia; and regional security of Southeast Asia with a focus on non-traditional security issues affecting the Association of Southeast Asian Nations (ASEAN) such as women's rights and the impact of religion. She has published in renowned journals and contributed to several books. In her free time, she volunteers at community-oriented projects and has served on several civic boards and panels. She is also actively engaged in fostering intra-faith dialogue.

TERENCE LEE is an associate professor in mass communication at the School of Media, Communication and Culture, Murdoch University (Australia). He is also a research fellow of the Asia Research Centre and a member of the Centre for Everyday Life, both at Murdoch University. His research and publications have centred on aspects of media, cultural and creative policies, and politics in Singapore. He holds a Ph.D. in politics from the University of Adelaide (Australia).

SYLVIA LIM, born in 1965, holds a bachelor of laws (honours) degree from the National University of Singapore and a master of laws degree in 1989 from the University of London (UK). From 1991 to 1994 she was a police inspector with the Singapore Police Force. She was active in investigation work (including supervision) at Central Police Division HQ and thereafter was a staff officer to the director of Criminal Investigation Department. In 1994, she returned to practising law in the private sector. For four years, she conducted both civil and criminal litigation in the High Court, Subordinate Courts, and Juvenile Court. In 1998, she joined Temasek Polytechnic as a law lecturer and is now manager of continuing education and training at Temasek Business School. Her main areas of teaching and research are in civil and criminal procedure, criminal justice, and private security. She joined the Workers' Party in November 2001 and has been chairman of the party since June 2003. In April 2006, she entered her first candidature at a general elections, leading a team of five candidates in Aljunied GRC and garnered 43.9 per cent of the valid votes cast, the highest polled among the losing opposition candidates. As provided by the constitution, and pursuant to a Workers' Party decision, she was declared a non-constituency member of parliament in May 2006.

EDWIN PANG is assistant director for youth development at the National Trades Union Congress (Singapore). An ex-journalist and former communications and teambuilding consultant, he has a masters degree in strategic studies and a postgraduate certificate in terrorism studies from the S. Rajaratnam School of International Studies, Nanyang Technological University (Singapore). He has been a member of the People's Action Party since 1996 and serves on the executive committees of the Young PAP and Kampong Ubi-Kembangan PAP Branch. A former voluntary senior police officer, he is also a member of the Kampong Ubi-Kembangan Citizens' Consultative Committee and sits on the board of the New Life Community Services Centre in Bukit Panjang.

KIRPAL SINGH is a writer and associate professor of English literature and creative thinking at the Singapore Management University. He is today recognized internationally as a creativity guru and is a frequent keynoter and plenary speaker at some of the world's most powerful conferences and seminars on creativity and innovation. As a writer of fiction and poetry he has an established reputation and he is always on the international reading and performing circuit. He is a boundary-breaking scholar who has published numerous essays, articles, and books. His latest book is *Thinking Hats and Coloured Turbans*. He is currently working on a book titled *Leadership Across Cultures: do we ever learn?*

ALVIN TAN is founder and artistic director of The Necessary Stage (TNS) (Singapore). Under him, TNS has grown from a society in 1987 to one of Singapore's most prominent and respected theatre companies. He initiated the company's Theatre For Youth Branch, the Marine Parade Theatre Festival, and M1 Theatre Connect. He has a bachelor of arts degree from the National University of Singapore, a diploma in education from the Institute of Education (Singapore), and a master of arts degree from the University of Birmingham (UK). One of the leading proponents of devising theatre in Singapore, he has directed more than 40 plays, which have been staged in Singapore and at international festivals in Glasgow, Cairo, Busan, Seoul, Sibiu, Hungary, Hong Kong, and Melbourne. In 1997, he was awarded a Fulbright Scholarship. The following year, he was conferred the Young Artist Award by the National Arts Council (Singapore). He is also deeply engaged in civil society work, representing Singapore in conferences and workshops around the world. He is the founder and co-artistic director of the M1 Singapore Fringe Festival.

TAN CHONG KEE is a well-known civil society activist in Singapore. He founded Sintercom, and was a founding member of The Working Committee (TWC) and vice-president of the Stanford Club of Singapore. He is the current chair of the board of The Necessary Stage. His research interests and publications range widely over fields such as queer studies, Chinese literature, Singapore theatre, and Singapore civil society. He received his BA (honours) in computer science from Cambridge University, his MA in Chinese Literature from National Taiwan University, and his Ph.D. in Chinese literature from Stanford University.

KENNETH PAUL TAN is an assistant professor at the Lee Kuan Yew School of Public Policy (Singapore) where he is assistant dean. He also teaches at the National University of Singapore's (NUS) University Scholars Programme, and was formerly a faculty member of the NUS Political Science Department. His research interests have included topics in social, cultural, and political theory, and aspects of society, culture, and politics in Singapore. In addition to several journal articles and book chapters on democracy, civil society, media, and multiculturalism, his publications include a forthcoming book *Cinema and Television in Singapore: resistance in one dimension (Brill, 2008)*. He is currently working on a book on the politics of Singapore as a global city. The recipient of the 1995 Lee Kuan Yew Postgraduate Scholarship, he received his Ph.D. in social and political sciences at the University of Cambridge (UK). In 1994, he obtained a first class honours degree in economics and politics at the University of Bristol (UK) on a Public Service Commission overseas merit (open) scholarship. He chairs the board of directors of the Asian Film Archive (Singapore), sits on the board of directors of theatre company The Necessary Stage (Singapore), and has composed music for some of its performances.

WOO YEN YEN JOYCELN received her doctorate from Teachers College, Columbia University (US), where she also worked as a lecturer and research fellow. In 2004, she participated in a UNICEF project to help in the rebuilding of Afghanistan's education system. She is now an assistant professor at the School of Education at Long Island University in New York (US) where she teaches curriculum development, theory, and history. Together with her husband Colin Goh, she co-founded *TalkingCock.com*, Singapore's highly popular and award-winning satirical humour website. They also produced a film based on the website that has been screened in numerous festivals worldwide, and co-authored the *Coxford Singlish Dictionary*, a bestselling lexicon of Singaporean vernacular English which the *Times of London* pronounced 'invaluable'. With their second film, *Singapore Dreaming*, Woo and Goh won the Montblanc New Screenwriters Award, the first Singaporeans to win a major international screenwriting prize.

In renaissance Singapore

KENNETH PAUL TAN

At a public forum held on 13 December 2003 at the National University of Singapore, a young lady in the 300-strong audience revealed that she had considered starting up a socio-political discussion website, but stopped herself from doing so for fear of the consequences of her actions. When asked by sociologist Kwok Kian-Woon what she thought would have happened to her had she gone ahead with her plans, she hesitated to give an answer, and eventually suggested in a tentative way that she feared the possibility of being arrested in the middle of the night (Teo and Ng 15 December 2003; Teo 14 December 2003).

The forum was organized for interested people and public intellectuals to explore critically the various meanings of widely perceived changes in Singapore's political system, practice, and culture. Words like 'change', 'renewal', and 'remaking' appear to have found a comfortable place in Singapore's public discourse, in which the most dazzling metaphor has been the 'renaissance city', a reference to a 'rebirth' of culture and the arts, the economy, and the physical city itself. And clearly, anyone who returns to Singapore today after being away for just 10 years or more will immediately perceive the extent to which the country has transformed physically and culturally. The big question, though, has been whether these sorts of cultural, economic, and lifestyle developments and aspirations would also include more fundamental political changes. Or put another way, can there be a 'new society' without 'new politics'?

The 'old politics' is a politics of apprehension – a ghostly kind of fear that, in a menacing way, haunts the minds of Singaporeans like the young lady at the forum who censored herself after dreaming up a plan to contribute meaningfully to society. But she was not alone in thinking this way. Even seasoned feminist and social activist Constance Singam, who was present at the forum, sympathized with the young lady and related passionately how she, too, had been warned by well-meaning people that her own actions were being closely monitored by the government. Several panellists at the forum, including Kwok, Cherian George (the author of *Singapore: The Air-Conditioned Nation*, a collection of critically reflective essays on Singapore politics), and Sylvia Lim (chairman of the opposition Workers' Party and author of Chapter 14 in this book) argued that this sort of apprehension in Singapore had taken on a life of its own – it was irrational, merely perceptual, and quite detached from reality. Nevertheless, it continued to cripple any attempts to mature as a political society. In fact, as some of the authors in this book argue, the crippling effect of apprehension extends well into any attempts – political or non-political – to revitalize society, culture, and economy, a development that needs to happen if Singapore is, at least according to official rhetoric, to meet the complex and highly global challenges of the twenty-first century.

The chapters in this book were written by public intellectuals from a wide range of backgrounds who had been invited to respond to the vision articulated so eloquently in the *Renaissance City Report* released amidst an uneasy mix of millennial celebration and pessimism from a prolonged economic downturn.

> Renaissance Singapore will be creative, vibrant and imbued with a keen sense of aesthetics. Our industries are supported with a creative culture that keeps them competitive in the global economy. The Renaissance Singaporean has an adventurous spirit, an inquiring and creative mind

and a strong passion for life. Culture and the arts animate our city and our society consists of active citizens who build on our Asian heritage to strengthen the Singapore Heartbeat through expressing their Singapore stories in culture and the arts. (Ministry of Information and the Arts 2000)

In practice, what lies within, beneath, and beyond this renaissance city vision is anything but clear. And this is particularly so where politics is concerned. Today, notwithstanding the visitor's casual observation of how much Singapore seems to have changed, is there anything really new about Singapore's society, its culture, and especially its politics? To realize the vision of Singapore as a renaissance city, would a radically 'new' kind of politics be necessary? What should 'new politics' look like? Is the government ready for it? Are the majority of Singaporeans ready for it? What are its prospects?

New economy / old politics

Official accounts assert that 'good governance' is the main factor contributing to Singapore's socio-economic success achieved in the remarkable span of four decades since gaining full independence. Good governance refers mainly to a pragmatic mode of administration, which could really mean anything from technocratic policy-making that is free from dogma to unapologetically unprincipled actions motivated by material profit and the national interest. Good governance also refers to meritocracy, a system through which the 'best' people are selected to form the government (and are rewarded fairly according to their talents and efforts). And since official history favourably records the PAP government's achievements in 'overcoming the odds' and transforming Singapore's status 'from third world to first', Singaporeans in general naturally believe that the PAP government is Singapore's best bet for the future.

At least three consequences arise from this vision of good governance. Firstly, it justifies the nearly half-a-century of PAP rule and provides compelling reasons for its continuance. Secondly, it effectively legitimizes the wide and deep powers exercised by the government. Thirdly, it creates passive citizens who are more used to the government taking charge of their lives than coming forward themselves to offer their arguments (no matter how unwanted they may appear to be) and actions for the benefit of themselves and much less others in Singapore. This is 'old politics' – old in the sense that it seems to sit uncomfortably with visions of a new society and new economy; but old not in the sense that it no longer persists in 'new times'. Today, new and fancy visions are trapped within old realities.

In Singapore's public imagination, the 'heartlander' has become a common-sense idea for thinking about politics in Singapore, not because of its demographic accuracy, but because of the way it has been ideologically constructed and summoned to sustain an old politics of apprehension, materialism, and conservatism. The persistence of old politics in new times depends to a great degree on the durability of the myth that a majority of Singaporeans are unready for any real political change because they believe, at worst, that this would cause the downfall of Singapore and, at best, that citizens should not need to ask for more responsibilities as citizens since the government is doing such a fine job of providing for their material needs. But this myth, as I argue in 'New politics for a renaissance city?', is balanced against a second one that acknowledges the need for cosmopolitan Singaporeans and foreign talent who, although threatening to destabilize the traditional nation-state, nevertheless bring in the necessary capital and skills for sustained economic performance in the global league of creative economies. The PAP government appears to be adopting a classic strategy of divide-and-rule to sustain the heartlander – cosmopolitan divide in order to retain the old politics of PAP dominance by appealing positively to the moral and patriotic sentiments of the ideologically constructed heartlander, and warning the ideologically constructed cosmopolitan that heartlanders are not yet ready for change. At the same time, it hopes to reap the economic gains from a more open and liberal elite workforce that is clearly separated from the heartlands. The PAP government's political legitimacy is, after all, based both on moral authority *as well as* economic performance.

Foreign talent, at least according to official rhetoric, is necessary for taking Singapore's economy up the technological ladder in order for it to transcend the kind of economic activity of the surrounding region in which Singapore will surely be unable to compete in terms of cost. In 'Odd man in', Janadas Devan discusses the implications of Singapore's position in relation to its Southeast Asian neighbours, to China and India, and to the United States' presence in the region. Singapore's destiny is very much tied to its location. Compared with other countries in the Southeast Asian region, Singapore appears to be losing its distinctiveness that has given the city-state an edge over the other less developed neighbouring countries. At the same time, the economic centre of gravity that anomalously moved in the 1980s to the Asian 'periphery' – a periphery made up of the 'tiger' economies of Hong Kong, Singapore, South Korea, and Taiwan – is beginning to shift back to the Asian mainland, and in particular to China and India. Devan's chapter sets the stage for thinking about how Singapore needs to change – to retain its 'oddness' – in order to extract itself from competition with its neighbours whose low-cost environments will give them a clear advantage. The renaissance city plans may, in this regard, be viewed as part of larger efforts to transform Singapore's old economy into a knowledge-based creative economy that will set it apart from its neighbours.

The prospects for such a transformation are explored in Terence Lee's 'Industrializing creativity and innovation', where he argues that talk about creativity in Singapore is really talk about 'industrializing creativity'. The government works on the fashionable rhetoric – and not necessarily the substance – of creativity as a way of keeping up with global trends in the media and culture industries, demonstrating also to mobile creative talent that Singapore is a tolerant place where they can live and work. The prospects of creativity and openness in Singapore are strongly limited by economic and political imperatives that have dominated the public imagination. But real creativity – involving a passionate and intrinsic motivation to generate new ideas that are relevant to a domain – can only really flourish in a climate that allows people to challenge conventional ideas and perspectives, a climate that sits uncomfortably with tight political control and an obsession with economics. Singapore's interest in creativity is somewhat limited to the creative industries of the arts, design, and media – industries that the government hopes will thrive within a 'depoliticized' environment animated by 'gestural politics', informed by a state-directed mass media, and surveilled by open-ended laws that allow for wide-ranging application.

National identity and values: Contradictions and contestations

Old politics is a largely authoritarian politics that privileges order, predictability, and security. In new times, order and security are certainly not irrelevant, but thoughts about economic recessions, terrorist attacks, and outbreaks of disease should not dominate all attempts to make sense of the world and Singapore's place in it. Certainly, an obsession with order and security in Singapore has created an anxious society that is apprehensive even of itself. It is an unforgiving society with narrow definitions of achievement. In such a society, people are unwilling to take any risks for fear of being labelled a failure. And so, ironically, experimentation, entrepreneurship, and innovation – identified as central to the new economy – will be extremely difficult to foster. In such a society, people are unwilling to tolerate any divergence from the norm as conformity signals predictability and order, difference deviance and criminality.

National identity is purpose-built; and any deviation from the norm is ignored, ridiculed, branded as extremism, or – if perceived to be really dangerous – exiled. A national ideology that claims to represent, enshrine, and protect the values that are unproblematically shared by a nation-community will almost certainly limit the possible range of what could constitute 'national identity'. Singapore's national ideology defines what it means to be a Singaporean. At various points, these modern efforts to formulate a national identity have turned to 'traditional' sources associated, through imagination and invention, with Confucianism and Asian values. At other times, these efforts have turned to the more pragmatic orientations that characterize Singaporeans as uninterested in dogmatic ideology and 'childish' ideals, but engaged in the material and utilitarian bases of nationhood that often collapse into angst-ridden talk about survival and success.

Placed at the centre of claims about preserving public order, protecting ethnic/religious groups and the institution of multiracialism, and maintaining society's moral standards and the nation's core values, the heartlander is often invoked to justify state censorship of the arts. In 'Censorship in whose name?', I discuss three case studies of how the dominance of old politics has prevented Singaporeans from developing into more self-reflective, self-critical, and creative citizens by censoring a more socially empowering, critically reflective, and intelligently experimental performing arts scene. The case studies are of forum theatre in 1994, the play *Talaq* in 2000, and performance art in 1994.

The practice of censorship extends well beyond the arts, scarring the work of cyber-satirists and filmmakers Woo Yen Yen and Colin Goh who reflect, in 'Caging the bird', on their experiences of editing the popular satirical humour website *TalkingCock.com* as well as producing the film and the comedy/music CD album that both sprang from the tremendously successful website. Their experiences have shown that the 'normal' (read 'official') image of the Singaporean – a depiction of a materialistic, apathetic, uncreative, and conservative heartlander – is a much distorted one that nevertheless features strongly in citizenship narratives that detail the shortcomings of Singaporeans as obstacles to the nation's progress. These are narratives that restrict the performance of citizenship to a narrow range of legitimacy. The officially favoured model of the Singaporean citizen is a mainly male professional with a good command of the English language who is invited to sit on national committees. Less qualified, Singlish-speaking Singaporeans are encouraged to be 'active citizens' by focusing on narrow municipal matters since these correspond with the deficient heartlander image that they have been labelled with. In thinking about Singapore's renaissance ambitions, one particularly acute irony that Woo and Goh point out is the government's censorship of Singlish, even though it is in this localized, multicultural, and hybridized linguistic medium that Singaporeans are, arguably, at their most creative. Ultimately, Singaporeans should not be described as 'inarticulate' but 'disenfranchised' by a narrow and limiting range of what counts as legitimately Singaporean. Woo and Goh are clearly in favour of extending and diversifying this range to include behaviour and characteristics that are currently devalued, even censored, by official pronouncements. In resisting these narrow accounts of legitimate citizenship through its brand of localized satirical humour, *TalkingCock.com* has indeed been a successfully political space – but not political with a capital 'P', since 'partisan politics', as Woo and Goh are at pains to point out, would draw the unwanted attention of the ever-present political censors.

It is not just the officials of the state who are deemed to be intolerant and censorious. An authoritarian personality, it might be observed, is perhaps just as much a feature of Singapore society. In 'Keeping vigil', Kirpal Singh explores the factors – including Singapore's small-nation status – that have contributed to Singaporeans' somewhat inadequate capacity for open-mindedness and multiculturalism. Singh discusses Singapore's lack of openness in terms of the poor quality of public (especially political) debate, the inaccessibility of certain kinds of information guarded by the civil service, and the negative response to any experimental ideas or suggestions that are not in line with the official rhetoric. Openness is also about attitudes to ethnic diversity. Singh observes that inter-ethnic mixing among Singaporeans takes place almost entirely at the workplace, and argues that the more important social dimension of interaction remains lacking. Longstanding educational policies that aim to create a cultural – mainly Chinese – elite will prevent future leaders from working towards a deeper and richer practice of multiculturalism in Singapore. A peaceful Singapore society of ethnic and religious communities that simply tolerate one another without any desire to engage at a more complex cultural level is grossly inadequate, and particularly so if Singapore genuinely wants to embrace the possibilities and contain the threats of globalization.

New politics in civil society

To survive and prosper, organizations and actors in Singapore's civil society have had to play clever games with the state. One game – and the one most favoured by the state – has involved leaving politics to the state, while thriving on private and civic activities, often with the state's encouragement and resources. A second has involved the 'sneaking' of politics into overtly non-confrontational private and civic activities: the goals of advocacy are in this way achieved through very small steps. A third has involved engaging with the state at the political level, but doing this behind closed doors or on the state's own terms of reference. The political stakes and risks increase with each of these games.

In renaissance Singapore, the political out-of-bound markers still remain unclear: with each new attempt to engage politically, the state responds in either surprisingly tolerant or surprisingly repressive ways. Uncertainty causes the risk-averse to retreat from politics. But the renaissance city vision suggests new opportunities for old civil society organizations and actors to work out strategies for new, more sophisticated levels of political engagement. Developments of this kind can clearly be seen in the complex tensions among Muslims, secularism, the nation-state, and democracy. Suzaina Kadir's 'Muslim politics, the state, and society' argues, centrally, that modernization, Islamization, and globalization have produced new 'horizontal' tensions within the Muslim community in Singapore, and new 'vertical' tensions between the community and the state. These tensions have generated new sites of contestation. The institutionalization and centralization of Islamic administration in Singapore have led to a conflation of Muslim and Malay identities that have in turn been represented almost exclusively by Malay politicians who also head the state-controlled Islamic Religious Council of Singapore (MUIS). At the horizontal level, global Islamic revivalism has not brought about homogeneity but pluralism within the Malay-Muslim community, as evidenced in particular by the spectrum of orientations – from fundamentalist to progressive – that is displayed by the *ulama* (Islamic scholars) community. Tensions between the 'Islamic pillar' (Islamic scholars) on the one hand and the state-administered 'Malay pillar' (Malay MPs and leaders of MUIS) on the other have created new and complicated political dynamics that Kadir explores in a discussion of the *madrasah* (Islamic religious schools) issue, the *tudung* (Islamic headscarf) issue, the debates about Muslims in a secular Singapore, and the proposal for an Islamic pillar in the leadership of the Malay-Muslim community.

New developments in 'face-to-face' politics are more than matched by complex new strategies made possible in and through cyberspace. The birth, life, and death of the *Singapore Internet Community* (*Sintercom*) are discussed by its main creator Tan Chong Kee in 'The canary and the crow'. Civil society organizations like *Sintercom* performed a 'canary' function that was useful to the PAP government as a means of deflecting criticism of the suppression of free speech in Singapore. But *Sintercom* and other civil society organizations also performed a 'crow' function that annoyed the government with well-articulated and well-organized critique. The government will tolerate – even support – any civil society actor, organization, or project whose canary value exceeds its crow value. *Sintercom*'s strategy was one of 'deliberate naiveté': the website justified its actions as a positive response to the government's call to come forward as active citizens. In fact, *Sintercom* was originally deemed by the government to be more canary-like in the way it aimed to be non-partisan in representing a range of views and positions, some supportive and others critical of the government. But when *Sintercom* began to take on more politically challenging roles, it was forced to register as a political website – a prospect that, Tan reveals, gave him no choice but to close down the website. Drawing from the *Sintercom* experience, Tan constructs a model to help explain the rise and fall of civil society organizations more generally. One pattern that the model explains particularly well is the way the government tries regularly to raise the people's morale through a more liberal rhetoric, but then turns around and disappoints. The lack of enthusiasm for the renaissance city rhetoric from the arts and academic communities is an example of how accumulated disappointment in the government's empty rhetoric can lead to irreparable disenchantment and withdrawal.

But some members of the arts community have been actively able to forge new strategies within renaissance Singapore. Alvin Tan, artistic director of professional theatre company The Necessary Stage (TNS), discusses the company's new artistic directions in 'Theatre and cultures'. Explaining how TNS' vision for theatre has moved away from the overtly political, he gives an account of the constraints that professional arts companies in Singapore face, mainly those that relate to funding and censorship regulations. TNS' new strategy takes its focus on indigenous and socially engaged theatre to the next stage. Since the renaissance vision appears to promote a global orientation without necessarily weakening a sense of nationhood, TNS too is seeking to leverage on cultural, artistic, and financial resources at the regional and international levels in order to boost indigenous and socially engaged productions. Intercultural collaborations drawn from across national boundaries will provide richer comparative perspectives and opportunities for developing more sensitive, critical, and fresh images and metaphors to bring about a better understanding of identities, influences, and how these are perceived across cultures. Through this 'globalized', collaborative, and socially motivated theatre, TNS wishes to engage diverse artists and audiences in a reflection of how their everyday lives are affected by the actions of others, and vice versa. Through a theatre practice that is research driven, interdisciplinary, and dialogical, TNS wishes to give articulation to the voices that have been silenced by official narratives. It can be argued that TNS' project is a 're-politicization' of theatre by creating a new fluidity and richness in the artistic language and by establishing a slippery global network of safe performing spaces where social and political critique can be protected from over-enthusiastic agents of censorship.

Fluidity and slipperiness would also seem to characterize quite well the political strategies of some new civil society organizations in renaissance Singapore. In the chapter on 'The Working Committees', Chng Nai Rui gives a highly personal account of his experiences as an active member of landmark civil society initiatives The Working Committee (TWC) and The Working Committee 2 (TWC2). He argues that the 'culture of fear' that is often proffered as a reason (perhaps even excuse) for civil society inactivity, risk-aversion, and inefficacy can in fact lead to a culture of creativity in which civil society actors are forced to find novel and creative ways to engage other citizens and the state. Identifying such novel features in the structure and strategy of TWC and TWC2, Chng paints an optimistic picture of civil society that is wholly in accordance with the renaissance city vision.

Youth and the future

Singaporeans seem to take almost pathological pleasure in lamenting that their youths are apathetic. Politically, this myth of youth apathy has been useful to the government when it 'explains' how the new generation of Singaporeans are practical in their concerns about achieving academic success and pursuing promising careers without the distraction of political activism. Images of student-led demonstrations in countries like South Korea and the Philippines, or in Singapore from the 1950s to the 1970s, are appropriated and projected to signal how 'lucky' today's Singaporeans are to live in conditions of peace, stability, and affluent comfort. But this myth has also made it difficult to encourage more young Singaporeans to become more civically engaged – that is to say, engaged in matters that affect the well-being of the larger community, but not those that involve overt political challenge to the establishment and the status quo. The PAP government – like any 'adult generation' – tries hard to connect with young citizens. But this – especially where teenagers and adolescents are concerned – is an always impossible connection, an impossibility that translates, as I argue in 'Youth: every generation's moral panic', into a sense of inefficacy, anxiety, and resentment that collectively take the form of public worry about and disappointment in the perceived – and constructed – inadequacies of the next genera-tion, and how these inadequacies will threaten the very survival of the nation. Youth are the hope of the future; but at the same time, they seem to escape the comprehension and control of adults who are constantly looking for youth 'folk devils' to blame for all or most of an essentially capitalist society's ills and negative prospects. As a result, the youth scapegoat is cornered and draped in descriptions of apathy, disloyalty, ungratefulness, ignorance, selfish materialism, superficiality, flabbiness, effeminacy, aimlessness, vulgarity, and violence. But this is only possible with historical amnesia, since every generation has needed to deal with its failings and anxieties in very similar ways.

In the new millennium, the PAP's youth wing – the Young PAP (YP) – has been attempting to 'refresh' itself by making the YP more relevant to young Singaporeans as a premiere platform where they can participate in the political and policy-making processes that take place at the national level. According to YP executive committee member Edwin Pang in 'Refreshing the Young PAP', this effort has meant increasing the space within the party for more diverse ideas and perspectives to be articulated by young Singaporeans, mainly through active discussion forums – face-to-face as well as online. Secondly, refreshing the YP has meant expanding the membership and building synergies within the larger PAP family. Members are being given more important responsibilities in recognition of their talents and abilities, and as a means of nurturing the future core of the PAP. While the YP aims to refresh its image including matters of style and rhetoric, it remains convinced of the PAP's core values that have stayed essentially the same since the party was established in the mid-1950s.

Since the early 1980s when the PAP's parliamentary monopoly was broken, electoral trends seem to point to the gradual demise of oppositional politics. Workers' Party (WP) chairman and non-constituency member of parliament Sylvia Lim, in 'The future of alternative party politics', identifies at least two important features of the electoral system – multi-member constituencies and a depoliticized citizenry – as serious obstacles to opposition prospects. Nevertheless, she remains 'cautiously optimistic'. One set of reasons for this optimism has to do with the WP's performance in the 2006 general elections that drew on the support of a younger, more globally-oriented, well-educated, and courageous generation of Singaporeans – the 'post-65-ers' – not only as WP voters but also as WP candidates. Another set of reasons for this optimism has to do with what can be described as an erosion of popular support for the PAP. This erosion results from a perception that the PAP government is no longer able to continue delivering the material goods, at least not to the extraordinary extent of the earlier decades of double-digit growth rates. This erosion may also result from the need to correct for unintended consequences of earlier policies, increasing doubts about meritocracy in Singapore, widespread cynicism towards government sponsored feedback channels, and the rise of the internet as a platform for information and dialogue that bypasses the state-controlled media. Significantly, Lim chooses the term 'alternative party politics' over the more familiar 'opposition party politics' as a means of signifying a more 'constructive' political contribution. The WP does not want to oppose everything that the PAP says simply for the sake of opposing it. Instead, the alternative party wants to give the PAP some healthy competition and thereby provide Singaporeans with alternative ideas that they can decide on through the democratic exercise of their right to vote.

Politics in the renaissance city: The new prince

In his 'swearing-in' speech on 12 August 2004 as Singapore's third prime minister, Lee Hsien Loong outlined – in no uncertain terms – a vision of a forward-looking, critical, open, unconventional, diverse, participatory, and inclusive society, a vision whose details were spelt out more concretely in policy-making terms during the National Day Rally speech two weeks after (Lee 22 August 2004). It is, of course, too early to make a fair assessment of these pronouncements in terms of sincerity, determination, or success.

The chapters in this book provide detailed and often very personal accounts of efforts in various domains of Singapore's economy, society, and politics to negotiate possibilities in the context of an apparent flowering of culture in Singapore. Many of these accounts suggest that Singapore can become a more open, inclusive, and vibrant place to live in. But more importantly, these accounts document the kinds of obstacles and inertias that would make this prospect extremely daunting. Cynics and realists will draw from these accounts more evidence to argue that change – especially political change – will never proceed beyond the rhetoric. Optimists will identify opportunities for making small changes in a positive direction, if for no other reason than the frequently articulated imperatives of globalization and economic development. From these accounts, the reader will find important data to calculate the trajectories of political change, and perhaps even predict if there will indeed be new politics for this renaissance city.

REFERENCES

Lee, H.L. (12 August 2004) Swearing-in speech as prime minister of Singapore on 12 August 2004, Singapore Istana.

Lee, H.L. (22 August 2004) Speech at the National Day Rally on 22 August 2004, Singapore.

Ministry of Information and the Arts (2000) *Renaissance City Report: culture and the arts in renaissance Singapore*, Singapore. Online. Available HTTP: <http://www.mica.gov.sg/renaissance/FinalRen.pdf> (accessed 22 December 2004).

Teo, H.N. and Ng, S.Y. (15 December 2003) 'Fear factor – is it just an excuse?', *Today* (Singapore).

Teo, L. (14 December 2003) 'WP sees better chance at hustings', *The Sunday Times* (Singapore).

PART I

NEW ECONOMY/OLD POLITICS

New politics for a renaissance city?

KENNETH PAUL TAN

This chapter is about the persistence of 'old politics' in 'new times'. It presents a broad account of the construction of old politics over the decades since Singapore's independence, and argues that the same old politics that has tightly controlled the possibilities and limitations of civil society in the 1980s and 1990s will continue to hold back any real transformation of Singapore into a renaissance city. Old politics has essentially been the means of emasculating any political threats that may accompany economically necessary liberalization in Singapore, mainly by asserting that Singaporeans 'are not yet ready' for deeper change.

Entrenching old politics

Old politics in Singapore has mainly been about shaping the public imagination with national narratives of permanent vulnerability and fragile success. Complaisant behaviour that conforms to these narratives has been encouraged – sometimes subtly, at other times dramatically – through a system of reward and punishment. These powerful narratives and systems set the conditions that make possible but at the same time severely constrain thought, speech, and imagination within both the public and private spheres. Events are explained and actions justified nearly always by resorting to the language of vulnerability and success. And, following from this, Singaporeans appear to others and to themselves as remarkably obsessed with fear and achievement – different sides, perhaps, of the same coin.

An important founding moment in these narratives has been Singapore's ejection from Malaysia in 1965 when the atmosphere, as described in standard historiography, was one of anguish and anxiety (Lau 1998; Lee 1998). The dominant belief at the time was that Singapore could not survive as an independent political entity, a belief that has grown into an enduring national culture characterized by a 'siege mentality' that actively reproduces narratives of vulnerability and crisis. The notion that the most capable leaders must take full charge of rapidly building a nation with limited resources and no room for failure has been the dominant way of thinking about the limits and possibilities of politics in Singapore, yielding justification for various kinds of political restrictions and self-restrictions. Today, the trophies of Singapore's economic achievements are prominently displayed not to signal that Singapore has arrived, but to remind its citizens of the fragility of this success and how continued hard work, thrift, sacrifice, and obedience to the 'best' political leaders Singapore can find are still fundamentally required to retain this success, surpass it, and only by doing so survive as a nation. At its best, this mentality could motivate each Singaporean to 'perform' optimally. At its worst, it could sustain a culture of repression, anxiety, and over-cautiousness that permeates nearly every level of society, economy, and government.

Colonial Singapore was governed with a very light touch, and this allowed civil society – composed, at the time, of wealthy philanthropists, clan associations, independent schools, and community hospitals – to flourish. In fact, several organizations were even able to advance their causes through political modes of action, though the more militant organizations that directly threatened British interests were forcefully restrained (Gillis 2005). With independence, the newly installed People's Action Party (PAP) government took a strong developmentalist approach, taking over many of the social and economic functions that had been performed by private individuals and organizations in colonial civil society. In effect, civil society was suffocated by the widespread belief that the government was able to perform these functions far better than the voluntary and less professional organizations in civil society. Singaporeans turned from being active voluntary members of community during colonial times into passive clients of the new PAP-governed state.

In the early years of independence, the PAP government addressed Singapore's defence needs by quickly organizing a regular armed forces with a reserve army that would consist of every able-bodied male Singaporean. Today, compulsory national service refers to a system in which males undergo full-time military training for up to two years (but up to 2004, the duration was two-and-a-half years) just before they turn statutorily into adults, and are subsequently called up annually for military training for up to 40 days each year for most of their adult life. National service has in this way also become an important political instrument for disciplining and controlling the male population whose aggressive energies are redirected from political expression into military regimentation that focuses these energies onto the perceived external, and sometimes internal, enemies (Tan 2001: 98–99). War – or the imagined threat of war – is, after all, one of the most fundamental organizing principles of any society. Excluded from compulsory military service, women, too, are disciplined into carrying out their unlegislated 'national service' as biological reproducers of the nation and nurturers of its young, all this while supplementing (on relatively lower remuneration) a male-dominated workforce that has been too limited in size. Gendered service to a modern nation in perpetual crisis supports and is supported by the patriarchal practices and institutions associated with Asian traditions and values (Tan 2001).

Another popular narrative describes a well-defended Singapore as necessary for the kind of stability that attracts foreign capital for economic development and growth. The control of militant trade unions through laws enacted in the late 1960s to ensure peaceful industrial relations has also been explained by the need to attract foreign capital. The National Trade Union Congress, an umbrella body formed by the PAP and led by many of its members, quickly co-opted the major unions in Singapore and constitutes one voice in the annual tripartite mechanism for issuing influential wage

recommendations. Employers (including foreign managers) and
government officials represent the other two voices in this partnership
that today is a powerful means of controlling and disciplining workers
in order to draw and keep foreign capital that is increasingly finding
its way into lower-cost and lower-wage environments in Singapore's
surrounding region.

In the 1950s and 1960s, the Malayan communists who were
outstanding organizers demonstrated to the PAP the great value of
mass support, secured largely through a well-developed and networked
grassroots sector. The PAP was originally a middle-class, English-
speaking party of overseas-educated technocrats, professionals, and
intellectuals. By cooperating with the communists, a risky strategy
that has come to be known by the analogy of 'riding the tiger', these
PAP leaders were able to gain access to the mostly Chinese-speaking
popular support base controlled by the communist movement. In
exchange, the public face of the underground Malayan Communist
Party would be concealed by a mask of legitimacy that the PAP could
provide. Riding the tiger was a strategy that the PAP adopted skil-
fully to emerge as the resounding winner in Singapore's short political
history. And as winner, the PAP gets to play a disproportionately
large part in the way official history is written, thereby – many would
argue – continuing to secure its political dominance.

Today, the grassroots sector, a wide range of overlapping organizations all linked in some way to the PAP government, has co-opted
traditional community leaders and is dominated by leaders and
members who are also affiliated in some way or other to the PAP
government. This creates an informal but reliable system of patronage.
The grassroots sector serves as a feedback mechanism and a mouthpiece for the government, also providing PAP politicians with a large
resource of manpower. For example, grassroots members help to run
the weekly meet-the-people sessions when constituents come to speak
to their elected representatives to ask for various kinds of help. In this
way, the grassroots sector presents the human face of a technocratic
government focused on the business of national administration. The
grassroots sector is also tasked with monitoring social and political
trends at the constituency level, including the behaviour of individuals
and groups of residents suspected of antisocial, subversive, or politically oppositional activities. The grassroots sector helps not only to

maintain internal security, but also to sustain a climate of surveillance and fear that can be harnessed both for nation building as well as political gain (Tan 2003a).

Nearly nine out of every 10 Singaporeans live in public housing estates carved into constituencies that are each served by a range of overlapping grassroots organizations all linked in some way to the PAP government. These estates, the geographical heartlands of Singapore's residential landscape, are maintained and upgraded by the government to considerably high standards. In this way, support for the government is significantly tied to these kinds of material benefits that continuing support for the government will ensure. At its worst, this is the kind of relationship that fosters a petitionary, materialistic, and politically apathetic public culture. In the popular imagination, the dominant image of the Singaporean has been one who remains interested in 'politics' not to pursue the larger ideals that govern questions of public concern, but to secure maximum material benefit for the self. Ironically, the government has both criticized and celebrated this Singaporean characteristic. The government criticizes Singaporeans who are over-dependent on it for welfare and who do not volunteer community service at levels that are anywhere close to those in the United Kingdom or the United States. But the government celebrates Singaporeans who are pragmatic in their choice of economics over democratic politics, 'common sense' materialism over democratic idealism.

The school system, in a society of mostly dual-career parents, remains a dominant instrument of socialization. As in many parts of the world, students in Singapore wear standardized uniforms, participate in the daily ritual of singing the national anthem in front of the state flag, and are required to take part in a sport or one of the many student uniformed groups such as the National Cadet Corp. The education system, for the most part science-biased, has been dominated pedagogically by methods of drilling students to perform well in examinations, since it is mainly their examination results that determine their school's position in the highly competitive school ranking system. Few schools have been able to break out of this bureaucratic constraint to provide a progressive learning environment that prioritizes process over outcome and that gives students the resources, encouragement, and space to reflect and discover for themselves where their interests and strengths might lie. Although the government has more recently been articulating a bolder and more progressive vision of diversity and autonomy in the education system (Shanmugaratnam 2004), the reality will take a much longer time to catch up with the rhetoric. In any case, the decades prior to these recent progressive changes saw the entrenchment of an unforgiving culture that privileges conformity and a narrowly academic model of competitiveness, and supports a myopic vision of education as only important for training young Singaporeans to join the workforce (from the national point of view) or to secure well-paying jobs (from the personal point of view).

An official history whose theme is how Singapore has – but also can and must continue to – overcome the odds, and an extensive social infrastructure consisting of national service, economic tripartism, the grassroots sector, public housing, and the school system are important components of the nation-building project, components that also lend themselves as political instruments to control and discipline Singaporean workers who reside predominantly in public housing estates, and who have evolved into what is now ideologically called the heartlander class. Through a thoroughly rationalized system of regimentation, training, bureaucratic administration, surveillance, material incentives, and affluence (classic features of Herbert Marcuse's (1964) 'one-dimensional' advanced industrial society), members of this class have been, and continue to be, socialized as individuals who are affirmative, conservative, fearful of both change as well as difference, and materialistic and consumerist in orientation. The system produces individuals who fit the authoritarian personality associated with vulgar accounts of Confucianism. Even if heartlanders do not actually behave in this caricatured fashion in everyday life, the widespread belief that they collectively do is sufficient to justify any resistance to change, and this would especially include political change. In effect, heartlanders are electorally significant, on the whole quite predictable, and therefore politically useful.

Old politics can therefore be described as heartlander politics. And the persistence of old politics in new times can, in the main, be attributed to the constant re-imagining of the majority of Singaporeans as conservative heartlanders unready for change, especially political change.

Ideological control and heartlander politics

The heartlander – and indeed heartlander politics – is as much constituted by ideology as it is a product of socio-political engineering through official history, national service, economic tripartism, the grassroots sector, public housing, and the school system. Up to the late 1970s, the ideal Singaporean was someone who was able to cope with the demands of rapid industrialization, an individual who was rugged, diligent, and self-reliant. This ideal was probably inspired by comparisons with western rationality, science, industry, and progress. The Singapore citizen needed to be proficient in English and transformed from 'lazy native' into modern capitalist worker who was rationally, industrially, and economically oriented.

Ironically, the PAP government's economic success story and the socialization that was needed to achieve it both produced a 'disenchanted' citizenry of *homo œconomicus* motivated mostly by material gain. Their love for and loyalty to country and government were a function of personal economic benefit. Such a basis for political legitimacy was soon felt to be too fragile and short-sighted as a political strategy. A more 'religious' kind of faith in the government and patriotism for the nation needed to be rekindled, and one way to do this was to 're-enchant' the materially rich but spiritually barren Singaporean caricature. By the mid-1980s, materialism as the basis of the government's political legitimacy was even less secure as Singaporeans were beginning to witness economic downturns that were largely beyond the control of a government that had always justified its claim to power in terms of its ability to deliver the material goods. The PAP government, therefore, has been increasingly concerned about directly controlling the less tangible and less 'pragmatic' questions of identity and values.

To forge a national 'Singaporean' identity out of a multiethnic society, the PAP government has assumed firstly that 'pre-nation-state' ethnic identities are primordial and so cannot be eliminated, and secondly that Singapore's short history needs depth. Nation building, therefore, took the form of preserving private spheres where these eternal 'Asian' ethnicities could flourish and provide the deeper historical, cultural, and moral resources for a stable and substantial overarching Singaporean identity. In the public sphere, there were to be secularism, equal opportunities for all, and common modes of communication and participation. The public sphere would be the 'common space' that with time and collective confidence should increase as Singaporeans give priority to their national over their ethnic identities.

In practice, the separation of private and public has not been – perhaps cannot be – entirely clear. In order to manage the cultural and moral Asianization of Singaporeans whilst attempting to increase the common space, Singapore's ethnic composition has been officially simplified into a four-part model known as Chinese-Malay-Indian-Other (CMIO). This simplification has in turn had the effect of exaggerating ethnic differences even further. Although state-sponsored self-help groups organized on ethnic lines often do share resources and carry out joint projects, the image of a divided Singapore where each ethnic community looks after its own is a difficult one to transcend.

It could be argued that the CMIO division that perpetuates the threat of interethnic conflict can nevertheless be instrumental to nation building. If Singaporeans believe that their society is prone to interethnic hostilities, it might be easier to convince them that they should never be complacent about nation building and this might mean having to forego some of the liberties enjoyed by citizens of other advanced countries since these liberties may make possible situations that ignite conflict in this dangerously portrayed multiethnic society. Some of these liberties may include real political choices and a genuinely competitive democratic system. It remains questionable, though, whether a nation built on fear and suspicion is a nation at all. It is nevertheless clear that the Hobbesian logic that drives Singaporeans to give consent to authoritarian government must be regularly nourished with sufficient evidence. The emblematic vision of a nation permanently divided along ethnic and religious lines provides such evidence.

'Re-enchanting' the nation has involved not only questions of national identity, but also national values. The vision of a heartland community has been politically cultivated as a complex means of coping with rapid capitalist-industrial modernization and the political disenchantment that attends it. The basis of political legitimacy had to be widened, and the way to do this was to cast the PAP government not only as transactional leaders but also as visionaries with the moral authority to govern. Nation building could not simply be about forging a formal national identity devoid of any substance other than pragmatism and materialism. National identity needed to be built from more primordial sources – fragments of the Chinese, Malay, and Indian 'civilizations' imagined as the origins of each major ethnic group in Singapore. From these fragments, contemporary Asian 'high cultures' could be constructed, then protected from a corrupting western Other, invented to secure antagonism between Singapore's moral conservatism, deference to authority, diligence, and thrift at one end, and western liberal democracy at the other.

In the early 1980s, secondary school students had to study one religious knowledge subject (Christianity, Buddhism, Islam, Hinduism, Sikhism, or Confucianism) as a compulsory and examinable component of the curriculum. Religious knowledge aimed to install cultural and moral ballasts to help the newly independent Singapore ship to stay afloat and on course in an increasingly uncharted and unpredictable ocean. Confucianism was generally regarded as the most important of these subjects as it was fashionable – though intellectually indefensible – in the 1980s to speak of the East Asian economic 'miracle' as evidence of an elective affinity between Confucianism and economic success. Confucianism was also useful for political reasons, since it provided the cultural and moral resources for legitimizing deference to authority. Properly Confucianized Singaporeans, it was thought, would be diligent and thrifty workers and obedient and respectful citizens.

By 1991, the emphasis on religious education was effectively replaced by a newly forged civil religion officially called the 'shared values' and consisting of five precepts that essentially codified the integrating aspects of Confucianism. Ethnically and religiously neutral on the surface, these precepts prioritized nation over community and community over the individual. They enshrined the family, religious and racial harmony, community support, and consensus as fundamental social principles, outlawing conflict as a mode of engagement. If these values were taken seriously as rules to live by, then the political consequences may not have been dissimilar to those of a properly Confucianized society. But generally excluded from the process of formulating these national shared values, few Singaporeans actually remember that such values exist, and fewer still know what they are. Nevertheless, Singapore is regularly described as a communitarian society with a communitarian – often 'Asian' – form of democracy that at its best is a viable, culturally sensitive alternative to western liberal democracy, but at its worse is a disguise and justification for authoritarianism that pervades government and a self-righteous society.

Civic society: New politics depoliticized

Other than striving to deliver on the socio-economic promises, and continuing to culturalize/moralize Singaporeans according to a Singaporean identity strengthened by Asian values, the PAP government has attempted to secure its political legitimacy also by promoting a stronger sense of ownership among Singaporeans, in particular those seen to be increasingly affluent, more highly educated, and internationally mobile. It is ironic how the PAP government's success story has produced a generation of affluent, better educated, and more wisely travelled Singaporeans who seem less willing to accept the heavy-handed ways of the same government. But the government needs to anchor Singaporeans who possess skills that are in global demand and an outlook that enables them to settle almost anywhere in the world, since these 'cosmopolitans' – together with similarly talented foreigners working in the country – are needed to fuel Singapore's new economy, of which the creative industries will make up a large part.

The loss of one and then two parliamentary seats to the opposition in the early 1980s came as a shock to the PAP government who had held all seats in parliament since 1968. A world recession in the mid-1980s tarnished the PAP government's internal image of infallibility. Also in the 1980s, the next generation of PAP leaders was being publicly groomed to take over from then-Prime Minister Lee Kuan Yew. Uncertainty was certainly in the air.

To decompress any democratic pressures that might be building up, the government began to institutionalize new constitutional checks and balances that, it suggested, would not require Singaporeans to 'waste' their votes on opposition politicians who, according to stereotype, lacked credibility. Also, the government established various official feedback channels and public consultation exercises, meant – at the very least – to produce in the citizenry a sensation of being heard and being involved in matters of public importance. From a human resource angle, consultative mechanisms provided the PAP government with more ideas and experiences from the frontlines that it could pick and choose in order to formulate the best policies. But consultative mechanisms would also set the stage for dispersing the blame for any huge policy failures in the increasingly complex future, failures that would erode the PAP government's authority.

Forging a sense of ownership and belonging has involved the careful cultivation of civic society. At his prime ministerial swearing-in ceremony in November 1990, Goh Chok Tong – who promised a kinder and gentler style of government – declared,

> I will use the collective talents of my colleagues, and the combined
> energies of all citizens, to help the Singapore team stay ahead ...
> Singapore can do well only if her good sons and daughters are prepared
> to dedicate themselves to help others. I shall rally them to serve the
> country. For if they do not come forward, what future will we have?
> (Goh 28 November 1990)

Less than a year later, Minister George Yeo made a landmark and much-quoted speech promoting what he called 'civic society',

> The problem now is that under a banyan tree very little else can
> grow. When state institutions are too pervasive, civic institutions
> cannot thrive. Therefore it is necessary to prune the banyan tree so
> that other plants can also grow ... we cannot do without the banyan
> tree. Singapore will always need a strong centre to react quickly to a
> changing competitive environment. We need some pluralism but not
> too much because too much will also destroy us. In other words, we
> prune judiciously. (Yeo 20 June 1991)

Notably, Yeo called for pruning the banyan tree, not chopping it down and planting a different kind of tree. Nevertheless, the speech was an indication – and to the nascent civil society organizations, a particularly promising one – that the political environment was ready for more openness, consultation, and participation, and that citizens could organize themselves to pursue their private and civic interests, and perhaps even discreetly political ones.

Almost a decade later, the government was not only allowing for civic society, but actually promoting a form of active citizenry. In the midst of Singapore 21, a nation-wide consultation exercise conducted to get Singaporeans talking about fundamental dilemmas facing the country, then-Deputy Prime Minister Lee Hsien Loong declared that

> it is not enough just to express unrestrained views over drinks, or even to write critical letters to the press. If you want to have a serious influence over policy, then you must put in the effort to understand the issues, debate them knowledgeably, and have useful contributions to make. If you are not satisfied with the way things are in your own communities, then you should come forward to organize community and grassroots groups and activities, spend many evenings and weekends doing voluntary work, and patiently change things for the better. (Lee 16 January 2000)

And in his speech to the Harvard Club of Singapore, Lee argued that

> [p]eople should debate issues with reason, passion and conviction, and not be passive bystanders in their own fate. Disagreement does not necessarily imply rebellion, and nor should unity of purpose and vision mean sameness in views and ideas ... Singaporeans should take an interest not just in areas that directly affect them, but also in broader issues such as trends in our society, our aspirations for the future, or our role in the region and the world ... We will encourage Singaporeans to participate more actively in solving their own problems, and to organize themselves to do their part for their community. An active citizenry will help us to build a national consensus, engender a sense of rootedness, and enable the Government to serve the people better. (Lee 6 January 2004)

As Singapore's third prime minister, Lee Hsien Loong has indicated clearly – both in a speech during his inauguration ceremony on 12 August 2004 and in his three-and-a-half-hour-long National Day Rally speech on 22 August 2004 – that in his vision, Singapore would thrive on public participation and debate, diverse views, unconventional thinking, innovative strategies, a spirit of adventure, and a forward-looking orientation. Rhetorically at least, these two speeches would seem to be the apogee of 'political liberalization talk' that began in the mid-1980s as a response to perceived pressures from the ground. But widespread scepticism – particularly amongst organizations and actors in civil society – has meant that many will continue to proceed on the side of caution. This scepticism is based on the experience of civil society actors who, in spite of the kinder and gentler rhetoric of the Goh administration in the 1990s, continued to witness repressive state actions that put vague – and sometimes surprising – limits on public and private behaviour that was acceptable to the government.

One way to explain these vague and surprising limits is to think about a line that, in theory, divides the 'civic' from the 'civil'.[1] According to liberal traditions, civil society is a space in which autonomous individuals protect their right to self-preservation and pursue their capacity for self-determination by associating with other individuals and organizations aligned to a diverse range of lifestyles, world-views, and value systems. Diversity of this kind provides the self-determining individual with many options and choices, so vital for fashioning and refashioning the self. Freedom of association, expression, and information, as well as a healthy regard for experimentation are crucial for autonomous self-determination of this kind. Individuals must enjoy the right to be wrong, so that they can learn through experience, self-critique, and deliberation about what they should believe, why they should believe the things that they do, and why not the things that they do not. Diversity and experimentation may cause friction in society and this can become a source of conflict. If conflict seriously threatens the very existence of civil society then the state must play a role in protecting it. Most liberals would agree that this is the basic role of the state, and libertarians would go further to say that this should be the very limit of legitimate state intervention.

When the state, a necessary evil, appears to be going beyond its basic role, liberals and libertarians become suspicious. In the 'real world' where states do in fact go beyond simply protecting the civil sphere, it is not surprising that liberals in civil society behave in a guarded and sometimes antagonistic and confrontational way towards the state. In other words, when the state intrudes into the private, self-determining, and autonomous affairs of like-minded individuals in civil society, these groups of individuals will put up resistance against the state and, in that way, they become 'politicized'. Since nation building in Singapore involved the PAP government exercising extensive and invasive powers over private citizens in order to manufacture a nation-state that, in its view, could survive and succeed, civil society of the liberal kind would certainly not be tolerated. With 'civic society' it would be a different story. The concept of civic society is less about individual rights than about the individual's duty to its community, society, nation, and perhaps even beyond this. Social capital – the widespread norms and networks of trust and reciprocity within society (Grix 2001) – can be built from its shared values. These values, norms, and networks, whether real, invented, or imagined, are iconic and emblematic of a community's efforts to forge a coherent and consistent code of conduct and ethics that is grounded on something larger than the self or the existing community – perhaps the collective wisdom of ages or the 'golden age' of a closely related civilization.

Civic society also maps onto the PAP government's long-running campaigns to forge a 'gracious society' (Lee, T. 2002). The annual courtesy campaigns since the 1970s, the activities of the Singapore Kindness Movement, the promotion of culture and the arts, the 4 million smiles campaign to welcome International Monetary Fund (IMF) and World Bank delegates to Singapore in 2006, etc. have all been directed towards making Singaporeans more gracious for a number of possible reasons. A gracious society is good in and of itself. A gracious society might attract more tourist dollars and investment into the country. And a gracious society might be respectful towards authorities, never even dreaming of asking the awkward question in public even if the question needed to be asked. Giving 'face', after all, is a much studied Asian quality, and one that the PAP government would certainly promote. In the government's ideal civic society, individuals and the communities to which they inextricably belong cooperate harmoniously with the state and come out enthusiastically to take up their civic responsibilities. But it is the state that sets the agenda and makes the final decisions.

In practice, civic society can easily turn into civil society, a more politically challenging form of which the government is deeply suspicious. Of great importance to the government has been its ability to maintain its moral authority and political legitimacy in the eyes of the electorate. All talk of active citizenship never extends to compromising this ability. In order to outlaw civil society, the government wields the power to define what counts as going 'out-of-bounds'. What does count as going out-of-bounds is determined on a case-by-case basis, and usually after the event. This kind of ambiguity has been a serious obstacle to active citizenship as it breeds a culture of apprehension and self-censorship, based on the existence of political instruments of coercion including public rebuke, the Internal Security Act (ISA) (Chapter 143), and the Societies Act (Chapter 311).

In 1994, the academic and novelist Catherine Lim was publicly rebuked by then-Prime Minister Goh for writing an article in which she described a tension in the PAP government between the more authoritarian strain of Lee Kuan Yew and the more liberal strain of Goh Chok Tong. She argued, however, that Goh was increasingly not living up to his promises to be more open, consultative, and participatory. In his reply, Goh insisted that if

> a person wants to set the agenda for Singapore by commenting regularly on politics, ... that person should do this in the political arena. Because if you are outside the political arena and influence opinion, and if people believe that your policies are right, when we know they are wrong, you are not there to account for the policy. (Chua 5 December 1994)

It is interesting to note how the speech conveys an extreme confidence about being right in any dispute with the people, and the discomforting notion that anyone who thinks differently from the government – and is therefore wrong – will have to be corrected in full public view.

The ISA, an inheritance of the colonial administration, empowers the minister for home affairs to detain for two years any persons found to be 'acting in any manner prejudicial to the security of Singapore or any part thereof or to the maintenance of public order or essential services therein'. The two-year detention periods can be renewed indefinitely, and detainees have no recourse to judicial review or to any higher authority outside of Singapore. In 1987, 22 people were detained under the ISA. The group – connected to the Roman Catholic Church in Singapore and consisting of social workers, lawyers, radical theatre practitioners, and members of an opposition party – were working towards improving the lives of migrant workers in Singapore, including foreign domestic workers. These mostly middle-class, socially conscious Singaporeans were charged with conspiring in a Marxist plot to overthrow the PAP government and turn Singapore into a Marxist state. The Church was described as merely a screen for these subversive activities. Confessions were extracted and the detainees were eventually released. But the memory of the 1987 episode remains a stark warning to any socially conscious Singaporean thinking about coming forward to work for a more just world.

According to the Societies Act, if 10 or more people want to form a society, they will need successfully to register it. Otherwise, the society will be unlawful. According to law, the Registrar of Societies can refuse to register a society that is believed to be 'used for unlawful purposes or for purposes prejudicial to public peace, welfare or good order in Singapore'. The society must not be contrary to Singapore's national interest. In the case of political associations, membership must be restricted to Singaporeans and the society itself must not be affiliated to foreign organizations. 'The national interest' and 'public peace, welfare and good order' are, however, such highly contentious terms. In 1996, a homosexual group calling themselves People Like Us applied to have their society registered. Its stated aims were:

> (a) to promote awareness and understanding of the issues and problems concerning gay, lesbian and bisexual persons; (b) in furtherance of the above object, the society may (a) hold small group discussions, (b) conduct research, (c) organise social events, and (d) circulate a newsletter among Ordinary and Associate Members. (People Like Us 2000)

The application was rejected, and subsequent appeals were also rejected, each time without any reasons offered. One might infer from this that homosexuality was believed to be detrimental to the national interest, public peace, welfare, and good order in Singapore. In the context of a conservative majority in Singapore – once again, real, invented, or imagined – recognizing homosexuality by registering a homosexual society might incur the wrath of what is in effect a 'moralizing' (and electoral) majority.

The continued presence of coercive state instruments like the ISA and the Societies Act, together with ambiguous ideas about public order and security that inform their use, will cast shadows over even the most rhetorically persuasive promises about liberalization.

The renaissance city: Globalization and the new economy

As Singapore moves closer to achieving its aspirations of being a global city, its citizens – and, in particular, the affluent ones who travel and have access to higher levels of education – will be exposed to a significantly wider range of ideas, values, and lifestyle options. This will expand their set of needs, with an increase in those that are higher up the Maslovian hierarchy. Rising affluence – although it at first may mean a preoccupation with consumerism and lifestyle needs – will eventually equip individuals with more personal resources and confidence to take part as active and informed citizens. Globalization will also increase the access of private citizens and groups to international resources – information, know-how, and funding – that can be leveraged for civic and political action within Singapore, or even from outside it.

Globalization also produces a class of cosmopolitans who will be directly responsible for Singapore's continued success in the knowledge-based economy. They will be joined by foreign talent, including the very geographically mobile creative class. To attract the creative class to a place like Singapore, and to anchor Singaporean cosmopolitans to their nation, the government will need increasingly to turn Singapore into a stimulating and more tolerant place with a greater variety of lifestyle options. As a space that celebrates diversity, a vibrant civil society can make Singapore more attractive. As a space in which Singaporeans are allowed to act upon their passions and carry out inventive projects that will be of service to others, civil society can help to give cosmopolitans a sense of belonging and ownership in Singapore.

Participating in the new global economy makes the work of national decision-making a lot more complex. Economic performance is much less controllable, and business cycles seem to be getting shorter. This could mean that the PAP government is likely to make more mistakes in the future. More mistakes and frequent crises will make it harder for the government to manage public perceptions in order to prevent an erosion of political legitimacy.

To do well in the new economy, the government may need to take the results of consultation with the public a lot more seriously, without dismissing feedback that it does not like to hear or ideas that come from people it does not think too highly of. The agenda cannot be exclusively set by the government. Input from the ground and frontline is important for making more well-rounded decisions, and for dispersing the blame should there be a policy mistake of significant consequence. To do well in the new economy, creativity, innovation, and a propensity to take risks must be cultivated in the people, and this may require a more open and diverse environment that civil society can provide.

This is a significantly different kind of Singapore from the one that created – and had in turn been reproduced by – heartlander politics. Heartlanders, as a constructed majority, continue to be ideologically hailed as moral, political, and electoral supporters of the government and its more conservative policies. However, these conservative values may, today, not be useful or conducive – may in fact be counter-productive – to the drive towards becoming a successful, globally oriented, and creative economy on which much of the government's political legitimacy will increasingly be staked. In the most conceptual terms, while heartlanders are necessary to secure the government's moral authority, cosmopolitans and foreign talent are increasingly necessary for the economic basis of its authority.

The assumption stated in this chapter and developed in Chapter 5 is that the heartlander – cosmopolitan distinction, shaped by the dialectic between globalization and decades of state coercion and socialization, is ultimately an ideological manoeuvre, not a static sociological reality. As an ideological manoeuvre, the distinction can neither be proved nor disproved by sociological data (income, occupation, education, housing type, ethnicity, etc.), but is nearly always activated according to the situation, whether this arises through leading questions in opinion polls or the insinuations of moral, religious, and political entrepreneurs. Most Singaporeans in ordinary situations are likely to bear characteristics of both the typical heartlander and the typical cosmopolitan, but the close analysis of particular moments will identify heartlander effects that arise from the workings of politics and ideology. These effects are unstable; people are sometimes more heartlander-like and sometimes more cosmopolitan-like depending on the issues or circumstances that provoke their response.

New politics for renaissance Singapore, therefore, may be little more than a matter of resource management to produce a more complicated political legitimacy based on simultaneously resisting and harnessing globalization. Insofar as this balance can be controlled by the government, it resembles a classic game of divide-and-rule, where heartlanders are praised for the way they uphold the nation against bad foreign influences, and cosmopolitans – described to heartlanders as a necessary evil – are provided with less restricted lifestyle options and told that Singapore cannot change too quickly because the heartlanders are not ready for it.

Old politics is about perpetuating the belief that Singaporeans are not ready. The myth of the heartlander is therefore a convenient ideological tool of controlling the nature and extent of political change. As long as old politics persists in new times, renaissance Singapore will be a goal that Singapore must achieve but one for which it will be eternally unready.

NOTES

1. Parts of this section have been adapted from Tan (2003b).

REFERENCES

Chua, M.H. (5 December 1994) 'PM: no erosion of my authority allowed', *The Straits Times* (Singapore).

Gillis, E.K. (2005) *Singapore Civil Society and British Power*, Singapore: Talisman.

Goh, C.T. (28 November 1990) Swearing-in speech as prime minister of Singapore on 28 November 1990, Singapore Istana.

Grix, J. (2001) 'Social capital as a concept in the social sciences: the current state of the debate', *Democratization*, 8(3): 189–210.

Lau, A. (1998) *A Moment of Anguish: Singapore in Malaysia and the politics of disengagement*, Singapore: Times Academic Press.

Lee, H.L. (16 January 2000) Speech at the Singapore 21 Forum organized by Ang Mo Kio-Cheng San Community Development Council on 16 January 2000, Grassroots' Club Singapore.

Lee, H.L. (6 January 2004) 'Building a civic society', speech by the deputy prime minister at the Harvard Club of Singapore's 35th Anniversary Dinner, 6 January 2004, Singapore. Online. Available HTTP: <http://www.newsintercom.org/index.php?itemid=34> (accessed 22 December 2004).

Lee, H.L. (12 August 2004) Swearing-in speech as prime minister of
    Singapore on 12 August 2004, Singapore Istana.
Lee, H.L. (22 August 2004) Speech at the National Day Rally on 22 August
    2004, Singapore.
Lee, K.Y. (1998) *The Singapore Story: memoirs of Lee Kuan Yew*, Singapore:
    Times Editions.
Lee, T. (2002) 'The politics of civil society in Singapore', *Asian Studies
    Review*, 26(1): 97–117.
Marcuse, H. (1964/2002) *One-Dimensional Man: studies in the ideology of
    advanced industrial society*, London: Routledge.
People Like Us (31 March 2004) 'The first application correspondence',
    People Like Us Website. Online. Available HTTP: <http://www.geo-
    cities.com/plusg1/index2.htm> (accessed 22 December 2004).
Shanmugaratnam, T. (29 September 2004) Speech by the minister for educa-
    tion at the Ministry of Education Work Plan Seminar on 29 September
    2004, Ngee Ann Polytechnic Convention Centre, Singapore.
Tan, K.P. (2001). '"Civic society" and the "new economy" in patriarchal
    Singapore: emasculating the political, feminizing the public', *Crossroads:
    An Interdisciplinary Journal of Southeast Asian Studies*, 15(2): 95–122.
    Online. Available HTTP: <http://www.niu.edu/cseas/seap/CROSSRO
    ADS%20Tan%20Reformat.pdf> (accessed 22 December 2004).
Tan, K.P. (2003a) 'Democracy and the grassroots sector in Singapore', *Space
    & Polity*, 7(1): 3–20.
Tan, K.P. (2003b) 'Singapore: de-politicising civil society', *The SEACSN
    Bulletin*, October – December 2003. Online. Available HTTP: <http://
    www.seacsn.net/publications/bulletin/oct-dec03/singapore.htm>
    (accessed 22 December 2004).
Yeo, G. (20 June 1991) 'Civic society – between the family and the state',
    NUSS Inaugural Lecture on 20 June 1991, World Trade Centre audi-
    torium, Singapore.

Odd man in

JANADAS DEVAN

What sort of world will Singapore find itself in over the next 50 or so years?

A good place to begin is the present. The most pithy, the most succinct, definition of Singapore's strategic and economic predicament that I know was offered, not by a Singaporean, but by a foreigner. Many years ago, in 1973, a New Zealand prime minister by the name of Norman Kirk told the then prime minister of Singapore, Lee Kuan Yew, that New Zealand and Singapore had one thing in common – they were both 'odd', sharing little in common with the rest of the region. But while New Zealand, with Antarctica as its largest close neighbour, was the 'odd man out', Singapore, Kirk said, was the 'odd man in'.

The most important determinant of a country's foreign policy is location. Where it is, who are its neighbours, whether it is landlocked or on the coast – these count for far more than ideals or principles. Ideals and principles are important, of course. But geography is coercive.

If Singapore were in the middle of Europe (like Switzerland) or next to Antarctica (like New Zealand), then its foreign policy would obviously be very different too. But this is a multiracial, multi-religious country, with a large Chinese majority, in the middle of an overwhelmingly Muslim archipelago. And Southeast Asia, itself sandwiched between North Asia and South Asia, is a collection of relatively small states stuck between two huge continental powers, China and India. For Singapore, being 'odd' is one thing. More significant is where you are odd in.

The United States in East Asia

Consider how different countries have answered one of the most controversial of foreign policy questions today, namely, 'what is to be one's position towards the United States?' There is no nation, not even hyper-loyal Great Britain, that is not to some extent uncomfortable about America's power. It is an unprecedented situation in world history to have such massive economic power, married to such an overwhelming technological lead, supported by such astounding military might. America spends more on defence than the next 20 highest spending nations in the world combined (Hellman 2003: 6). What sort of position should one adopt towards such a power?

Obviously, one's answer to that question will depend on where one is, literally. France and Germany have been able to adopt an anti-American position, at least on Iraq, because they are in Europe – in a middle-class and upper-middle-class neighbourhood, as it were – with no overwhelmingly huge disparities in wealth or power. Adopting an anti-American position has also been possible because the Cold War is over, and France and Germany do not need the US to protect them against the Soviet Union.

By contrast, the Japanese and South Korean governments have responded quite differently, though opinion polls show that the majority of Japanese and Koreans oppose the war (Reuters 19 January 2004; British Broadcasting Corporation 21 June 2004). This is because they, unlike the French, still need the US security umbrella.

Similarly, in the case of Singapore, why is its government supportive of the US position? Singapore leaders have been open and frank about their reasons. Firstly, they believe Singapore – as the 'odd man in' – is also a potential target of terrorism. And they believe the best form of defence is offence. And secondly, Singapore wants the US to remain a presence in East Asia, serving as a counter to a resurgent China. For more than half a century after the Second World War, its presence in East Asia has served a reassuring purpose. And Singapore wants to keep it that way.

These broader security concerns provide the backdrop for the Free Trade Agreement (FTA) that Singapore signed with the US in 2003. The primary purpose of the agreement is of course economic. But it also has a political purpose. How do you keep Southeast Asia relevant even as China and perhaps India emerge as mighty forces? One answer, the answer the FTA offered, is that it should make itself attractive to US investors. From the point of view of a small nation like Singapore, the worst thing that can happen is for it to be trapped in a closed-in regional system dominated by one overwhelming economic and political power.

Keeping the US interested and engaged in the region is a means of avoiding that possibility. In the assessment of Singapore's leaders, no conceivable grouping of nations in East Asia – not even if all East Asian countries (excluding China) were to combine – will be able to match China without a US presence. Dreams of an East Asian Union, modelled on the European Union, will be just that – dreams – unless the two major regional powers, China and Japan, establish a *modus vivendi* with each other, just as Germany and France did after the Second World War. But just as European post-war stability was conditional upon a US presence, the same will hold for Asian stability in the coming decades.

As long as the US maintains a presence in East Asia, it will mean that no one power can dominate the region. As long as Southeast Asia remains attractive to investors, it need not fear being squeezed by China and India. And as long as Singapore can be useful to the world, being the odd man in need not be too unpleasant – all other things being equal.

But then all things are never equal. Over the next few decades, Singapore will face two challenges simultaneously. Firstly, it will become less odd, relative to its Southeast Asian neighbours (Indonesia, Malaysia, Thailand, the Philippines, Cambodia, Vietnam, Laos, and Burma); and secondly, the neighbourhood as a whole will become more odd, relative to the Asian mainland (China and India). Less odd and more odd: it is not clear which is worse, but both conditions will pose their peculiar challenges.

Singapore becoming less odd

First, the less odd. Anyone who has been to Kuala Lumpur or Bangkok in recent years will realize that Singapore's achievements over the past 40 odd years are not *sui generis*. The policies, strategies, and systems that it adopted are replicable. And they are, indeed, being replicated to a great extent. Twenty years ago, Singapore's competitors were other global cities relatively distant from it – Hong Kong, Tokyo, London, Frankfurt, etc. Fifty years from now, Singapore may have competitors near and dear.

Kuala Lumpur, for instance, has become one of the most exciting cities in Asia. Young Singaporeans visit it often. They take off on weekends for short trips. The Bangsar area is the magnet. I remember that place from my childhood. It was a largely Chinese area then, with a sizeable Indian population. Part of it was a congested extension of old Kuala Lumpur, and part of it was rubber estates. Now it is one vast cosmopolitan version of Holland Village, the enclave in Singapore that has been very popular, particularly among the expatriate community, for its concentration of restaurants, pubs, antique shops, and handicraft shops. But Bangsar might even be better than Singapore's Holland Village: the music is better, the restaurants more varied – an altogether messier, grittier, glitzier, and cheaper place.

In the long-term, if Malaysia remains politically stable, Kuala Lumpur may pose a challenge to Singapore. And it is not just Kuala Lumpur anymore. It is one vast metropolis, a sort of Los Angeles. Kuala Lumpur actually starts somewhere in Seremban in the south and ends somewhere in Rawang in the north. It covers more or less the entire Klang Valley, encompassing Petaling Jaya, Subang Jaya, Damansara, Putrajaya, Shah Alam, etc. When you drive around, you cannot really tell where one district ends and the next begins. It is like driving around Los Angeles, from Hollywood to Beverly Hills to Venice Beach – you cannot tell where the boundaries are. The estimates vary, but about 30 per cent of the population of peninsular Malaysia reside in the Klang valley (Department of Statistics Malaysia 2000). Thirty years from now, the metropolitan area may contain as many as 15 to 20 million people. Singapore expects to be able to support a population of 8 million, but only in several decades' time (Teo 3 April 2004). Eventually, Singapore may be to Kuala Lumpur what San Francisco today is to Los Angeles. That would not be the end of the world, though. San Francisco, after all, spawned Silicon Valley. But it may not necessarily be the top of the world either. Does size matter? Historically, cities have always been important because they have brought together large numbers of people, making the mobilization of capital, talent, and resources easier. All things being equal, Kuala Lumpur and Bangkok may be in a position to challenge Singapore's historical status as the premier city in Southeast Asia within the next 30 years. Bangkok may actually have a better chance, for Thailand's population (64 million) is more than double that of Malaysia's (24 million) and the kingdom has a larger hinterland, Indochina, whose economic potential remains largely untapped.

To cite one example, Bangkok's new mega-airport, Suvarnabhumi Airport, may – assuming its early problems do not reflect systemic faults – provide competition for Singapore's Changi Airport, just as the Port of Singapore Authority may face competition from Tanjung Pelepas in Johor. When long-haul aeroplanes come on stream, there will be no need for an airliner flying from Sydney to London, or Tokyo to Sydney, to stop in Singapore. And if they do stop in Southeast Asia, Bangkok may have as strong a claim to be a hub as Singapore.

I do not believe Singapore cannot cope with these challenges. But I think one would be wise not to assume that superior organization, better infrastructure, and efficiency of production can, much longer, be the sole sources of Singapore's competitive advantage. Development will tend to make these virtues common. What appeared like an unusually expensive carpet 20 years ago will look like linoleum 20 years from now. To be different, to survive economically, Singaporeans will need to become more agile, more resourceful, more independent, more entrepreneurial, more creative. In other words, make common what are at present not altogether common virtues for a variety of reasons. Nevertheless, it seems to me that Singapore becoming less odd, less unusual, will force a renaissance.

Southeast Asia becoming more odd

That other quandary – the region becoming more odd – has much to do with the rise of China and, not far behind, India. The rise of China is an epochal event of staggering proportions, as significant in modern history as the emergence of the United States as a major power in the early twentieth century, or Germany in the late nineteenth. In terms of purchasing-power parity, China accounted for 25 per cent of global growth between 1995 and 2002, compared to America's 20 per cent. The extraordinary thing is that China achieved this feat despite growing at a slower rate than Japan, Taiwan, South Korea, and Singapore at comparable periods in their respective take-offs. As Martin Woof has pointed out,

> If China's savings and investment performance have been exceptional, returns have been far less so. If China obtained the same increase in output for each unit of investment as South Korea in its days of super-fast growth, its trend rate of growth would be at least 12 per cent a year, not a 'mere' 8 per cent or so as now. (Woof 8 December 2003)

What this means is that China has not quite got its act together, and yet it has become this juggernaut. When it does, then what? Juggernaut squared? It is like what someone said of George Bernard Shaw, who was a vegetarian: 'God help us if he eats meat'. The Chinese will eat meat; in fact, they already do.

For 150 years or so, since the Meiji Restoration, the centre of gravity in Asia has been on the periphery. In the second half of the twentieth century, the first nations to emerge economically were all on the periphery: South Korea, Taiwan, Hong Kong, and Singapore; and later, Malaysia and Thailand. Historically, this was an anomaly. For thousands of years, the centre of gravity in Asia had been in the mainland. As recently as the fifteenth century, all three of the major powers of that era were in the Asian mainland: Ming China, Mughal India, and of course the Ottomans in what is now known as the Middle East. Singapore is in many respects the product of the mainland's decline; for otherwise, the nation's forefathers from China and India would have had little reason to emigrate to this part of the world in the nineteenth and twentieth centuries. The twenty-first century will witness a slow reversal to the historical norm. The mainland will again dominate. The periphery will again become what it had always been before this brief interregnum in the twentieth century: the periphery. Small may still be beautiful; but in the longue durée, size is king.

This radical shift in Asia's centre of gravity raises a number of implications. Firstly, the Association of Southeast Asian Nations

(ASEAN) has no alternative but to come together as an economically effective regional grouping. Four million people in Singapore, or even 250 million in Indonesia, cannot provide a more attractive market than China or India. Four hundred and fifty million in ASEAN can. Secondly, to a lesser degree than even Europe 100 years ago, Asia continues today not to exist as a unitary concept; not, at any rate, in any form that answers to the grandiose invocation of 'Asian values' some years ago. It has no political arrangement resembling the European Union, no economic arrangement resembling the North American Free Trade Agreement, and no security arrangement like the European Conference on Security and Cooperation to mitigate potential conflicts. Asia today resembles the Europe of the nineteenth century, with its major powers seeing one another as opponents and threats.

Thirdly, the fact that Asia is becoming economically interconnected does not guarantee peace. It is a delusion to believe that economic interests can by themselves moderate strategic tensions. We forget this now, but Europe was more economically integrated in the nineteenth century than it was for much of the twentieth. Today's European Union, in large part, merely restores the economic regime which existed prior to the First World War. Passports were unnecessary then, capital markets were open, and tariffs were minimal. And yet, Europeans found themselves butchering each other in 1914.

Europe's experience since 1945 suggests that the existence of supranational political organizations makes a crucial difference. Asia would benefit enormously if it had similar structures. Thus far, it only has the Association of Southeast Asian Nations (ASEAN) and the Asia-Pacific Economic Cooperation (APEC) – neither a well-oiled machine.

Conclusion

Singapore has always been rather odd. For 40 years, that oddness helped it to survive. Over the coming decades, Singapore's becoming less odd in the region will pose a challenge. But the greater challenge will be posed by the region, as a whole, becoming more odd as Asia reverts to its historic norm, and the centre of gravity shifts to the mainland. You cannot argue with gravity. All you can do is to accommodate yourself to the landscape that gravity forms, much as the planets in the solar system do – but hopefully, not exactly as in our solar system, with only one sun predominating.

REFERENCES

British Broadcasting Corporation (21 June 2004) 'South Korean ruling, opposition parties demand hostage's release', *BBC Monitoring Asia Pacific.*

Department of Statistics Malaysia (2000) 'Data awal banci 2000' (Preliminary Data Census 2000 Malaysia). Online. Available HTTP: <http://www.statistics.gov.my/English/DatawalCensus.htm> (accessed 2 August 2004).

Hellman, C. (2003) 'The Pentagon's fiscal year 2004 budget request: still growing strong', *The Defense Monitor*, 32(2): 2, 5–7.

Reuters (19 January 2004) 'Japanese troops due in Iraq, opinion split at home', *Reuters News.*

Teo, A. (3 April 2004) '8 million population for S'pore will provide critical mass – NTU economist', *The Business Times* (Singapore).

Woof, M. (8 December 2003) 'The long march to prosperity', *The Financial Times.*

Industrializing creativity and innovation

TERENCE LEE[1]

Introduction: 'Opening-up' Singapore

On 9 March 2004, the Singapore Tourism Board (STB) launched its 'Uniquely Singapore' branding to market Singapore as a premier tourism destination, with the primary aim of achieving a target of 7.6 million visitor arrivals for 2004 (Singapore Tourism Board 9 March 2004). Comprising a range of media advertisements for different global markets, this new branding strategy was developed in the wake of the city-state's 'recovery' from its economically crippling encounter with the severe acute respiratory syndrome (SARS) viral epidemic during the first half of 2003. The strategy also coincided with the wider circulation of a broad 'new' rhetoric that speaks of a 'more open' and 'creative' Singapore (Leo and Lee 2004: 205), designed to (re)package the city-state as a vibrant place where local and foreign talents can, according to a contemporary catchphrase in Singapore, 'live, work, and play' (Lee and Lim 2004: 150).

In a STB advertisement placed in an Australian newspaper, the image of a socially and culturally revitalized Singapore is evident as the nation is presented as a 'cool' and 'funky' city of excitement and thrills.

Things change fast in Singapore. These days, nightlife stretches to daybreak. And at many pubs, dancing on the bar is actually expected. On the shopping front, new boutiques continue to pop up islandwide, and an ever-growing alfresco dining scene is a treat if you love the tropical outdoors. With thrills like reverse bungee, exciting cabaret acts and so many international concerts, no two visits to Singapore are alike. In fact, your travel guide may already require a reprint. (*The West Australian* 19 June 2004: 32)

The reader – or prospective visitor – is 'instructed' to burn travel guides on Singapore that are old and outdated (defined in the advertisement as 'more than 8 months old'). These inscriptions signal a form of radicalness that is intended to displace old mindsets about Singapore's colourless cultural landscape, its lacklustre creative scene, as well as its notoriety as a 'police state' (Lee 2002a, 2002b). In the advertisement are still-strong echoes of McCarthy and Ellis' widely-publicized *Time Magazine* cover story which presented the city-state as 'competitive, creative, even funky' (McCarthy and Ellis 19 July 1999).

The fashionable rhetoric of creativity has been mobilized to demonstrate to the world that Singapore has become more open and innovative. Some of these publicized changes have included the prospective appointment of homosexuals to certain civil service positions, the legalization of 'bar-top dancing' in pubs and nightclubs, and the auto-registration of societies, clubs, and interest groups. In March 2004, amidst animated and polarized public debates, the government informed Singaporeans that it will 'keep an open mind' on whether to build a casino in Singapore with the primary aim of diversifying and boosting the domestic economy (Tan 13 March 2004; Teo 20 April 2004). The eventual decision to build not one but two licensed gambling/gaming venues in Singapore – a lucrative option that the government had resisted since the time of Singapore's independence – has been interpreted as another sign of Singapore's opening up.

The vision of a creative Singapore follows a government-commissioned report entitled *Creative Industries Development Strategy: propelling Singapore's creative economy* (Creative Industries Working Group 2002). This report, unveiled in September 2002 in the wake of Singapore's worst economic performance year since independence, identified the voguish 'creative industries' as one of the future economic growth sectors that Singapore should embrace. The concept of the creative industries has its formal origins in the United Kingdom in 1998 as one aspect of British Prime Minister Tony Blair's economic revitalization strategy, and has since been adopted by many developed countries in Europe as well as Australia (Flew 2005: 116–17). Captivated by the apparent success of the British experiment, the Singapore government jumped on the bandwagon and adopted the creative industries label, believing that the development of a 'creative cluster' – a creative network comprising the arts and cultural sector, the design sector, and the generic media industry – would propel Singapore's new innovation-driven economy by encouraging risk-taking and entrepreneurship, and attracting creative talents into Singapore (Lee and Lim 2004: 150). By liberalizing the creative industries and embracing openness, Singapore would not only prosper economically, but would also become, as the Creative Industries Working Group (CIWG) report puts it, the 'new Asia creative hub' of the twenty-first century (Creative Industries Working Group 2002: v).

As liberalization strategies and policies surrounding creativity and innovation were being introduced, there were also signs that open mindsets existed only in what Lee and Lim describe as the 'non-political margins of society' (Lee and Lim 2004: 150). As they explain,

> the Singapore government continues to forewarn individuals and groups to steer clear of controversial political issues. Such behaviour is consistent with the ruling People Action Party's (PAP) approach to political administration and governance, where strategies of diversion have been variously applied to depoliticize the citizenry since it came into power in 1959. (Lee and Lim 2004: 150)

The deliberate depoliticization of creativity, along with its attendant discourse of openness, suggests that the Singapore government is not interested in creativity per se, but in industrializing creativity and innovation for economic gains. These creative proposals are also designed, as Kenneth Paul Tan puts it, to 'sex up' Singapore so that it would 'produce a fertile, stimulating, innovative and risk-taking climate conducive to success in the new global, knowledge-driven and entrepreneurial economy vital for staying competitive' (Tan 2003: 406).

The paradoxical notion of openness was well captured in an address by then-Deputy Prime Minister Lee Hsien Loong to the elite Harvard Club of Singapore on 6 January 2004. In what was widely perceived as his maiden speech as prime minister-designate, Lee declared

> I have no doubt our society must open up further. The growing participation and diversity over the two decades have been vital pluses for Singapore. ... Looking ahead, the important task of the Government will be to promote further civic participation, and continue to widen the limits of openness. (Lee, H.L. 6 January 2004)

Lee's speech provides an excellent demonstration of the effectiveness of the PAP government's *realpolitik.* By foregrounding 'vital pluses for Singapore' in terms of the nation's growing tolerance for diversity, Lee could then subtly yet unmistakably reassert the importance of instituting parameters – otherwise known as 'out-of-bound' or OB markers (a golfing terminology) – to stifle political debate and commentary (Lee 2002a: 109–11; Lee and Lim 2004: 151). Lee cautioned that OB markers, designed to ensure that government authority remains unchallenged, would continue to apply in a more open Singapore under his premiership because the majority of Singaporeans 'still do not play golf' (Lee 6 January 2004).

Not unlike many other government policy directives, this one contained contradictions. The government-initiated notion of openness meant to pave the way for a new creative outlook was likely to conform to the more controlled terms and tenets of political engagement and economic imperatives (Leo and Lee 2004; Throsby 2001: 10–12). Such a conformist-cum-pragmatic approach would arguably limit the flowering of 'real' creativity, or the type that requires one to operate with an open and questioning disposition and to challenge status quos so that original and innovative outcomes may be produced (Leo 2003: 8). As Leo and Lee have noted most explicitly, such a position is highly problematic in the context of a government-made Singapore, where upsetting the preferred states of power relations is hardly an option for creativity and its industrialization (Leo and Lee 2004: 209–10).

In Chapter 3 of this book, Janadas Devan argues that Singapore's economic survival will depend on its ability to stay 'different' from the region; and to do that, it will have to become 'more agile, more resourceful, more independent, more entrepreneurial, more creative'. This chapter will begin with an examination of the psychological and socio-cultural motivations for creativity. It will then consider the wider question of whether the government's ambitious plan to open up and industrialize creativity can succeed in the light of its overtly economic focus as well as Singapore's notoriously censorious and politically rigid climate. While noting that Singapore has typically thrived on various social, cultural, and political ambivalence and contradictions, this chapter will attempt to consider how, if at all, a truly open and creative society can be fashioned without the loosening of what Cherian George has described as 'centralized control' (George 2000).

Creativity uncovered

In a review essay on the rise of creativity as a cultural discourse, media and creative industries scholar Terry Flew declares somewhat ominously that creativity has become 'both big business and a lot of different things to different people' (2003: 90). The upsurge of interest in the area since the late 1990s appears to stem from the pace and extent of take-up of the notion of creativity within government, policy, and corporate circles (O'Keefe 2004: 34; Flew 2004: 161), notwithstanding the fact that researchers from diverse disciplinary domains have for years attempted to understand the complex workings of creativity in humans (Lee and Lim 2004; Florida 2002; Hesmondhalgh 2002; Howkins 2001). Richard Florida's (2002) bestselling book *The Rise of the Creative Class*, in which he argues that economic growth is a by-product of creativity and that the nurturing of what he calls the 'creative class' is the key determinant of an economy's success or failure, is perhaps the most prominent contribution to the debate in recent years.

Widely employed, creativity remains a nebulous concept, not unlike the concept of 'culture', which Raymond Williams (1976) describes as one of the most complex and complicated in the English language. 'Creativity' is described by experimental psychologists Teresa Amabile and Elizabeth Tighe as 'too ill-defined a quality to be studied properly' because it is a vacuous concept that defies ordinary thinking (1993: 8). In order for a product or response to be considered creative, it must be extraordinary and 'different from what has been done before' (Amabile and Tighe 1993: 9). The most widely accepted conceptual definition of creativity is 'the ability to invent and develop new and original ideas' (adopted by popular dictionaries such as the *Collins Cobuild English Language Dictionary* (1993) and the *Little Oxford Dictionary* (1998)).

But creativity involves more than just a new idea or invention, since not every original idea can be construed as creative. According to Margaret Boden, a professor of cognitive science, creativity should also be 'valuable' both aesthetically and pragmatically (Boden 2004: 10). In other words, creativity must be appropriately applied to a situation that would be well-received – or regarded as valuable – by its audience. This is referred to as 'domain-relevance', the first of three basic components of creativity advanced by Amabile and Tighe (1993: 14). While the first marker of creativity has to do with the originality-cum-appropriateness of an idea, solution, or product, the second relates to the level of passion for the creative activity (Lee and Lim 2004: 152). Amabile calls such passion 'intrinsic motivation', or the ability to engage with a creative activity due to genuine fervour for the task (Amabile 1990: 78–79).

> People will be most creative when they feel motivated primarily by the interest, enjoyment, satisfaction, and challenge of the work itself (intrinsic motivation), and not by external pressures (extrinsic motivation) ... [and] people will achieve the level of deep task involvement that is essential to creativity. (Amabile and Tighe 1993: 16)

Although it may be possible for intrinsic motivation to coexist some-what with extrinsic motivation, one of the two tends to emerge as the primary driving force for a given task (Lee and Lim 2004: 152). Based on Amabile and Tighe's (1993) principle, it is the task undertaken with intrinsic motivation that tends to be the more creative.

The third element of creativity relates to 'creativity-relevant skills' which include cognitive and personal styles that tend towards independence, risk-taking, innovation, non-conformism, and toler-ance for ambiguity and diversity, all of which are seen as 'conducive to generating novel and useful ideas in any domain' (Amabile and Tighe 1993: 15). Indeed, Florida elaborates on this aspect of creativity by championing the promotion of tolerance (in addition to technology and talent, collectively known as the '3 Ts') as one of the keys to harnessing creativity (Florida 2002: especially Chapter 14). Florida specifically cites 'bohemianism' and 'homosexuality' as two non-conformist cultural practices that test the limits of tolerance of a society, and suggests that creativity presents itself in intellectuals or individuals within the 'creative class' who are motivated, even empowered, by such diversities (Lee and Lim 2004: 153).

Kirpal Singh, Singaporean creative-thinking professor, poet, and author of this book's Chapter 7, recommends that in order for creativity to flourish, workers need to be given the freedom to offload baggage-laden restrictions of the past and tread into uncharted territories to discover and generate new ideas (Singh 2004: 16). As summarized by Lee and Lim (2004: 153), 'creativity ventures into uncertain territories for the purpose of challenging workers to discover novel alternatives, and, as such, is typically found in places open towards social plurality and cultural diversities'. Although the term 'social' tends to be used in place of 'political' in debates surrounding creativity, various studies have shown that 'political openness' has a direct, as well as indirect, socio-cultural bearing on creativity (Lee, T. 2004).

Drawing from the work of leading psychologist Dean Keith Simonton, Florida puts forth the case that creativity flourishes best in places and times marked by four characteristics: 'domain activity, intellectual receptiveness, ethnic diversity, [and] political openness' (cited in Florida 2002: 35). Whilst not endorsing political dissidence or social rebellion against establishments, prominent Fulbright fellow Mihaly Csikszentmihalyi (1999) makes a complementary point in arguing that creative insights are necessary for cultural change and differentiation in social and political thought. The implication here is that without diversity and tolerance coupled with political openness and participation, creativity will be impeded in a society where rules and knowledge are the 'monopoly of a protective class or caste [to which] others are not admitted' (Csikszentmihalyi 1999: 320–21).

In the context of Singapore, the government has played the role of the 'protective class' by steering Singaporeans away from autonomous political discussion via the enactment of societal and political laws and regulations. As many of such laws are vague and open-ended, they allow for wide-ranging applications, resulting in the 'creation' of a (self-)censorious climate of fear (Gomez 2000: 68; Lee 2002b: 6). Not only do these measures impact negatively on Singaporean creative workers, especially those involved in the arts, cultural, and media industries, they also put in place various psychological barriers that blunt the creative edges of many Singaporeans. The creative industries strategy launched in September 2002 and the promise of openness made by the prime minister himself (Lee, H.L. 6 January 2004) are steps towards repairing the damage caused by past cultural policies that are best described as myopic. Nevertheless, this chapter contends that only a genuine embrace of an open society that espouses non-violent political and democratic freedoms of speech and association can deliver a truly creative and innovative Singapore.

The pragmatics of creativity

The Singapore government's swift adoption of the creative industries 'phenomenon' demonstrates its pragmatism in latching onto a sector that looks set to become a key economic deliverable. The creative industries, as determined by Britain's Creative Industries Taskforce (1998) and adopted into Singapore's own creative industries strategy document, is defined as 'those industries which have their origin in individual creativity, skill and talent and which have a potential for wealth and job creation through the generation and exploitation of intellectual property' (Creative Industries Taskforce 1998: 5).

If creativity is about the development of new and original ideas, then the *Creative Industries Development Strategy* (Creative Industries Working Group 2002) falls short of the very marker it tries to set. Not only does it fail to offer its own 'localized' definition of the creative industries, the statement is essentially regurgitation couched as a 'creative clustering' of earlier cultural and media policies, including the *Renaissance City Report: culture and the arts in Renaissance Singapore* (Ministry of Information and the Arts 2000) and *Media 21: transforming Singapore into a global media city* (Singapore Broadcasting Authority 2002), aimed at enlivening the arts, culture, and media scenes in Singapore (Bereson 2003). This denotes what I would describe as the pragmatics of creativity in Singapore, where an existing policy or practice should *always* be extrapolated or re-used, especially if it had worked previously or in other contexts.

The well-rehearsed doctrine of pragmatism, in dictating that there is no need as it were to 'reinvent the wheel', clearly defies some of the tenets of creativity. The creative cluster, developed to propel Singapore's creative economy, consists of three broad groups – the arts and culture, design, and media industries (Creative Industries Working Group 2002). The creative cluster idea is drawn very heavily from the work of Florida, who notes that creative workers have become the decisive source of competitive advantage in the contemporary economy and society (Florida 2002: 5–6). With the understanding that businesses seek to situate themselves in places where clusters of creative people reside, Singaporean authorities embarked on a long-term campaign to re-brand Singapore as the 'renaissance city' where creative people can 'live, work and play' (Lee, T. 2004: 291; Oon 16 November 2004). The Singapore Tourism Board's Uniquely Singapore campaign, highlighted at the start of this chapter, is one example of this.

In Singapore's case, the first creative cluster initiative took the form of a minor revision made to the original *Renaissance City Report* (Ministry of Information and the Arts 2000), mainly to include innovation as a key policy outcome within the arts and cultural sector. In the Creative Industries Working Group's report (2002: Chapter 2), the revised version was codenamed *Renaissance City 2.0*, which is to be read as Version 2.0 of the original report. Such nomenclature reflects once again Singapore's ability to keep up with cool management trends and technological buzzwords. In essence, however, this is mostly a rehash of old policy statements pertaining to Singapore's 'Asian renaissance' vision (Bereson 2003: 6), in which every Singaporean is imagined to be civic-minded, 'attuned to his [sic] Asian roots', and an 'active citizen who is not just a mere actor in a vast nameless play, but a co-writer of the Singapore Story, with the latitude and responsibility to input his own distinctive [and creative] ideas' (Ministry of Information and the Arts 2000: 39). To be sure, the Singapore Story – as defined by Singapore's founding father (now Minister Mentor) Lee Kuan Yew in his highly publicized dual-volume memoirs – is a politicized account of the economic miracle of Singapore fashioned by Lee himself (Lee 1998, 2000). Hence, the creative and innovative Singaporean must be one who 'participates' in enhancing the economic competitiveness of Singapore by industrializing his or her artistic and creative talents, just as Lee in the past had done for Singapore.

The second vision of the creative industries policy is to spearhead a Design Singapore initiative, so as to position Singapore as a global hub of multimedia design capabilities (Creative Industries Working Group 2002: Chapter 4; *The Straits Times* 21 March 2003). Apart from a general recognition of the importance of good commercial design, particularly in product packaging, architecture and urban planning, fashion and jewellery design, and the (re)branding of Singapore as a high-tech and global hub city, not much else has been articulated about the significance of a Design Singapore initiative under the rubric of the creative industries. In August 2003, the Ministry of Information, Communications and the Arts (MICA) formed a high-level Design Singapore Council (DSC) to spearhead a national initiative to develop and promote design in Singapore. Although the DSC website (http://www.designsingapore.org) tries to spell out, in very broad and fluid terms, the roles and strategies of the Design Singapore initiative, the descriptions are far too cryptic. It claims, nevertheless, that the 'design services cluster' contributed about 1.9 per cent of Singapore's gross domestic product in 2001 and directly employed some 25,000 individuals. In response to projections that the economic output from design initiatives is poised to flourish, the government announced plans to invest in design education within the tertiary and vocational institutions (Creative Industries Working Group 2002: 24–25). In spite of these measures, I would argue that conceptual inadequacy, coupled with the lack of both quantitative and qualitative data to measure their success or shortcomings, makes it virtually impossible to assess the impending contributions of this supposedly creative sector. More fundamentally, whether the foregrounding of design as a viable economic pursuit will invoke 'creative shifts' in the mindsets of Singaporeans remains a question that may never be answered (Lee, T. 2004).

While it appears as though the inclusion of design within the creative industries document is a visionary 'step' of faith, since it is not based on any specific or substantial previous policies, there are signs that the younger technologically-savvy generation are developing an interest in multi-media tools, interactive games, and computer-based design. In September 2004, a Games Creation Community (GCC), an initiative of Singapore's Economic Development Board, was established to capitalize on what is believed to be a fast-growing global electronic games sector. Housed at Nanyang Polytechnic's School of Design, the GCC is essentially an innovative start-up venture with a broad base of foreign and local financial backers, including the three main internet service providers in Singapore – SingTel, StarHub, and Pacific Internet (Ho 25 September 2004: 1). The economic motivation here is to direct talents towards a nascent but potentially bustling industry of the future, not unlike the government's drive since the late 1990s to embrace biosciences research and development in Singapore.

'Media 21' – the third and final cluster initiative – 'envisions Singapore as a global media city, a thriving media ecosystem with roots in Singapore, and with strong extensions internationally' (Creative Industries Working Group 2002: 37). The reference to 'ecosystem' within Media 21 is intended to link the Singapore media sector within a broader creative network that includes the arts, multimedia design-cum-digital technologies, as well as media exchange and trading. A media park, meant 'to capture public and industry imagination' and to 'underscore government commitment to develop [the media] sector' (Creative Industries Working Group 2002: 39), is in the process of being constructed within 'one-north', a 200-hectare development set aside for people 'to inspire and be inspired to push the boundaries of knowledge and turn ideas into groundbreaking innovations' (one-north 2003). This media park contains buildings with voguish names like Fusionpolis, and is defined as a 'state-of-the-art work, live, play and learn environment for media and info-communication companies, and the artistic community' (Singapore Broadcasting Authority 2002: 7). Official statements and documents claim that the intention behind this physical 'creative-clustering' of media and media-related professionals into a single township is to increase economic vibrancy and to inspire the wider community toward greater creativity and social vitality (Creative Industries Working Group 2002: 2), not unlike the recently launched Creative Industries Precinct of Queensland University of Technology in Brisbane, Australia (http://www.creativeindustries.qut.com). The precinct in the inner Brisbane suburb of Kelvin Grove was completed in 2004 and has been hailed as a breakthrough for education and research as well as a shining example of inner city urban renewal, described by Glover and Cunningham (2003) as the rise of a new and creative Brisbane.

The new emphases on creativity in Singapore tend to approach the so-called creative sectors not so much from cultural or artistic viewpoints. Rather, the approach is overwhelmingly and unashamedly economic (Toh et al. 2003). Although the term 'creative industries' clearly suggests a consideration of the commercial in policy-making, Singapore's uptake of the concept is an extraordinary case study in that it privileges economic returns over all else (Lee and Lim 2004: 157). In a study on cultural policy in Singapore, Lily Kong calls this the 'hegemony of the economic in Singapore' (Kong 2000: 423). Unlike the 'original' Renaissance period in Florence that emphasized social, political, intellectual, and emotional development of the individual, the Singaporean renaissance is designed to industrialize creativity so that every individual with creative potential can and will become economically productive (Lee, T. 2004: 290). In actuality, the Mediapolis/Fusionpolis concept is intended to replicate cluster centres such as New York's Silicon Alley and San Francisco's world-renowned Silicon Valley, in the belief that it would be a draw card to lure creative talents for the sake of economic prosperity and longevity (Chang and Lee 2003).

Since creativity is predominantly associated with the evocation of new ideas, solutions, or products that have not previously been explored, the primacy of economics in conceptualizing the creative industries is highly problematic. As Lee and Lim (2004: 157) have pointed out, the island-state's virtual absence of natural resources has turned it into a trading port with an overt dependency on imported goods for consumption. This has in part led to the favouring of cultural and creative products from foreign sources (usually the west) over local ones. After all, it is economically more viable to import such products than to produce them 'in-house' for only 4 million people (Chang and Lee 2003: 137). The corollary is that such an economic rationale leads to decreased creativity, with local or indigenous cultural workers robbed of their physical and metaphysical creative spaces to explore and nurture their crafts (Lee and Lim 2004: 157). Alvin Tan makes a similar observation of local theatre in Chapter 10 of this book, but he delineates specific creative efforts to get around the problem.

The building of the S$600-million mammoth Esplanade – Theatres on the Bay, opened amidst a multi-million dollar extravaganza in October 2002, was regarded by local arts practitioners and critics as a dual 'economic-cum-tourism' strategy to attract world-class acts to perform in Singapore (Lee 2004: 284). Only such 'surefire successes', as measured by box-office takings, would be able to afford the space (Kong 2000: 419). Local artists were thus deemed unimportant, or at least secondary, when compared to their foreign counterparts. Yet, a city that professes to be creative would only be truly so if it developed local art forms, instead of building empty shells through which global acts transit. While the state currently attempts to nurture its creative industries, its inherent bias towards foreign art forms – the result of its pragmatic focus on immediate economic returns – makes the notion of creativity as the harnessing of new ideas, solutions, or products untenable in Singapore (Lee and Lim 2004: 157–58). As Singaporean cultural theorist C.J.W.-L. Wee (2003: 87) puts it, the highly publicized and commercialized Esplanade is nothing more than a 'statist attempt to create a commercial Cult of the Beautiful' for the Singaporean 'community' comprising mainly visitors and expatriate business executives (and a few locals) desiring 'high culture' while residing, often temporarily, in Singapore.

The economic pragmatism that has been drilled into the Singaporean psyche hinders the development of creativity by setting extrinsic and overwhelmingly economic inducements as motivations, rather than encouraging a more humanistic approach to the sector (Chang and Lee 2003: 133; Leo and Lee 2004). As discussed earlier, a creative society can only be nurtured if people are intrinsically motivated (Amabile and Tighe 1993). In a country where 'economic growth is the anchor without which all issues become irrelevant' (Birch 1993: 4), the meanings behind nurturing a creative, enlightened, and appreciative society have been rendered secondary to sustaining economic deliverables. While it is true that the broad creative industries can benefit the economic gross domestic product (GDP) by uncovering 'new economic value' (Toh et al. 2003: 51), the 'capacity to unleash social and cultural vibrancy can be easily shackled by an uncompromising focus on the commercial' (Tan 2003: 418). The authorities, as well as the people, must lean towards a more liberal interpretation of 'pragmatism' – one that allows political openness, social plurality, and cultural diversity to flourish, before creativity and innovation can begin to emerge.

Creative politics and the politics of creativity

The PAP government's political legitimacy has been largely founded on economic performance and management. Indeed, under its leadership since attaining administrative independence in 1965, Singapore has been transformed into a thriving metropolis (Neher 1999: 39). As founding prime minister Lee Kuan Yew (2000) wrote in his memoirs, Singapore has progressed from third-world to first-world status in just one generation. This 'success' is largely attributed to the PAP's aggressive adoption of pragmatic strategies to 'create' a people focused on economic productivity, which in turn led to a 'steady and systematic depoliticization of a politically active and aggressive citizenry' (Chan 1975: 51).

While the government is loath to admit it, the overwhelming success of pragmatism has become problematic for the cultivation of creativity. This is because creativity requires a socio-cultural environment that is not only tolerant enough to cultivate new ideas (even in their possibly politically subversive manifestations) (Florida 2002: 35), but also one that encourages autonomous civic and political participation among its citizenry. Singapore's reputation as a no-nonsense authoritarian regime – with its political leaders ultra-sensitive to political criticisms and its citizens highly subservient and docile (Lee 2002a and 2002b) – is somewhat incompatible with the discourse of creativity, even making it futile. After all, creativity requires not passive and mechanical individuals, but thinkers who constantly challenge the status quo to achieve originality and innovation (Leo 2003: 8). Rather than make substantial changes at the ideological level, the government has sagaciously opted to make some frivolous – but nonetheless strategic – allowances to demonstrate to the world that Singapore is 'opening up' (Lee and Leo 2004: 159).

For example, on 27 August 2004, local daily *The Straits Times* announced that Singapore would soon be 'on the world map of extreme sports' when it hosts a blockbuster 'made-for-television' extreme sports event in October 2004 (Fong 27 August 2004). Described as a 'cross between the hot TV serials *Survivor* and *The*

Amazing Race', the Action Asia Challenge puts 'athletes through a challenging course that will see them jumping off bridges and perhaps zipping down the Esplanade' (Fong 27 August 2004). Not only will such an event allow television viewers and potential tourists around the world to view Singapore as a vibrant city and hopefully be drawn to its shores, it will enable the government to make broad claims about its openness and creative shifts (Lee, T. 2004). As the editorial in *The Sunday Times* (29 August 2004) noted with cogency in response to the announcement,

> [Singapore] is on the brink of a renaissance in diverse areas. From the departure of some of the policies that have structured its economics and society, to the appearance of political space that may allow Singaporeans to reinvent themselves, the only continuity here is change. Sports plays a real role in this national transition. A sense of adventure, a desire to take rational risks, a need to push back the boundaries of the possible – these characteristics of sports are markers of what Singapore can yet be. (*The Sunday Times* 29 August 2004)

Despite the high levels of publicity surrounding the liberalization of such activities, the government continues to enforce OB markers and other state-defined conditions (Lee 2002a: 110). Such concessionary changes, I would argue, hardly constitute 'the brink of a renaissance'. Rather, this 'national transition' is about softening the impact of authoritarian and rigid rules in the hope of obscuring their continued existence. This entails the 'politically creative' practice of 'gestural politics', where on the one hand, the government seems to accommodate greater socio-cultural plurality, but on the other, it suppresses the emergence and development of an independent civil society (Lee 2002a). These token concessions are thus intended to further depoliticize the citizenry by appearing to increase the vivacity of a society without running any risk of the ruling party's authority being challenged or undermined. In short, these measures to liberalize Singapore do not possess much practical or political significance because they are in essence gestural (Lee 2002a: 111; Lee and Lim 2004: 159).

Before the advent of the creative industries project, the government had vehemently rejected the so-called immoral and liberal values of the 'decadent west' – particularly homosexuality and other contrary vices – in terms of 'Asian values' (Tan 2003: 408). However in July 2003, despite the fact that homosexuality remains a criminal offence in Singapore under the Penal Code (*Reuters* 15 November 2003), then-Prime Minister Goh Chok Tong made a peculiar declaration that the Singapore government was prepared to hire gays in 'certain positions of government' (Nirmala 4 July 2003; Elegant 7 July 2003). Lest one gets too caught up with governmental 'spin', this seemingly liberal statement needs to be read in the context of the authority's continued refusal to grant Singapore's most prominent gay rights group, People Like Us, a legitimate and licensed existence (*The Straits Times* 6 April 2004), using the convenient Asian values conservatism argument as a justification for its austerity (Lee and Lim 2004: 159–60). As Kenneth Paul Tan suggests in Chapter 2, the myth of a conservative majority is strategically employed to justify the limits of liberalization.

Whether the majority of Singaporeans actually adhere strictly to Asian values or whether the myth of a conservative and moral majority is simply 'politically useful fiction' remains an open-ended issue (Tan 2003: 410). What is clear, however, is that the PAP has historically associated homosexuality with western 'baser instincts', and resistance towards such behaviour indicates an unrelenting move to insulate Singapore against any subversive conduct that may threaten the government's authority and electoral standing (Lee and Lim 2004: 160). By buying into Florida's (2002) assertion that creative people are mostly found in places that are tolerant, diverse, and accepting of gay lifestyles, Singapore has sought pre-emptively to assuage the fears of creative workers that they would be taken to task for their 'bohemianism' or alternative lifestyles (*Today* 13 April 2004). As *The Straits Times* columnist Chua Mui Hoong (9 July 2003) has clarified most unequivocally, 'It's not about gay rights – it's survival!' In other words, deviance is an acceptable component of creativity only if workers choose either to support the PAP government openly or stay apolitical, and if they are able to industrialize their creative skills to boost the economic bottom line.

In addition to the concept of Asian values, OB markers remain potent in ensuring the political docility of the population. Through communitarian ideological reasoning and deference to authority, the PAP government moralizes the Asian cause of self-reduction in the name of a collective national interest, to ensure the depoliticization of the citizenry (Lee and Lim 2004: 160). The PAP government summons the use of OB markers publicly to rebuke political transgressors or troublemakers, a tactic that is highly effective in a society where personal 'face' should be preserved at all costs (Lee 2002a). By refusing to define the limits of OB markers, the government bestows itself the power to use them in a catch-all manner, often retrospectively, resulting in a sophisticated mode of auto-regulation that enforces mass subjugation and discipline (Lee 2002b: 10–11). The ambiguity of OB markers thus creates a culture where people are prone to err on the safe side of the apolitical, or non-political. In Chapter 9, *Sintercom* webmaster Tan Chong Kee recounts his experiences of closing down Singapore's first political website to avoid the frightening consequences of inadvertently walking into the nebulous OB zone. As Lee and Lim surmise,

> [All of] these laws, codes, and rules – whether written or unwritten, real or imagined – combine to create a climate of fear and excessive caution in Singapore, resulting in the enactment of psychological barriers that prevent people from 'pushing the limits' for fear of being incarcerated or 'blacklisted'. Singaporeans are thus dis-incentivized from 'thinking outside the box', a common element of creativity, preferring instead to remain in secure boundaries. Even if a creative individual has no wish to rebel against the political establishment, the ability to explore freely uncharted territories is often inhibited. (Lee and Lim 2004: 111)

While the introduction of extreme sports might encourage a minority of Singaporeans to take calculated physical risks, it is really the widening of genuine political and ideological space(s) to allow individuals to think, speak, and act openly and autonomously that would contribute to the real creative process (Csikszentmihalyi 1999).

One of the key avenues for a truly open and creative discourse is the media. In spite of Singapore's professed desire to become a 'global media city', as envisioned by the Media 21 statement (Singapore Broadcasting Authority 2002), state leaders have repeatedly echoed Lee Kuan Yew's credo that the media's role is to act as the government's mouthpiece and thereby assist in nation building (Leo and Lee 2004; Birch 1993). This means that the liberal democratic model of the press as the fourth estate and the media as society's watchdog is frowned upon in Singapore (George 2002). Even as the key deliverables of the creative industries strategy – such as the Mediapolis within the one-north site – start to materialize, there are signs that Singapore under the premiership of Lee Hsien Loong will continue the 'tried and tested' media policy of containment. As Lee declares in his 'open up Singapore' speech,

> [t]he [Singapore] media should report news accurately and fairly, in order to inform and educate the public. It should adopt a national perspective on issues, educating Singaporeans on the reality of global competition, or the need for healthy habits during the SARS outbreak. But it should avoid crusading journalism, slanting news coverage to campaign for personal agendas. This way, the media helps the public to decide and judge issues for themselves, and provide a valuable channel for them to voice news and opinions. (Lee, H.L. 6 January 2004)

The term 'global media city' implies a relevance to the wider world. Yet the government-mandated and overtly nationalistic role of the Singapore media contradicts Singapore's aspiration to be a 'media city'. The absence of 'crusading journalism' and 'slanting news coverage' in the media means that alternative ideologies – and indeed subversive and innovative ideas alike – will find it hard to circulate in Singapore (Lee 2002b: 10). Yet, in the context of the creative industries, a socio-cultural and political environment that is open to difference and diversity does not appear to be an option. Unless the authorities are prepared to rescind the OB markers and other open-ended laws, 'gestures' of openness will remain inconsequential and Singapore's vision of creativity would likely fall short of its ideal.

Conclusion

On 12 August 2004, the nation witnessed its second political leadership transition when Lee Hsien Loong, the elder son of Singapore's elder statesman Lee Kuan Yew, was installed as Singapore's third prime minister. In his speech delivered at the swearing-in ceremony, Lee reasserted his 'new' mission to remake Singapore as an open and creative society,

> We will continue to expand the space which Singaporeans have to live, to laugh, to grow and to be ourselves. Our people should feel free to express diverse views, pursue unconventional ideas, or simply be different. We should have the confidence to engage in robust debate, so

as to understand our problems, conceive fresh solutions, and open up new spaces. (Lee, H. L. 12 August 2004)

Lee's call for a more open and diverse Singapore is not so much to declare an open season under his premiership, but to project Singapore as a mature, progressive, and creative society to the rest of the world. The target audience consists of those cosmopolitans who belong to Florida's (2002) 'creative class', expected to respond in three economically productive ways: visit Singapore as big-spending tourists, relocate in Singapore and contribute towards the industrialization of the nascent creative industries, or invest in any aspect of Singapore's new economy.

While it is fair to say that there are 'new spaces' in Singapore that do open up from time to time, I have argued here that most of the creative shifts and modifications since the release of the *Creative Industries Development Strategy* in 2002 have been cosmetic and inconsequential – or, in a word, gestural (Lee 2002a). The government's obdurate insistence on measuring the success of various sectors almost solely on economic outcomes may have worked in the past, but such an approach has the potential to limit the development of creativity as Singapore moves towards a differentiated economy, needing in this way to become, as Janadas Devan describes in Chapter 3, 'more odd'. Although the industrialization of creativity, along with cognate fields and industries, is to be expected as the Singaporean economy and society become more developed and sophisticated, Singapore as a polity needs to move beyond such token gestural changes (Lee 2002a; Lee and Lim 2004: 162).

In conclusion, I suggest that the repackaging of Singapore as a 'creative' place for Singaporeans 'to live, to laugh, to grow and to be ourselves' – and also as a 'unique' and 'thrilling' place to visit (Singapore Tourism Board 2004) – should coincide with the loosening of political rigidity in order for 'diverse views' and 'unconventional ideas' to surface in the main (Lee, H.L. 6 January 2004: 6). For Singapore to realize its 'new Asia creative hub' ambition, the government must demonstrate its courage to take real political risks by truly opening up Singapore society. As Cherian George (2000: 207) puts it, 'centralized control' must 'give way to individual autonomy' for creativity and innovation to flourish. All other gestures and rhetoric will not do.

NOTES

1. An earlier version of this paper was presented at the Cultural Studies Association of Australasia's (CSAA) annual conference at Murdoch University, Perth, Australia on 9 December 2004. I am grateful for the constructive comments received at the conference. The research assistance of my former student Denise Lim (Murdoch University), with whom I co-authored an earlier piece analyzing the economics and politics of 'creativity' in Singapore (Lee and Lim 2004), is hereby acknowledged.

REFERENCES

Amabile, T.M. (1990) 'Within you, without you: the social psychology of creativity, and beyond', in M. Runco and R. Albert (eds.), *Theories of Creativity*, California: Sage, pp. 61–91.

Amabile, T.M. and Tighe, E. (1993) 'Questions of creativity', in J. Brockman (ed.) *Creativity*, New York: Touchstone, pp. 7–27.

Bereson, R. (2003) 'Regurgitation or renaissance? arts policy in Singapore 1957–2003', *Asia Pacific Journal of Arts and Cultural Management*, 1(1): 1–14.

Birch, D. (1993) *Singapore Media: communication strategies and practices*, Melbourne: Longman Cheshire.

Boden, M.A. (2004) *The Creative Mind: myths and mechanisms*, 2nd edn, London: Routledge.

Chan, H.C. (1975) *The Dynamics of One Party Dominance: the PAP at the grassroots*, Singapore: Singapore University Press.

Chang, C.T. and Lee, W.K. (2003) 'Renaissance City Singapore: a study of arts spaces', *Area*, 35(2): 129–41.

Chua, M.H. (9 July 2003) 'It's not about gay rights – it's survival', *The Straits Times Interactive* (Singapore). Online. Available HTTP: <http://www.straitstimes.com.sg> (accessed 9 July 2003).

Collins Cobuild English Language Dictionary (1993) London: Harper Collins.

Creative Industries Taskforce (1998) *Creative Industries Mapping Document*, United Kingdom.

Creative Industries Working Group (2002) *Creative Industries Developmental Strategy: propelling Singapore's creative economy*, Report of the Economic Restructuring Committee Services Subcommittee, Singapore, September 2002.

Csikszentmihalyi, M. (1999) 'Implications for a systems perspective for the study of creativity', in R.J. Sternberg (ed.) *Handbook of Creativity*, Cambridge: Cambridge University Press, pp. 313–35.

Design Singapore Council (2003) Website. Online. Available HTTP: <http://www.designsingapore.org> (accessed 12 December 2004).

Elegant, R. (7 July 2003) 'The lion in winter', *Time Asia*, 161(26). Online. Available HTTP: <http://www.time.com/time/asia/covers/501030707/ sea_singapore.html> (accessed 4 September 2003).

Flew, T. (2003) 'Creative industries: from chicken cheer to the culture of services', *Continuum: Journal of Media and Cultural Studies*, 17(1): 89–94.

Flew, T. (2004) 'Creativity, the "new humanism" and cultural studies', *Continuum: Journal of Media and Cultural Studies*, 18(2): 161–78.

Flew, T. (2005) *New Media: an introduction*, 2nd edn, Melbourne: Oxford University Press.

Florida, R. (2002) *The Rise of the Creative Class, and how it's transforming work, leisure, community and everyday life*, New York: Basic Books.

Fong, T. (27 August 2004) 'S'pore on world map of extreme sports', *The Straits Times Interactive* (Singapore). Online. Available HTTP: <http://www. straitstimes.com.sg> (accessed 27 August 2004).

George, C. (2000) *Singapore: the air-conditioned nation*, Singapore: Landmark Books.

George, C. (2002) 'Singapore: media at the mainstream and the margins', in R.H.K. Heng (ed.) *Media Fortune, Changing Times: ASEAN states in transition*. Singapore: Institute of Southeast Asian Studies, pp. 173–200.

Glover, S. and Cunningham, S. (2003) 'The new Brisbane', *Artlink* 23(2): 16–23.

Gomez, J. (2000) *Self-Censorship: Singapore's shame*, Singapore: Think Centre.

Hesmondhalgh, D. (2002) *The Cultural Industries*, London: Sage.

Ho, K.W. (25 September 2004) 'Singapore eyes big slice of games pie', *The Straits Times* (Singapore), p. 1.

Howkins, J. (2001) *The Creative Economy: how people make money from ideas*, London: Allen Lane.

Kong, L. (2000) 'Cultural policy in Singapore: negotiating economic and socio-cultural agendas', *Geoforum*, 31: 409–24.

Lee, H.L. (6 January 2004) 'Building a civic society', speech by the deputy prime minister at the Harvard Club of Singapore's 35th Anniversary Dinner, 6 January 2004, Singapore. Online. Available HTTP: <http:// www.newsintercom.org/index.php?itemid=34> (accessed 22 December 2004).

Lee, H.L. (12 August 2004) Swearing-in speech as prime minister of Singapore on 12 August 2004, Singapore Istana.

Lee, K.Y. (1998) *The Singapore Story: memoirs of Lee Kuan Yew*, Singapore: Times Editions.

Lee, K.Y. (2000) *From Third World to First: the Singapore story 1965–2000*, Singapore: Times Editions.

Lee, T. (2002a) 'The politics of civil society in Singapore', *Asian Studies Review*, 26(1): 97–117.

Lee, T. (2002b) 'New regulatory politics and communication technologies in Singapore', *Asia Pacific Media Educator*, 12/13: 4–25.

Lee, T. (2004) 'Creative shifts and directions: cultural policy in Singapore', *International Journal of Cultural Policy*, 10(3): 281–99.

Lee, T. and Lim, D. (2004) 'The economics and politics of "creativity" in Singapore', *Australian Journal of Communication*, 31(2): 149–65.

Leo, P. (2003) 'Creative restructuring of Singapore media: research lacunas', *Asia Pacific Media Educator*, 14: 4–25.

Leo, P. and Lee, T. (2004) 'The 'new' Singapore: mediating culture and creativity', *Continuum: Journal of Media and Cultural Studies*, 18(2): 205–18.

Little Oxford Dictionary (1998) 7th edn, New York: Oxford University Press.

McCarthy, T. and Ellis, E. (19 July 1999) 'Singapore lightens up', *Time Magazine*, pp. 17–23.

Ministry of Information and the Arts (2000) *Renaissance City Report: culture and the arts in renaissance Singapore*, Singapore. Online. Available HTTP: <http://www.mita.gov.sg/renaissance/FinalRen.pdf> (accessed 22 December 2004).

Neher, C.D. (1999) 'The case for Singapore', in M. Haas (ed.) *The Singapore Puzzle*, Westport: Praeger, pp. 39–54.

Nirmala, M. (4 July 2003) 'Government more open to employing gays now', *The Straits Times Interactive* (Singapore). Online. Available HTTP: <http://www.straitstimes.com.sg> (accessed 4 July 2003).

O'Keefe, B. (17 November 2004) 'Suits can profit from a spell in the sandpit', *The Australian*, p. 34.

one-north (2003) Website. Online. Available HTTP: <http://www.one-north.com/> (accessed 22 December 2004).

Oon, C. (16 November 2004) 'Tap region's "cultural DNA" to get new Asian feel', *The Straits Times Interactive* (Singapore). Online. Available HTTP: <http://www.straitstimes.com.sg> (accessed 16 November 2004).

Reuters (15 November 2003) 'Singapore does some soul searching over sex', *Reuters*.

Singapore Broadcasting Authority (SBA) (2002) *Media 21: transforming Singapore into a global media city*, Singapore: SBA.

Singapore Tourism Board (STB) (9 March 2004) 'Singapore launches its new destination brand "Uniquely Singapore"', Press release.

Singh, K. (2004) *Thinking Hats and Coloured Turbans*, Singapore: Pearson.

Tan, A. (13 March 2004) 'Top-draw resort for southern isles', *The Straits Times Interactive* (Singapore). Online. Available HTTP: <http://www.straitstimes.com.sg> (accessed 13 March 2004).

Tan, K.P. (2003) 'Sexing up Singapore', *International Journal of Cultural Studies*, 6(4): 403–23.

Teo, L. (20 April 2004) 'Casino decision in 6 to 9 months', *The Straits Times Interactive* (Singapore). Online. Available HTTP: <http://www.straitstimes.com.sg> (accessed 20 April 2004).

The Straits Times (21 March 2003) 'Govt has designs on the next big thing', *The Straits Times Interactive* (Singapore). Online. Available HTTP: <http://www.straitstimes.com.sg> (accessed 21 March 2003).

The Straits Times (6 April 2004) 'Gay group fails again to register as society', *The Straits Times Interactive* (Singapore). Online. Available HTTP: <http://www.straitstimes.com.sg> (accessed 6 April 2004).

The Sunday Times (29 August 2004) 'Extreme spin-offs', *The Straits Times Interactive* (Singapore). Online. Available HTTP: <http://www.straitstimes.com.sg> (accessed 29 August 2004).

The West Australian (19 June 2004) 'If your guide book is more than 8 months old, burn it', Singapore Tourism Board 'Uniquely Singapore' advertisement, *The West Australian Weekend Extra*, p. 32.

Throsby, D. (2001) *Economics and Culture*, Cambridge: Cambridge University Press.

Today (13 April 2004) 'What's so subversive about People Like Us?', *Today* (Singapore).

Toh, M.H. et al. (2003) 'Economic contributions of Singapore's creative industries', *Economic Survey of Singapore First Quarter 2003*, Singapore: Ministry of Trade and Industry, pp. 51–75.

Wee, C.J.W.-L. (2003) 'Creating high culture in the globalized "cultural desert" of Singapore', *The Drama Review*, 47(3): 84–97.

Williams, R. (1976) *Keywords: a vocabulary of culture and society*, London: Fontana.

PART 2

NATIONAL IDENTITY AND VALUES
CONTRADICTIONS AND CONTESTATIONS

Censorship in whose name?

KENNETH PAUL TAN[1]

Nearly every justification offered for both general principles and individual acts of censorship in Singapore is linked in some way or other to a social category that has come to be known as the 'heartlanders'. Popularized by then-Prime Minister Goh Chok Tong in his 1999 National Day Rally speech, the word in its most literal sense refers to the great majority of Singaporeans – more than 80 per cent – who live within vast public housing estates. However, this chapter argues that the heartlanders should not be thought of in straightforwardly demographic terms. It is an ideological category that creates in the public imagination an absolute connection between the massive geographical heartlands and some notion of a conservative majority whose ontological horizons are, typically, limited to the boundaries of the nation-state. Firmly rooted to Singapore in a geographical sense, the heartlanders are also supposed to form the bedrock of values, community, and identity, all linked in some reductive way to ethnicity, religion, and nationality.

The heartlander's Other – or what the heartlander is not – is the 'cosmopolitan', described by Goh (19 March 2000) as possessing 'the skills and the global outlook that enable him to do well almost anywhere in the world'. Singapore, as a small nation-state plugged into a complex global network of possibility and threat, keeps in elegant balance these binary categories, casting the majority of Singaporean individuals as 'loyal' subjects whose horizons are local, and a minority as 'creative' subjects whose horizons lie further away. The nation, according to this myth, needs both. And to have both, the nation needs a strong enough government to coordinate the separate advantages that can be reaped from heartlanders and cosmopolitans, while keeping the peace between them. Somewhere in this design is a strategy of 'divide-and-rule' for securing political legitimacy (Tan 2003).

The heartlander as an ideological category provides the state's censorship policies with their terms of reference, including notions of 'public order', 'vulnerable multiracialism', and 'core social values'. The state censors in this way because, it claims, that is exactly what the majority of Singaporeans – the conservative heartlanders – want. Democracy is about being accountable to the majority of voters; and politics more generally is about gaining power by winning the support of the most influential persons or groups of persons in any polity. And so, engineering a conservative majority of Singaporeans and then acting in ways that suggest faithful representation of their interests is a powerful political strategy, but not one that goes completely unnoticed in Singapore. For instance, theatre practitioner Sim Pern Yiau observes that

> when the government talks about who it pretends, consciously or unconsciously, to represent, who is it that they are talking about? It becomes dangerous and limiting when they talk about social mores, because what society are you talking about? Singapore is more than one community, if you talk about offending somebody, who is it that you are talking about? (Bereson 2001: 50)

Louis Althusser's (1971) notion of 'interpellation' offers a useful way of understanding the ideological nature of the heartlander category, which should not be confused with 'sociological realities' based on fixed categories quantifiable by demographic data. In the public sphere, the ideology of nation building – and in particular the ideological instrument of censorship – 'calls out to' concrete Singaporean individuals who are then constituted as nationalized/

moralized subjects belonging to an imagined citizenry dominated by a conservative majority. The ideologically constructed response of the conservative majority to the 'threat' of liberalization has nearly always been offered as justification against calls for change, especially change that may threaten the PAP government's political longevity and wide-ranging powers. In communicating reasons against change, the government has sometimes insinuated that the conservative majority of Singaporeans are ignorant, closed-minded, prudish, self-righteous, repressive, intolerant, oppressive, parochial, xenophobic, incapable of learning, resistant to change, and even boorish – but, it claims, there is absolutely nothing the government can do about it. Censoring the arts is part of a larger government-controlled nation-building project – clearly an ideological project – that re-creates the myth of the heartlander, complete with deficiencies, needs, value system, and political threat to which the government claims it must respond or else lose its moral authority and political legitimacy.

While I argue here that the government has defined the heartlander in terms of qualities that resist change, Woo Yen Yen and Colin Goh argue in Chapter 6 that the government has also belittled – even outlawed – the more creative qualities of heartland Singaporeans such as their use of the local English variant known as Singlish. This, Woo and Goh believe, has effectively excluded the Singlish-speaking heartlander from effective public participation. And yet, as I argue here, the abstract heartlander is constantly invoked in the government's public explanations against change that it does not want.

In response to an interviewer from *The Straits Times* who asked if the Censorship Review Committee's job was to identify the middle position occupied by the 'silent majority' and to censor accordingly, then-Acting Minister for Information, Communications, and the Arts David Lim replied:

> No, leadership is not taking the sum and saying, 'Where does the centre of gravity lie?', and that's what we will do. Leadership is about listening, sensing and then looking beyond the horizon and thinking through as best you can. And getting other people to think through, and help you think through as best they can what lies beyond that horizon. And then making choices. And they're not always easy choices. They sometimes go against the grain. (Tan 13 May 2002)

Lim's vision of thinking 'beyond that horizon', though noble in theory, really falls short in practice where politics, bureaucracy, and prejudice effectively limit the capacity of art and art criticism to enrich the public sphere of communication. The very act of censorship re-creates the arbitrary conditions for its own justification.

Arts censorship: Principles, policies, and practice

The Censorship Review Committee, headed by the chairman of the National Arts Council (a statutory board whose primary aim is to nurture the arts in Singapore), published its report in 2003, presenting a comprehensive series of recommendations based on a year-long public consultation process that involved more than 1,000 Singaporeans whose responses were captured mainly in a survey, from focus group discussions, and through written submissions received from representatives of various communities.

David Lim insisted that his ministry did not intend to play off conservative Singaporeans against the increasingly liberal ones (Tan 13 May 2002). But clearly, the censorship review exercise did seek to determine a new balance between control and liberalization – control to reassure the so-called conservative majority exhorted into being by the nation-building project, and liberalization to satisfy mobile Singaporeans and foreign residents who might demand a more open, liberal, and cosmopolitan range of lifestyle options.

In general, the committee recommended the exercise of greater control over materials that are broadcast directly to homes and displayed in public places, and the relaxation of control in the case of materials that demonstrate artistic and educational merit, appeal to niche audiences, and can be consumed in relative privacy. Conservatives, it could be assumed, desired positive freedom where wisely- and morally-emplaced constraints, defined by 'the community', would serve to elevate the individual from a 'lower' to 'higher' (and therefore 'freer') self. Liberals and cosmopolitans, it could also be assumed, desired negative freedom of the kind that could only be enjoyed in the absence of external human constraints (Berlin 1958).

The 2003 report is the third of such reports that aim, roughly every decade, to review censorship principles, policies, and practices in Singapore. Taken in succession, the three reports chart out the evolution of censorship over the decades, an evolution that one might confidently describe as a very gradual process of liberalization. But the fundamental objectives of censorship, in spite of these changes, appear to remain doggedly intact.

Firstly, censorship aims to help maintain public and social order in a multiethnic and multi-religious society faced, it is frequently asserted, with external and internal security threats. So censorship, according to this view, is in Singapore's national interest. The public discourse, controlled by the People's Action Party (PAP) government and its full complement of ideological instruments, presents Singapore's multiethnic composition as, above all else, a constant source of threat, but one that has historically been contained only through the durable, extensive, and intrusive powers of the government. Censorship is one such instrument by which the government wields these necessary powers, but it is also used in ways that prevent its *raison d'être* from being questioned. In other words, censorship erases arguments against censorship.

The second fundamental objective of censorship is the protection of the vulnerable in society, including the young as well as the (usually minority) ethnic and religious communities that, according to this view, depend on censorship to protect themselves from being misrepresented, disrespected, objectified, debased, exploited, and discriminated against, all out of ignorance, insensitivity, mischief, or malice.

The third objective is the need for censorship to protect the communities' moral norms and standards that are thought to form the basis of Singapore's core social values. These have often included imprecise references to family values, respect for elders and authority, moral integrity, etc. According to this view, the types of censorable content would include pornography, deviant sexual practices, sexual violence, child pornography, bestiality, violence, gore, horror, sexual content and nudity, coarse language, drug consumption, exploitative and promotional homosexuality, race, and religion.

A slow and gradual process of cultural liberalization is consistent with the popular perception that more Singaporeans are gradually becoming more highly educated, affluent, well-travelled, and globally connected; in short, more 'cosmopolitanized'. Technological development and Singapore's desire to become a media and communications hub will mean that Singaporeans will have access to an increasingly diverse range of communications and arts media. Censorship, for this reason alone, would become much more difficult, if not impossible, to enact with any reasonable degree of consistency and stability. The ability to attract talented foreigners to make up for the dearth in indigenous skills necessary for higher order economic development also depends to a great degree on Singapore's ability to sustain for its residents a reasonably stimulating social and cultural life, with greater lifestyle options including those that may appear to contradict the more narrowly conservative value system associated ideologically with Singapore's heartlanders.

The resulting 'liberalized' and 'cosmopolitanized' mindset change could exert political pressure to modify the prevailing value system, allowing for a more sophisticated, diverse, and tolerant cultural environment conducive to the development of an economy driven by world-class talent, creativity, and high technology (Florida 2002). As long as the government recognizes the centrality of global talent, creativity, and innovation in Singapore's new economic environment, it has good reasons to at least reconsider the impact on its own political legitimacy of ideologically constituting a highly censorious society through a rigid nation-building project, since its authority has always been based to a larger extent on economic performance than on moral leadership (Tan 2003).

Beyond the economically determined prospects for arts liberalization, cosmopolitan and liberal Singaporeans celebrate the emergence of a less rigid and closed society in which individuals can make informed choices from a wider array of lifestyle and consumer options, at least in private. Such prospects for liberalization could transform society into a developmental sphere of inquiry, debate, discussion, and experimentation, providing citizens with the intellectual and communicative resources to make, unmake, and remake personal and collective decisions according to a more inclusive notion of rationality.

Many of the changes recommended in the Censorship Review Committee's report, in fact, point towards such a society. For instance, it recommends, firstly, that acts of censorship be discussed in a 'rational and transparent' manner among arts regulators, industry, the community, and artists. Secondly, these stakeholders should all be seen as holding shared responsibility for the arts. Thirdly, discussion about censoring content should be sensitive to the context of each work. Fourthly, opening access to controversial media or content should not necessarily mean endorsement by the government. Fifthly, the report recommended the introduction of more diverse methods of censorship: rating, zoning, and belting, for instance, are means of differentiating a single artistic or cultural product, its availability, and the audience or market. Together with more accurate and detailed consumer advice, these censorship methods, rather than imposing blanket decisions, instead help to enable adult Singaporeans to decide whether they want to see anything that might possibly cause offence. As journalist Tan Tarn How (16 June 2002) argues, censorship 'should be a matter of choice'.

At an arts dialogue held in 2000, then-Minister Lim (in Bereson 2001: 13–18) cautiously spelled out his policy on censorship, arguing that:

1. Artists must act within the law, and not engage in lewd behaviour or commit acts of defamation and sedition;
2. Artists must not threaten social peace in multiracial Singapore, and exceptions to the law can only be made for good artistic reasons;
3. The government should be advised by committees that consist of ordinary citizens;
4. Censorship standards should be set according to the context of each work;
5. There should be a shift from censorship to self-regulation; and
6. Government support must be given based on the quality and commitment of artists to develop the arts in Singapore.

In the same speech, Lim sought a balance between artistic integrity and social responsibility, urging artists to be patient and sensitive to Singapore audiences who might not be sufficiently mature or prepared to engage with difficult and offensive work. He also encouraged audiences to approach experimental work with a 'critical but open mind' (Bereson 2001: 13–18). Although this might be read as a sign of liberalization of the arts, Lim's speech nevertheless contained enough ambiguities to impede any real progress. Phrases such as 'lewd behaviour', 'sedition', 'threaten social peace', 'good artistic reasons', 'ordinary citizens', 'quality', and of course 'artistic integrity' and 'social responsibility' are so ambiguous as to severely discourage artists from breaking new ground in an environment that is ultimately intolerant and punitive.

The constant patronizing and self-fulfilling assertion that Singapore audiences, since they are not sufficiently mature, will not be ready for experimental and challenging work ironically denies artists any real opportunity to challenge audiences in ways that are really quite vital to the latter's development.

The moral voice of the people

The government frequently makes glib references to surveys and regular 'morality polls' carried out by the local media over the years, in order to conclude all too conveniently that Singaporeans are still mostly conservative (for example, Chong 7 July 2002), and from this observation that at least two prevailing assumptions must continue to hold. Firstly, the process of liberalization, though unavoidably brought on by globalization and technological development, must nevertheless be controlled and slowed down to a gradual process. Journalist Koh Buck Song (1996) argues that 'in the liberalization of censorship, patience is the first lesson to be learnt'. The second assumption supported by these surveys and polls is that the majority of Singaporeans, characterized as conservative and moralistic, expect the government to play a leading role in censorship.

At the same time, however, it is the government that hails Singaporeans as a conservative majority forming the bedrock of national identity, which is presented nearly always as unstable and threatened by the ineluctable forces of globalization. By constructing the conservative majority as an unquestionable – even valuable – given, the government claims its moral authority to continue exercising power in a paternalistic, perfectionist, and thoroughly pervasive manner, all performed in their name.

Surveys and polls are among the most tangible of hailing mechanisms. By and large, people do not have finite, well-articulated opinions – much less arguments – about most things. When specific questions are asked, respondents produce opinions resulting from a milieu of diverse dispositions, orientations, experiences, memories, leanings, influences, linguistic competence, etc. And these 'on-the-spot' opinions may enjoy some durability, but not necessarily. Survey questions, for reasons of economy, rarely allow for nuanced answers. And the questions themselves are reduced to propositional stimuli that again restrict the range of possible responses. Since questions cannot, realistically, be framed in value-neutral language (any utterance, after all, immediately assumes a position), surveys and polls can easily suggest the right answers, even without intending to.

Although it is not suggested here that opinions are completely dictated by lines of questioning, it is argued that survey results on such topics as 'morality' will exaggerate certain dispositions; and so one ends up with repeated claims about the higher-than-average extent of conservatism amongst Singaporeans (Tan 2003: 410). If the ordinary citizen is constantly bombarded with these figures, he or she will almost certainly think twice about whether to utter in public any views that might depart too much from the imaginary norms of 'the community'.

Public and social order, and the national interest

The image of conservative heartlanders obsessed with public order and the national interest has been cultivated over the decades through national narratives about permanent vulnerability and fragile success, and through the pervasive economic, social, cultural, and political institutions that discipline Singaporeans to behave according to the imperatives set up by these dominant narratives.

The basic argument that censorship helps to maintain public and social order (for example, Storck 1996) in ways that are consistent with the national interest can be broken down into smaller components.

1. There are ideas that are erroneous, and therefore bad.
2. These ideas can be communicated through art.
3. Art that communicates erroneous ideas is itself erroneous, and is therefore bad art.
4. Bad ideas and bad art can directly influence the behaviour and action of individuals who receive them.
5. The individuals' bad behaviour and action can bring harm to themselves, and also to society, thereby threatening public order. Erroneous ideas and erroneous art are therefore dangerous.
6. Censorship of erroneous ideas and erroneous art will therefore protect individuals and society from danger.

Forum theatre in Singapore

In 1994, the government stopped funding forum theatre performances in Singapore, following a sensationalized media report (Soh
1994) that characterized them as by nature provocative, agitational,
politically motivated, and therefore dangerous. By most accounts,
the termination amounted to a *de facto* ban on this theatre form
that had been introduced to Singaporeans only a year earlier by
theatre company The Necessary Stage. (Its artistic director Alvin Tan
describes in Chapter 10 the company's current 'global strategy' to get
around the censors.)

Forum theatre was founded in Brazil by radical arts practitioner,
social activist, and politician Augusto Boal (Boal 1979; Schutzman
and Cohen-Cruz 1994). In a typical performance of forum theatre, a
short scene – the anti-model – is presented usually in intimate spaces
or public places. In this scene, whose main theme or issue is normally
of immediate relevance to the target audience, the protagonist is
prevented from arriving at his or her desired destination because
the way is blocked by an antagonist who presents and represents
obstacles and oppressions in life. At the end of the performance,
the same scene is replayed. But this time, members of the audience
are encouraged to intervene by stopping the scene at any point,
physically taking on the role of the protagonist, and then acting out
alternative actions that might lead to better outcomes. Through this
vital participation in the unfolding of the work, audiences become
'spect-actors' – passive spectators activated into actors. A facili-
tator – known as the 'joker' – then leads the audience in discussion
to assess these alternative solutions.

Alternative realms of possibility, grounded in the material reality
of the present situation, are articulated, played out, and deliberated in
a structured, voluntary, and purposeful manner. Forum theatre, theoretically at least, activates passive audiences and provides them with
theatre space as a rehearsal for dealing with obstacles and oppressions in real life. Theoretically, it is a social activity that empowers
individuals with opportunities for critical self-reflection that may
lead, through collective verbal and bodily articulation, to higher levels
of consciousness, that in turn can generate the will and capacity to
liberate the self from life's seemingly insurmountable yet often difficult to locate problems. Forum theatre, again at least theoretically, can

be a means of developing communicative intelligence, courage, and social responsibility. These are in turn skills and dispositions necessary, it might be argued, for healthy democracy.

Academic Sanjay Krishnan (1997), who was present at the 1993 forum theatre performances of *MCP* and *Mixed Blessings* by The Necessary Stage, claims that he had 'never seen a group of people [the audience] so engaged by a literary work, or so excited by a theatrical experience, in Singapore' (p. 202). TNS' artistic director Alvin Tan (quoted in Chew 22 February 2006) describes how his works have empowered audiences by getting them to find the 'interconnections, getting people to fill in the gaps themselves ... when people did get it, they couldn't stop talking about it because they filled in the gaps with their own information'. *MCP* and *Mixed Blessings* were about spousal abuse and inter-racial relationships respectively. Both plays ended in tragedy for the protagonists. Both plays, very local and recognizable in setting, could serve not only as critiques of patriarchal orientations and the superficial practice of 'multiracialism' in Singapore's mainstream culture, but also as an educational resource for dealing with obstacles that may arise from such taken-for-granted cultural orientations in everyday life. Instead of regarding forum theatre as an opportunity for critical thinking (which generally has a positive resonance in Singapore), the censors decided to view it as a source of danger to Singapore's fragile stability.

The arguments for censoring forum theatre might be reconstructed in this way:

1. It is a mistake to interrogate the principles and practices of multiracialism (even if it conceals systematic racial prejudice) and patriarchy (even if it normalizes violence against women) since these have thus far helped to achieve and maintain order and stability in a Singapore that continues to face ever-present threats.

2. Forum theatre not only promotes the articulation of these order-threatening (and so erroneous) alternatives but, as a largely unscripted form of performance, also does this in a most unpredictable and uncontrollable manner.

3. Forum theatre performances are therefore erroneous, and they are examples of bad art.

4. Exposure to erroneous alternatives through forum theatre can directly influence the behaviour and action of each participant.
5. Individuals who are influenced by these erroneous alternatives can act in ways that bring harm to themselves and to society, threatening public order that is based on a 'deliberately' taken-for-granted, unproblematic, and uncritical practice of multiracialism and patriarchy.
6. Censoring forum theatre, an inherently transgressive form that is dangerous to individual and society, will therefore protect Singapore for the conservative community who make up the majority of its population.

Apart from the circularity of this argument, there are other weaknesses too. Firstly, there can never really be any certainty about truth, if at all there is such a thing as an absolute truth. Even if 'truths' are determined by the consensus of a community, there is no real sense in which any community, much less a Singaporean community consisting of several smaller ethnic and religious communities, can be monolithic and coherent in its beliefs and values. Calling such a community of communities 'Asian' is also meaningless, as 'Asian' has increasingly become, or perhaps has always been, a historically conditioned notion at best, and an empty signifier at worst. This is not just a problem that arises from philosophical scepticism, but one that draws from concerns about how a community that becomes rigidly conventional, losing its self-critical ability, will ossify into a fragile and hollow shell. A living community needs to be open to ideas not just from without but from within, recognizing instead of denying or feeling threatened by its natural diversity.

The argument that individuals are directly and uncritically influenced by the ideas and images they encounter in their daily lives is too simplistic. There must, of course, be some influence – for example, ideas and images might provoke unconventional thought – but to assume that they will necessarily lead to harmful actions that destroy the individuals and their society is something of an exaggeration motivated by self-sustaining paranoia. It reflects a deeply insecure community built on mistrust. To view as bad influence any art work that conveys 'bad' ideas diminishes the sense in which art of this kind might be doing the useful work of identifying and reflecting deep problems in society that go unnoticed in everyday life – deep problems that, if ignored, may one day erupt and cause much greater damage beyond anyone's expectation and control. An art form that enables critical thinking and discussion can be a vital component of a living community.

If there were such a thing as 'absolute truth', perhaps it may emerge more easily from conditions of free critical debate than dogmatism. No one has the monopoly on knowing for certain what is true; and advances in media and communications technology have made it impossible to censor completely and uniformly. All censorship, even with the best of intentions, is therefore arbitrary. Furthermore, as art critic Lee Weng Choy argues, 'censorship is always an arbitrary exercise of power' (Davis 2004: 296): censorship is a basic form of thought-control, thought-control is a basic tool of dictatorial government, and the assumption that censors are not unintelligent or malicious is often questionable. According to Salman Rushdie, whose novel *The Satanic Verses* has been banned in Singapore,

> a free society is not a calm and eventless place – that is the kind of static, dead society dictators try to create. Free societies are dynamic, noisy, turbulent and full of radical disagreement. Skepticism and freedom are indissolubly linked. (Rushdie 18 April 1996)

Protecting multiracialism

Dynamism, noise, turbulence, and radical disagreement have not generally been welcome in Singapore, where the focus since independence has been on the task of forging a sustainable national identity out of a multiethnic society consisting of a large majority of ethnically Chinese Singaporeans (75 per cent), a numerically significant minority of Malays (14 per cent), and the remainder made up mostly of Indians (9 per cent) and a much smaller contingent of Eurasians.

However, the nation-building strategy – particularly since the 1980s – has been to retain ethnic divisions, with the effect sometimes of exaggerating them. In a society that is kept ethnically divided, the levels of sensitivity in the public space become extraordinarily heightened, so that any utterance that makes even tangential reference to ethnicity and religion is treated with deep suspicion and hostility. Ironically, this 'over-sensitivity' has produced a public sphere that is anything but sensitive to and critical of the deeper issues that continue to prevent Singaporeans from better understanding their own society, culture, and politics. In this context of exaggerated ethnic division, it would be unsurprising to learn that cautious Singaporeans choose a 'calm and eventless place' over a free society that is 'dynamic, noisy, turbulent and full of radical disagreement'.

On interethnic matters, the government secures its role as sole umpire, often using censorship in ways that also do not give depth to the practice of 'multiracialism', but instead respond to various degrees of hypocrisy, where the moral high-ground is articulated in public, whilst prejudices continue to proliferate in private. Ironically, a critical sensitivity at the social level has been so blunted by these public acts of censorship that the flood of negative ethnic stereotypes on local film and television go practically unnoticed. The solution should not be to censor every ethnic stereotype that appears in any work of art or popular culture, but instead to use these actively and critically in order not to reinforce the prejudices from which they spring, but to question society's latent assumptions that are the real source of fear and social depthlessness in Singapore. Otherwise, the opportunity to correct and criticize latent prejudices, bigotry, and hypocrisy will be buried (Tan 2004).

The practice of multiracialism has been largely an escapist's fantasy, a refusal to acknowledge real problems that need to be addressed at the public level, choosing instead to whitewash over them in the hopes that they will disappear. Art work that challenges this fantasy is viewed unfavourably.

Talaq, *violence against women, and religious sensitivities*

In 2000, theatre company Agni Koothu was refused a licence to perform *Talaq*, a play that explored 'oppression, marital violence and rape and the culture of silence forced on [women] by their families' (*Channel NewsAsia* 29 October 2000). The play was based on real-life personal accounts given by several Indian Muslim women. Earlier performances in Tamil had received very favourable reviews, although there were protests (including some death threats) issued by religious groups over the sensitive content of the play. What seemed to be most offensive about the play was the way it appeared to present Islamic marriages in unfavourable light. In the final scene, for instance, the protagonist shed her black robe and walked into a green light, depicting, according to the director, a rejection of patriarchal violence and oppression in favour of a purer Islam that accorded women great respect (green is the colour of Islam). Critics from some religious organizations, however, chose to interpret this as a rejection of Islam itself (Hamilton 26 March 1999).

According to an account published in local arts journal *Focas*, a private preview for the fourth run was attended by some members of the Public Entertainment Licensing Unit (PELU), the National Arts Council, the Drama Review Committee, the Islamic Religious Council of Singapore (MUIS), and the South Indian Jamiathul Ulama (SIJU), the last two representing the 'complainants'. Following discussions, PELU took the cautious move of not issuing a licence for performance. This prompted a series of manoeuvres between Agni Kootthu and the authorities that at its height saw the arrest of the theatre company's president (Chua 29 October 2000; *Talaq* documents 2000). The events drew considerable media attention locally and internationally (Liew 2000), and have become iconic of the view that Singapore has little room for the arts as long as it remains paranoid about itself.

The ban on *Talaq* was a lost opportunity to deal constructively and concretely with a real social problem – violence against women – that goes beyond religion or ethnic group. It was also a lost opportunity to discuss and possibly correct ethnic stereotypes and misunderstandings in an open, rational, and critical public space not limited by political correctness and mistrust. Instead, the ban leaves Singaporeans more fearful of their ethnic Other, believing additionally that ethnic minorities are too weak to stand up for themselves and their beliefs, preferring the heavy hand of government censorship to protect them from engaging with the larger society. An over-reliance on government censorship for protection not only weakens a minority community's resilience and sense of self-worth, but may also backfire when an over-censorious climate makes censorship very available to the majority for use against minority expression. Censorship re-creates the conditions that call for (more) censorship.

Moral standards and core social values

The third principle of censorship in Singapore is based on the argument that censorship must protect the community's moral standards and society's core values that are based on these standards. Censorship is needed to eliminate ideas and artistic content that are immoral, indecent, obscene, demeaning, and violent, preventing them from promoting actions and lifestyles that are also immoral, indecent, obscene, demeaning, and violent. Shared standards of morality, which are the basic structure of any society, will determine exactly what should be censored.

According to this overtly communitarian view, it is permissible for censorship and the more punitive application of obscenity laws (Chan 1996) to be used as a means of enforcing conformity to society's shared morality, even if the basis for this morality turns out to be mistaken. As a basic structure, shared morality is as essential to society's existence as its government. If the common standards of morality are not safeguarded, society will simply disintegrate, and since individuals can only find true fulfilment through social membership, there can be no valid argument against the censorship of anything that threatens the integrity of society and community (Devlin 1965). By protecting and even strengthening a community's shared standards of morality, censorship – consistent with arguments for positive freedom – forces individuals to be free of their baser selves.

In Singapore, the idea of a 'community' is once again ideologically linked to the heartlander class – whose members are really the products of state control and discipline – as well as the construction of national values for a 'new' and 'multiethnic' nation. Community has been situated firmly within romanticized notions of the 'ethnicized' or 'Asianized' national heartlands, where Singaporeans are flatteringly defined as patriotic keepers of core values that have helped Singapore to survive and become prosperous in a dangerous world full of negative, destabilizing, and disintegrating influences that come with modernization and globalization. The report of the Censorship Review Committee 2003 (p. 36) even refers to the need to protect the 'wholesome ambience' of public housing estates.

Josef Ng and performance art

The monomaniacal emphasis on building a pure Asianized heartland community coupled with hegemonic accounts of Singapore as an exemplary but fragile success story have to a large degree generated a puritanically self-congratulatory society that, when provoked, can be quite intolerant of difference, change, and experimentation, viewing these as threats to society's basic structure.

Journalist Alejandro Reyes (2000) describes Singapore as a 'buttoned-down society that [is] boring and obsessed with rules, results and founding father Lee Kuan Yew'. In this society, art works that bring audiences discomfort by representing 'degraded' aspects of life and not conforming to familiar and popular artistic formats often draw expressions of outrage, ridicule, and censure, but seldom from any critically informed position. For these kinds of reasons, the Censorship Review Committee 2003 recommended that R21 films (with an age 21 restriction) should not be screened in cinemas located within the heartlands to avoid 'offending residents in HDB estates' (p. 13). These films often contain nudity, violence, and homosexual content, deemed offensive to the conservative majority. How art actually offends the heartlanders is a somewhat complex matter that transcends questions of morality, decency, and obscenity.

In 1994, the government terminated funding not only for forum theatre but also for performance art, a site- and time-specific, multi-disciplinary form that often features multimedia and the artist's own body and activity. The government's reaction followed sensationalized coverage in the local media of artist Josef Ng's licensed performance in a public shopping centre. Ng's piece was a protest against earlier media reports that sensationalized the arrest of twelve men for homo-sexual solicitation. Ng was banned from performing in Singapore: his work regarded as offensive to public decency (Lee 1996). What drew public attention was a section in the work when Ng uttered 'I have heard that clipping hair can be a form of silent protest', turned away from the audience, snipped off his pubic hair, and placed it on a tile for the audience to see.

The obsession with decency and obscenity prevented the public from even trying to understand what the artist had intended by his performance, much less the artistic complexity, sociological-anthro-pological origins, and historical significance of performance art itself (Langenbach 1996; Goldberg 2001). The critical possibilities of Ng's work, the opportunity for professional development in a more diverse arts community, and the potential for widening the critical vocabulary of Singapore audiences were all obscured by the spectacle that the outraged Singaporeans only chose to see, and eliminated by state censorship that was based on a hypothetical expectation that Singaporeans would have been offended by such a work if they had seen it in its entirety.

It could be argued that a conservative majority with limited artistic horizons will not have the intellectual capacity to make sense of art work that goes beyond the facile. This is not just a story of the culture industry that demands a regressive audience to whom it can efficiently sell standardized, pre-digested, highly patterned, pseudo-individual-ized, and mimetic art work, commodified into light entertainment that delights workers in their leisure hours, preparing them for the next work day (Adorno 1941). This is also a story about the way heart-landers might choose to cope with or respond to the alienation that comes from encounters with difficult art work, in the absence of a crit-ical vocabulary to make sense of it. Difficult and critical art can often be an affront to the heartlands; and so heartlanders will violate art that appears to violate them, or that makes them feel stupid, deceived, or challenged. Without the (socially located) knowledge to decode an art work, how will the heartlander be expected immediately to engage with the art work itself rather than what is thought to be represented by the work, or aesthetics rather than morality, or form rather than function, or manner rather than matter (Bourdieu 1984)?

An uncritical exercise of state censorship actually reinforces the preconceptions and prejudices that defined the 'offence' in the first place, further restricting in this way the heartlanders' access to a richer body of critical resources to make sense of art, and even what it might represent. In his keynote speech at the Second World Summit on the Arts and Culture held in Singapore, Ho Kwon Ping argued that art installations and performance art were undeserving of public funding.

> As we all trudge respectfully through some of the most ridiculous art installations, intimidated into grudging silence, it's usually the children who ... have the honesty to say what they really think ... Some years ago, a young performance artist in Singapore snipped his pubic hair and urinated in public. Perhaps this would have been considered revolutionary and lionized in London, but this is Singapore, so the authorities banned the performance, which was probably as silly as the act itself. (Ho 2003)

Ho's words, unfortunately, encourage people to refuse to engage with difficult art, and so close the door to intellectual resources that can help to develop sensitivity, critical faculties, imagination, and a wider and more diverse appreciation for the arts.

If the conservative majority can get past the obsession with decency, and not resort to calls for censorship every time there is an aesthetic encounter that is unfamiliar and uncomfortable, perhaps the process of maturing as an audience can begin. A vibrant society is one that is alive with imagination and alternative visions and possibilities. To help achieve this, the arts should not simply affirm the status quo, but actually transcend it through experimentation and critique. A vibrant living community cannot be based on self-congratulatory ignorance of alternatives secured through rigid and self-imposed censorship.

Renaissance Singapore in the heartland grip

The *Renaissance City Report*, launched in 2000, articulated a vision of renaissance Singapore as 'creative, vibrant and imbued with a keen sense of aesthetics' (p. 5). Although terms like 'Asian heritage', 'Singapore Heartbeat', and 'Singapore stories' continue to be present in the renaissance city rhetoric in ways that might appeal to the ideologically conceived heartlanders, it is clear that less rigidly communitarian and nationalistic values are emerging in the discourse with the use of 'creative culture', 'global economy', 'adventurous spirit', 'passion for life', and 'active citizens'. The report, promising – in quite concrete terms – policies that would facilitate the development of a vibrant arts scene, was nevertheless met with a degree of scepticism; not least because of the way the arts continue to be valued as positive adjuncts to the larger global economy. Within such a framework, the ideologically conceived heartlanders with 'middle-class aspirations' would want to consume art work for light entertainment or prestige value, rather than experience art as powerful opportunities for active critical self-reflection.

In the 'old' politics, the heartlands were constructed as conservative; their fear of change and difference would prop up the status quo, a society protected against itself by a paternalistic, perfectionist, and pervasive PAP government synonymous with the state and perhaps even with the nation. Nurturing the heartland majority in this way provided the PAP government with a reliable source of political (and especially electoral) support. The principles, policies, and practices of censorship, justified by the conservative community's interest in public order, multiracial harmony, and moral and social values, re-established the heartland majority as conservative in orientation and unchangingly so.

Arts administrator T. Sasitharan argues against the simplistic notion that artistic transgressions must be confined to what is regarded narrowly as social responsibility.

> On the one hand, you say that art should be allowed to challenge the status quo and on the other, you say that you have to be socially responsible... You have to accept the fact that if the artist challenge[s] the status quo, then at the point at which the challenge is most effective and intense, where it is being most pertinent, he is being irresponsible. (Sasitharan, in Bereson 2001: 52)

If Singapore artists are to be more passionately adventurous and crea-tive, then censorship needs to be freed from the ideological 'heartland grip', so that a new multi-vocal community of artists, audiences, and government can emerge and build new trust, respect, social capital, and intellectual and artistic resources. In such a community, censorship itself could be transformed into something that is more productive than restrictive. For instance, if it is 'in the nature of art to challenge convention' (Censorship Review Committee 2003: 40), then *some* censorship can in fact reveal more clearly to artists (and audiences) the objects of critique; it may force artists to become more inven-tive, sharper in their critique, and more resourceful. Censored artists may become celebrated figures and censored works may become the objects of wider discussion beyond what their own merits might have been able to generate. Without any censorship at all, art and artists might in fact stagnate. But if censorship is enforced too rigidly – and with the full force of the state – as a powerful instrument of intoler-ance, prejudice, and ignorance, then the arts will be suffocated.

The renaissance city idea might be part of a cautious strategy to renew Singapore society and prepare it for the kinds of skills and dispositions needed for success in the new creative economy. At the same time, the government risks losing the support of 'old economy'

Singaporeans who make up the conservative heartlands and who rely on a predictable 'old politics' of control, discipline, and order. Finding the right balance in order to maintain its position in power is a complicated task for the government. But sanitizing the inherently problematic nature of the arts through technocratic methods will not lead to cultural and artistic vibrancy. As arts educator Sandy Philips explains,

> the arts have to grow and develop and because you or we try to please everyone all the time, we are going to end up with compromise. Compromise is something which is going to lead to bland theatre, bland arts and a total lack of creative integrity. (Philips, in Bereson 2001: 52)

Minister David Lim had pointed out that in the arts, and indeed in everything else, the government had to make difficult choices that 'go against the grain'. This chapter argues that 'going against the grain' to unleash the considerable power of art for self-understanding and critique will not be possible as long as intolerance, lack of experience, and superficiality remain the unavoidable by-products of a nation-building project whose laws, policies, and practices have been based on fear, enforced consensus, and narrowly defined economic and political goals.

NOTES

1. I wish to thank my former colleagues at the National University of Singapore's Political Science Department, especially Alan Chong and Benjamin Goldsmith, who provided helpful comments and suggestions during a seminar where an earlier version of this chapter was presented.

REFERENCES

Adorno, T.W. (1941) 'On popular music', in J. Storey (ed.) (1994) *Cultural Theory and Popular Culture: a reader*, Hertfordshire: Harvester Wheatsheaf, pp. 202–14.
Althusser, L. (1971) *'Lenin and Philosophy' and Other Essays*, London: New Left Books.
Bereson, R. (ed.) (2001) *Artistic Integrity and Social Responsibility: you can't please everyone!*, Singapore: Ethos Books.
Berlin, I. (1958) *Two Concepts of Liberty* (an inaugural lecture delivered before the University of Oxford on 31 October 1958), Oxford: Clarendon Press.

Boal, A. (1979) *Theatre of the Oppressed*, trans. C.A. and M-O.L McBride, New York: Urizen Books.

Bourdieu, P. (1984) *Distinction: a social critique of the judgement of taste*, trans. R. Nice, Cambridge: Harvard University Press.

Censorship Review Committee 2003 (2003) Report, Singapore: Ministry of Information, Communications and the Arts. Online. Available HTTP: <http://www.mda.gov.sg/MDA/documents/Censorship_Review_2003.pdf> (accessed 22 December 2004).

Chan, W.C. (1996) 'Obscenity and the law', in S. Krishna et al. (eds.), *Commentary: looking at culture*, Singapore, pp. 116–22.

Channel NewsAsia. (29 October 2000) 'President of drama group behind Talaq play arrested', *Channel NewsAsia* (Singapore).

Chew, D. (22 February 2006) 'A necessary revolution', *Today* (Singapore), 42–43.

Chong, C.K. (7 July 2002) 'Young Singaporeans more liberal in their attitudes', *The Straits Times* (Singapore).

Chua, C.H. (29 October 2000) 'Head of arts group arrested', *The Straits Times* (Singapore).

Davis, L. (2004) 'State of censorship Singapore post-CRC 3', *Forum on Contemporary Art & Society*, 5: 295–308.

Devlin, P. (1965) *The Enforcement of Morals*, Oxford: Oxford University Press.

Florida, R. (2002) *The Rise of the Creative Class, and how it's transforming work, leisure, community and everyday life*, New York: Basic Books.

Goh, C.T. (22 August 1999) Speech at the National Day Rally on 22 August 1999, Singapore. Online. Available HTTP: <http://app.sprinter.gov.sg/data/pr/1999082202.htm> (accessed 28 February 2003).

Goh, C.T. (19 March 2000) 'CDCs: local authorities and community governance', keynote address by the prime minister at the Community Development Council Seminar on 19 March 2000, Singapore.

Goldberg, R. (2001) *Performance Art: from Futurism to the present*, London: Thames & Hudson.

Hamilton, A. (26 March 1999) 'The rights of marriage', *Asiaweek*.

Ho, K.P. (23 November 2003) 'Global trends: arts, people & policy', keynote speech at Second World Summit on the Arts and Culture on 23 November 2003, Singapore.

Koh. B.S. (1996) 'Liberalising the arts', in S. Krishna et al. (eds.) *Commentary: looking at culture*, Singapore, pp. 107–150.

Krishnan, S. (1997) 'What art makes possible: remembering forum theatre', in *Nine Lives: 10 years of Singapore theatre: essays commissioned by The Necessary Stage*, Singapore: The Necessary Stage.

Langenbach, R. (1996) 'Leigong da doufu: looking back at "Brother Cane"', in S. Krishna et al. (eds.) *Commentary: looking at culture*, Singapore, pp. 123–38.

Lee, W.C. (1996) 'Chronology of a controversy', in S. Krishna et al. (eds.) *Commentary: looking at culture*, Singapore, pp. 63–72.

Liew, K.K. (2000) 'Between sensationalism and information: *Talaq* and the media', *Forum on Contemporary Art & Society*, 1: 173–80.

Ministry of Information and the Arts (2000) *Renaissance City Report: culture and the arts in renaissance Singapore*, Singapore. Online. Available HTTP: <http://www.mita.gov.sg/renaissance/FinalRen.pdf> (accessed 22 December 2004).

Reyes, A. (24 March 2000) 'Agents of change', *Asiaweek*. Online. Available HTTP: <http://www.asiaweek.com/asiaweek/magazine/2000/0324/cover.4people.html> (accessed 22 December 2004).

Rushdie, S. (18 April 1996) '"Respect" and the thought police', *Los Angeles Times*.

Schutzman, M. and Cohen-Cruz, J. (eds.) (1994) *Playing Boal: theatre, therapy, activism*, London: Routledge.

Soh, F. (5 February 1994) 'Two pioneers of forum theatre trained at Marxist workshops', *The Straits Times* (Singapore).

Storck, T. (1996) 'A case for censorship', *New Oxford Review*, 70(5).

'Talaq documents' (2000) *Forum on Contemporary Art & Society*, 1: 181–211.

Tan, K.P. (2003) 'Sexing up Singapore', *International Journal of Cultural Studies*, 6(4), 403–24.

Tan, K.P. (2004) 'Ethnic representation on Singapore film and television', in A.E. Lai (ed.) *Beyond Rituals and Riots: ethnic pluralism and social cohesion in Singapore*, Singapore: Eastern Universities Press, pp. 289–315.

Tan, T.H. (13 May 2002) 'A remaking of rules on censorship', *The Straits Times* (Singapore).

Tan, T.H. (16 June 2002) 'In censorship, it should be a matter of choice', *The Straits Times* (Singapore).

Caging the bird

TalkingCock.com and the pigeonholing of Singaporean citizenship

WOO YEN YEN JOYCELN AND COLIN GOH

It was 6 September 2001, and we had finished conducting auditions at the Substation[1] for *TalkingCock The Movie*, a film based on our increasingly popular website, *TalkingCock.com*.

We were amazed by the over 200 Singaporeans who had turned up. Instead of drama queens and aspiring MediaCorp[2] stars, the majority were ordinary folk – students, teachers, insurance agents, and even civil servants. This was especially surprising because only a couple of weeks earlier the government had considered in parliament the question of whether *TalkingCock.com* needed to register as a political website (*TalkingCock.com* n.d.). Some came to the auditions with complete comedy routines, some with original songs, and some simply to say hello and thank us for daring to post our satirical humour articles.

The find of the night, however, materialized when we sat down for a nightcap at the 'S-11' food court at the foot of the now-demolished National Library. At an adjacent table, surrounded by around 15 young people, was a large, jovial man with mischievous eyes, big hair, and a scraggly beard. He was clearly holding court, sending his companions into fits of giggles with tales told in his sonorous and laughing voice. It was as if we had witnessed Shakespeare's Sir John Falstaff reincarnated in a polo T-shirt. We just knew he had to be in our film. Approaching him, we learned that his name was Ron, that he was a taxi driver, and that his audience were members of his online chat group. After some cajoling, Ron agreed to a screen test.

When he arrived the next day with his posse from the night before, we knew we were in the presence of a major comedic talent. He had no routine; he was simply witty, effervescent, and irreverent as he spoke in Singlish and Hokkien. His posse – and indeed, we ourselves – seemed to find everything that tumbled from his mouth hilarious. We asked him to play Professor Lai Piah Chwee (Hokkien for 'come and fight'), the dean of Hoot U, the university for *ah bengs* (defined by TalkingCock.com's *Coxford Singlish Dictionary* as 'unsophisticated young Chinese hoodlums'). Ron's skills seemed endless. On the set, he was the undisputed king of the ad lib, extemporizing his lines into the most energetic Hokkien we had ever heard. It was all the cast and crew could do to keep from laughing and ruining each take. The most amazing incident, however, came when we asked him to speak a few lines for a song we wanted to mix into our soundtrack (later remixed into an original comedy CD album, *TalkingCock SingingSong* (Woo and Goh 2002)). Within two minutes, he crafted a rap which not only fit the meter of the track, but also rhymed – in Hokkien. It was spectacular.

Chance meetings with talented, creative, and spontaneous Singaporeans like Ron have been the story of *TalkingCock.com*. It was how the website (online since 4 August 2000) got started – over the dinner table with friends, wondering why there wasn't the Singaporean equivalent of *The Onion* or *Mad Magazine*, or even a simple website where people could share the same irreverent stories as we did in real life, seated in a coffee shop, over a convivial cup of coffee and a slice of toast with *guyu kaya* (Hokkien for 'butter with coconut and egg jam'). Hence the name 'talking cock', a Singlish phrase that means 'to engage in idle banter or to talk nonsense', a phrase that has also been uttered at least three times in Singapore's parliament. The first time was when David Marshall was chief minister (Josey 1982). The second time was when opposition member Ling How Doong was reprimanded for exclaiming 'Don't talk cock!' at his colleague

Chiam See Tong. The third time was when *TalkingCock.com* itself was debated in parliament in August 2001 (*TalkingCock.com* n.d.).

TalkingCock.com soon connected us with a battery of funny and incisive Singaporean writers from all over the world, working under poultry-related pseudonyms such as Kway Png, K.K. Cheow, Chicken Little, Jane Hencock, Lau Cheow, Phoenix Klaw, and Kok Kok Kway, as well as various computer whizzes who kindly donated technical support.

There were also the 109 Singaporeans who, like Ron, made their screen debuts in *TalkingCock The Movie*. Even Ramli Sarip, the Malaysian rock guru who is actually Singaporean, contributed a cameo. Many musicians and voice artistes from different generations and ethnicities also came forward to share their talents in *TalkingCock SingingSong*, our music and comedy CD album (Woo and Goh 2002). On the one hand, we had the band Boredphucks (now called the Suns, they are Singapore's answer to the Ramones), and on the other, Thubten Kway, of the famous 1970s band the Flybaits, who took leave from his job as a tennis centre manager in Germany to make his reappearance on the Singapore music scene with us.

Meeting all these people through *TalkingCock.com* has been a very strange experience. Firstly, everyone who works on *TalkingCock*-related events either does not get paid, or gets paid a token sum that is probably just enough to buy coffee and toast with *guyu kaya*. Secondly, many of those who got involved had never done these things before. Singaporeans taking risks, and for nothing but the fun of it? How strange!

Normal Singaporeans

Strange, at least, when compared to the portrait of Singaporeans that is usually proffered.

On 22 February 2003, we were invited to speak at a symposium on 'remaking' Singapore organized by Singaporean students at the University of Pennsylvania, many of whom were well-spoken, from middle-class homes, and on government scholarships. The panellists were discussing how Singapore needed a more open political culture when an articulate male undergraduate raised his objection to that sentiment. He said it was easy for us – the 'elite' – to sit around in

North America, talking about change, when we had no idea what the average 'heartlander' who lives in a HDB estate really wanted. 'They', the heartlanders, did not really care about a more open society, but for the bigger flat and bigger car, and 'we', the elite minority, had no right to make decisions about their political culture for them. This student's perception of problematic heartlanders – Singaporeans of a lower socioeconomic status who are *kiasu* (a Hokkien adjective literally meaning 'afraid of losing'), dependent, and materialistic, and who resist change – is consistent with the political leadership's portrayal of the majority of Singaporeans, as Kenneth Paul Tan discusses in Chapters 1 and 4.

In 1999, for instance, then-Prime Minister Goh Chok Tong talked about the divide between the 'cosmopolitans' who have access to global opportunities and the 'heartlanders' who do not (Chua 28 August 1999; Balakrishnan 2000). In 2001, he gave the example of a well-dressed young man who felt that the S$200 he had been given as aid for Hougang's needy constituents was 'not even enough' to meet the monthly mortgage payments on his car. And then in 2002, Goh pilloried a retrenched man who refused to take a cleaner's job because it meant lowering his expectations. More recently, in a speech to the Harvard Club of Singapore on building a 'civic society', then-Deputy Prime Minister Lee Hsien Loong highlighted how only a minority of Singaporeans are concerned about a more open political culture, while the majority – the 'less articulate majority' of Singaporeans who 'do not play golf' – are more interested in bread-and-butter issues. They are assumed to be more concerned with the material issues of 'jobs, security, and a better future for their children' and less with issues that will benefit the broader community (Lee 6 January 2004).

The narrative of citizenship that emerges from governmental sources has been a narrative that details the shortcomings of Singaporeans, especially heartlanders who are resisting the changes necessary to meet the perceived realities of globalization. Singaporeans have been told that they are not 'realistic' enough, not 'engaged' enough, not 'gracious' enough, not 'cosmopolitan' enough, and not 'civic-minded' enough (Goh 18 August 2002, 17 August 2003; Ministry of Information and the Arts 2000; Lee 6 January 2004). The list of Singaporean deficits – and its correlative exhortations to change – goes on.

So who's right?

Clearly, there is a mismatch in experiences. By getting involved with politically marginal social commentators like us, Ron the Hokkien-rapping taxi driver as well as the various actors, crewmembers, musicians, and writers clearly cannot be described as apathetic. Also, while many of them could easily be characterized as of a lower educational and socioeconomic status, they nevertheless demonstrated a 'creative mind' capable of 'acquiring, sharing, applying and creating new knowledge'; a connection with their roots in engaging with activities whose objectives were unrepentantly Singaporean; and an 'adventurous spirit' by being part of a creative project in which most had no prior experience. These are the very traits the government has deemed indicative of a 'renaissance' citizenry (Ministry of Information and the Arts 2000). Further, by being concerned about the preservation of Singaporean culture and organizing ourselves for little monetary reward, we must be the 'active citizenry' that then-Deputy Prime Minister Lee Hsien Loong identified with the Americans, whom Singaporeans should emulate (Lee 6 January 2004).

While we do not deny that bourgeois political dilettantes and materialist monomaniacs exist, we believe that gross generalizations and polarizing labels hinder rather than help. Our encounters with policies and practices through *TalkingCock*-related activities also suggest that the government has imagined citizenship in such limited and often contradictory ways that it is hard for the performances of sincere and spontaneous citizens to find legitimacy. Thus, Singaporeans who are actually demonstrating vital citizenship traits might nevertheless find themselves bumping up against existing cultural policies. We believe a more constructive approach is to ask how we can make the space for citizenship performance more inclusive and ensure a diversity of expression.

Citizenship by committee

So far, the definitive statement on citizenship performance is to be found in Lee Hsien Loong's speech entitled 'Building a Civic Society' (6 January 2004). In the speech, Lee recounted the steps taken by the ruling People's Action Party (PAP) in the wake of the 1984 general elections, when the loss of two seats and reduced voter share were interpreted as an act of protest by the electorate. According to Lee, to remedy its image of being insufficiently consultative, the PAP set up – over the years – the Feedback Unit, the Economic Committee, the Singapore 21 Committee, the Economic Review Committee, and the Remaking Singapore Committee. He cited the decisions to permit bar-top dancing and bungee jumping as evidence of successful consultation and growing liberalization. Lee also spoke of the need to open up further and explained that the government had placed a high priority on the promotion of civic participation and the progressive widening of the limits of openness. He said the government would 'pull back from being all things to citizens' and encouraged people to debate issues – and not just 'minor municipal' ones – 'with reason, passion, conviction'. He also pledged to continue more public consultation exercises, for which he laid out a series of 'terms of engagement' that asked both government and citizens to be tolerant of each other's views.

The sentiment in Lee's speech is admirable, and is the clearest sign yet of an outstretched hand. The question, therefore, is whether the average citizen will grasp this hand, believing it has been extended in genuine collaboration, or whether he or she, based on bitter experience, will recoil, believing the hand will only deliver a slap in the face. In this regard, Lee's speech is riddled with indications of equivocation. For instance, despite expressly stating that the government wants community guidance not just on 'minor municipal issues', an entire section of his speech seems to suggest that active civic participation actually involves voting on the colour of public housing blocks and reporting broken down lifts and mosquito nuisances.

Then there is the creeping intimation that serving on or speaking before government-initiated committees is the pinnacle of citizenship contribution. Committees present significant barriers to the participation of ordinary Singaporeans. We met several members of the Economic Restructuring Committee and Remaking Singapore Committee in the period between 2002 and 2003. A couple of them contacted us in New York to discuss the work of the committee, and a few others we knew as friends. All those we met are male professionals, invariably from elite schools, and speak excellent English. Our conversations with them about their work in the committee were always punctuated by statistics about economic growth rates, immigration rates, and the shaking of heads over Singapore's future. This performance of citizenship resembles the utopian 'public sphere' of the Enlightenment project, a sphere in which rational, logical, mostly male people discuss matters of the state (Habermas 1962/1989, 1987). In fact, this is precisely how Lee envisions public debate over policies: 'it has to be issue-focused, based on facts and logic, and not just on assertions and emotions' (Lee 6 January 2004).

If only government- and committee-led consultations are valued when thinking about citizenship performance, one must ask to what extent the average Singaporean's views are being considered, since these Singaporeans are unlikely to sit on such committees; are generally unable to access the required substratum of data to meet Lee's demand that they first have 'a good understanding of the issues at hand before they can sensibly take part in discussions'; and may be impaired by their lack of facility with the English language. Are they only allowed to make minor decisions in relation to their own lives such as what colour they want their public housing flats to be painted? How can we avoid policy being determined in ways that recall a scene out of the Platonic dialogues, with political elders and wealthy, connected, male scholars discussing how to secure a happy concord for citizens over dinner in a rich merchant's house? The debate may be intellectual, sincere, and data-driven, but its exclusivity will invariably undermine its legitimacy and responsiveness to the needs of different groups of Singaporeans.

If it is thus accepted that diverse views should be sought on issues that go beyond the municipal, and that committees and public consultation exercises have a limited reach, then one must ask what alternative channels exist for citizens to express themselves? That *TalkingCock.com* continues to exist and that our film made it to the screens suggest that alternative channels are available. Our experiences, however, indicate that pursuing such channels inspires a surprising degree of resistance and suspicion from the authorities, and this in turn threatens to undermine the potential for greater citizen participation.

Taking flight, clipping wings

When we founded *TalkingCock.com* in 2000, the aim was merely to share satirical jokes and vent our collective spleens. It was meant to be a private site, known only to friends, though we knew that in this age of search engines, it was only a matter of time before someone stumbled upon us. None of us, however, anticipated the response.

One morning, we awoke to find that our hit counter had surged. Before we could figure out what had happened, the press were on to us – especially the late *Project Eyeball*, whose journalists seemed determined to characterize us as a 'political website'. Granted, we did poke fun at policies and policy-makers with articles like 'Three days insemination leave for civil servants' and 'DPM Tony Tan agrees: commando *mm si lang*' (Hokkien for 'Commandos are not human', which is in fact a compliment), but similar publications and programmes such as America's *The Onion*, *Mad Magazine*, and *Saturday Night Live*; Britain's *Private Eye*; and Russia's *Krokodil* also lampoon their leaders, and they are hardly deemed political organs. The job of any satirical publication is to poke merciless fun at the topic *du jour*. If Lee himself acknowledges the omnipresence of the government in Singaporean life, it should come as little surprise that most of the content of a Singaporean satirical website should be aimed at the government.

We found ourselves arguing with journalists over the difference between politics with a small 'p' (i.e. general social comment) and politics with a capital 'P' (i.e. engaging in partisan politics). We also emphasized how there was no case for misrepresentation or defamation, as we had a conspicuous disclaimer on our home page reiterating the humorous and fictitious bent of the site. While convinced of the soundness of our arguments, we were also deeply aware that the history of Singaporeans' constitutionally protected right to free speech was capricious at best. There are, in fact, laws that undermine citizens' rights to free speech and assembly (Tay 2002). We recalled the whirlwind that novelist Catherine Lim unexpectedly set off when she first criticized ministerial salaries in 1994 (Lim 20 November 1994). The threatening words of then-Senior Minister Lee Kuan Yew echoed in our minds: 'Everybody now knows that if you take on the PM, he will have to take you on' (Ng 3 February 1995). And recently, we were reminded again of the leadership's defensiveness when Lee Hsien Loong warned of the ramifications of 'criticism that scores political points and undermines the government's standing, whether or not this is intended'. He claimed that the government will be obliged to 'rebut or even demolish' any opposition that 'criticizes an action or policy' (Lee 6 January 2004). We were scared, and we debated whether to continue the site. *TalkingCock.com* was fun, but none of us wanted to wind up in the cold room over some jokes. We sought out and canvassed the views of civil society activists, constitutional law experts, academics, and even civil servants in order to assess the state of the ground. The common response was a rather unhelpful, 'Well, there's a lot of talk about how things are changing, and they are in some small measure, but you never know'. As one legal expert put it, 'If they want to catch you, nothing can stop them'. True or not, this was the feeling amongst those we consulted.

Curbing participation

Indeed, as we soon discovered, 'catching' us was not beyond the government's contemplation. In August 2001, to our horror, opposition MP Low Thia Khiang asked in parliament if *TalkingCock.com* fell within the jurisdiction of the Singapore Broadcasting Authority, and Minister Lee Yock Suan replied:

> Well, we will have to study the law. But my impression is that they are liable. Of course, they are outside Singapore, and whether we can catch them is something else. But whoever targets Singaporeans, our laws will apply to them. (*TalkingCock.com* n.d.; see also Lim, Vasoo, and Chia 14 August 2001)

Minister Wong Kan Seng's interjection that we were not considered a political site yet, but we would be if we engaged in political discussion, gave us the coldest of comfort (*TalkingCock.com* n.d.). Firstly, because the government provided little clarity on what constituted political discussion; and secondly, why was it necessary to 'catch' us, since we were mere jesters?

In the end, we decided to run with the ball, for reasons not entirely rational. At some level, we agreed with some civil society activists that if the government was promising change, then we had some duty to hold them to their word and advance things. Another factor was that a modest video we had shot on a whim, *eAhLong. com*, had unexpectedly won the Special Achievement Award at the 2001 Singapore International Film Festival. This emboldened us to consider producing a feature film, and people were openly offering support, providing us with services, facilities, and plain old helping hands.[3] Our website's name notwithstanding, it seemed churlish to chicken out now. Being debated in parliament, however, was nothing compared to our clash with the censors over language.

Curb your language

Singlish is Singaporean vernacular English, a polyglot of English, Malay, Tamil, and various Chinese dialects. Closer to Cockney and Creole than to pidgin, Singlish is often characterized by humorous wordplay that cuts across multiple languages. Extremely popular, it may be the only uniquely Singaporean cultural identifier.

The government, however, seems bent on eradicating it. *TalkingCock.com* was formed partly as a response to the government's anti-Singlish stance. In 1999, then-Prime Minister Goh lamented the popularity of the sitcom *Phua Chu Kang*, which he attributed to the lead character's use of Singlish. Goh said that if Singlish were allowed to proliferate, the nation's global competitiveness would be affected (Chua, Ng, Long, Osman, Koh, and Andrianie 24 August 1999). When we founded *TalkingCock.com*, we felt Goh's reasoning was simplistic. While a greater facility with English would help our standing in the world of global business, we felt that instilling greater confidence in ourselves would go an even longer way in enabling success in life and international interactions. After all, many heads of state, world-class business leaders, and international artistes speak languages other than English. Instead of taking pride in citizens' creativity in mixing languages and celebrating the linguistic hybridization brought about by different groups of people encountering each other, the government embarked on an exercise in censorship.

Our media friends began reporting that television and radio programmes were now being vetted for Singlish, thus ensuring that naturalistic dialogue was eradicated. When even British and American programming has dialogue which is not grammatically perfect, why did the government feel this had to be the case for the Singapore media? It would in any case seem strange to criticize Singlish for being a mongrel language when English itself is a polyglot of Germanic and old Romance languages, and continues to add new foreign terms every year. Singlish is merely a localized extrapolation of English's promiscuous nature. We saw no compelling argument why Singlish and standard English could not co-exist. We also felt Singaporeans were intelligent enough to differentiate between the different registers of English in different situations. And in cases where we could not, there were many complex reasons – educational backgrounds, socioeconomic class, and language teaching in schools – that would not be ameliorated by the mere banning of Singlish in the media.

Concerned about the disastrous effects of gagging something so critical to our 'living culture' and capacity to invent 'new myths, new ceremonies' (da Cunha 1995: 288) as a multicultural immigrant society, we decided to make Singlish the cornerstone of *TalkingCock. com*. Our articles would be in perfectly grammatical English, but any dialogue within those articles would be free and natural. Similarly, we decided to uphold the principle of naturalistic dialogue in our feature film.

We never anticipated the resistance. The battle began when we submitted *TalkingCock The Movie* to the censors – the Ministry of Information and the Arts' Film and Publications Department (FPD), which has since merged with the Singapore Broadcasting Authority and the Singapore Film Commission to become the Media Development Authority. The FPD demanded that one scene be cut and that the film should bear a rating of NC-16, thereby preventing Singaporeans below the age of 16 from watching it. We appealed, availing ourselves of a new procedure that allowed a filmmaker to address the Appeals Committee directly. Colin Goh thus became the first filmmaker to argue before the Appeals Committee. The scene to be cut was known as 'The Turbanator sketch' which depicted a Chinese man making a racist joke against Sikhs, whereupon a tall, leather-jacketed Sikh man, in the mould of Arnold Schwarzenegger's 'Terminator' character, exacts revenge for this abominable slur. The FPD felt it was racially insensitive. We managed to convince the Appeals Board otherwise, arguing that any sensible person would be able to distinguish between a racist joke and a joke that invokes racism in order to critique it. We also bolstered our case with letters of support from Professor Kirpal Singh – an eminent Sikh academic

who is also the author of Chapter 7 of this volume – as well as the
youth wing of the Central Sikh Gurdwara, the highest Sikh temple
in Singapore, attesting that they took no offence whatsoever to the
scene. We managed to persuade the Appeals Committee to restore
the cut. But we lost, however, on the ratings point.

The FPD informed us that there were six issues they scrutinized
in any film: race, religion, depiction of drug use, sex, violence, and
profanity. We had won the race point in restoring the cut scene. There
were no religious issues in our movie, or depictions of drug use, or
sex, or violence. There were, however, several instances of Hokkien
profanity, which we had judiciously chosen to bleep out with bird
sounds. Astoundingly, however, the censors argued that despite
the profanities having already been bleeped out, the NC-16 rating
had to remain, presumably because people could still lip read and
decipher what was being said. We could understand if the rationale
for the policy was to prevent impressionable young children from
learning offending language, but instead, we were being penalized
for people's foreknowledge of the phrases! More galling was the
fact that *Chicken Rice War* (Lim, Leong, and Cheah 2000), a movie
made by MediaCorp's filmmaking subsidiary, had more fully audible
instances of the use of the English expletive 'fuck' (yes, we counted)
and still obtained a PG rating. We might have been willing to accept
a blanket policy against profanity, but we could not accept being told
that English profanity is somehow more acceptable than our own
homegrown version. What made it doubly ridiculous was that the
offending phrases had already been bleeped out. We felt the FPD
were displaying a severe case of post-colonial hangover.

The ratings decision had huge consequences. Firstly, cinemas
were less willing to set aside screens for a film with a restricted audience. Secondly, our advertising options were severely reduced. For
instance, Power 98 FM – a radio station for the Singapore Armed
Forces Reservist Association (SAFRA) – said they had to obtain a
special written waiver from the Singapore Broadcasting Authority
(SBA) before Colin Goh could be interviewed, because of the NC-16
rating. We were told that it was SAF policy not to support any films
with a rating over PG. It struck us as bizarre that the military – where
teenagers smoke, drink alcohol, and are taught to kill – would be
squeamish about movie ratings, especially when premised on foul

language that is nowhere near the level employed by most soldiers. Colin Goh was also told that the songs on the soundtrack could not be played, because they contained Singlish or dialect content. This was an omen, for several days later, our lone television trailer on Channel i was pulled off the air by the SBA for 'excessive use of Singlish and dialect'. The trailer, a mere 15 seconds long, had this script:

> Eh, come see our film, leh! Got animal, got pretty girl, got action. It's pao ka leow! Kuah si mi? Kuah *TalkingCock The Movie*. [In standard English, 'Come and see our film. It features an animal, a pretty girl, and it has action. It includes everything. What are you staring at? Come and watch *TalkingCock The Movie*'.]

The trailer contained less Singlish or dialect content than the then-prime minister's National Day Rally speeches, which he liked to pepper with colloquialisms. In the 2003 speech alone, Goh used '*Kah tak hoi, chew liak her. Hoi zao, her liu, aiyah, bor her hay ah hor*', and '*lao quee buay xi, bo quee jia eh xi*'. In the 2002 speech, he used '*bo chap*', '*bng tang*', and '*chin kang kor*'. In the 2001 speech, he used '*cheena*' and '*ang moh*' (Goh 17 August 2003, 18 August 2002, 19 August 2001). But when it came to our trailer, the SBA would not budge. We were also unable to find any restrictions on Singlish in media-related legislation. Our trailer was pulled despite having broken no law. We can only surmise that the SBA was just toeing the new anti-Singlish line.

The problems continued even after the movie finished its theatrical run. We were informed that the FPD had banned our film from being released on VCD and DVD, as only PG-rated films were allowed on these formats. The FPD informed us that to secure a PG rating, we had to remove the instances of our bleeped out Hokkien profanity. With great reluctance, we dubbed over with nonsensical English words the bird sounds that we had used to dub over the Hokkien words. It was a deeply symbolic final act.

Seeking the renaissance government

Just a few years after the government rattled its sabres before us in parliament and after we clashed with the censors, Prime Minister Lee Hsien Loong began talking about a commitment to more openness. However, the conditions that presented barriers to alternative performances of citizenship still have not changed.

The government has not resiled from its position on what constitutes 'political discussion', thus keeping the Sword of Damocles
dangling over every webmaster's head. Singlish restrictions continue
to be enforced – *TalkingCock The Movie* has been denied airing on TV
because, as our distributor explained to us, of 'excessive Singlish and
dialect'. Lee's speeches, in any case, seem to limit citizen participation
to mere municipal matters and submissions before government-initiated committees. Further, many contradictory demands continue to
be made on Singaporeans, leaving little space for self-defined forms
of citizenship performance. For instance, juxtaposing the National
Day Rally speeches (2001–2003) with the new prime minister's 'civic
society' speech produces a series of contradictory propositions on
what constitutes legitimate participation:

- Singaporeans are too materialistic, and that is why they are
  politically and socially inactive;
- But if Singaporeans get involved with politics or society, then
  their activities only count if they are profitable. (For instance,
  Goh (18 August 2002) disparages people from writing national
  song parodies and instead asks them to emulate filmmaker Jack
  Neo for his 'two successful films', while neglecting to mention
  Neo's less commercially successful ones. He also goes on to
  suggest Singapore needs more millionaire entrepreneurs like
  Sam Goi and Kwek Leng Beng.)
- Singaporeans are urged to be more like the Americans, with
  their active citizens and spirited debates;
- But Singapore should not be like the US where active citizens
  are allowed to engage in debates or activities which may
  undermine the government's standing.
- Singaporeans should speak up or act if they see a problem with
  their environment;
- But they must recognize there are limits (the so-called 'out-of-
  bound' markers or OB markers), which the government refuses
  to define.
- To meet the needs of the global economy, Singaporeans must
  be more cosmopolitan and abandon cultural traits such as
  Singlish or dialects;

- But to buffer themselves against the capricious winds of globalization, they must hang on to their unique cultural identities.
- To foster a more civic society, the government will pull back from being all things to all citizens;
- But the government must dictate what civic society can look like.

As the *TalkingCock.com* experience has demonstrated, these contradictions exist not only at the level of talk, but also as a web of rules and practices, both explicit and implicit, that proscribe citizenship performances when they do not fit within the government's imagination. The continued existence of these rules and practices makes highly questionable the government's persistent reiteration of Singaporeans' shortcomings. The development of a 'renaissance' citizenry demands a review of governmental discourse. We propose that the government develop a more inclusive approach, by reviewing its policies and practices to deconstruct two fundamental assumptions which unduly restrict citizenship performances.

Firstly, the assumption that heartlanders are by nature politically apathetic must be deconstructed. Considerable research on citizenship in international settings support Carole Pateman's (1989) argument that it is wrong to suggest that certain segments of society – especially citizens of a lower socioeconomic status and women – are naturally politically apathetic (Arnot and Dillabough 2000; Buckingham 2000). Instead, there are structural reasons which make women and working-class citizens feel that 'it is not worth being active', especially when their words are rendered 'meaningless' (Pateman 1989: 13).

In Singapore, the recent relaxation of restrictions on bungee jumping and bar-top dancing has been cited as manifestations of 'new directions for social and political development' (Lee 6 January 2004). To us, however, bungee jumping and bar-top dancing are hardly activities that will change the landscape of civic participation in Singapore, because they only invite Singaporeans to be consumers rather than engage in more meaningful acts of self-expression. Deconstructing the assumption that heartlanders are naturally apathetic must also translate into substantive practices, including concerted efforts to evaluate current forums for citizenship participation. For example, governmental committees should be evaluated for the extent to which they serve as adequate channels for all Singaporeans. Demographic statistics such as race, gender, education, and income levels of participants in these channels should be obtained and publicized to facilitate evaluation. Further, creative methods for eliciting the participation and trust of groups of citizens left out of extant feedback channels should be considered.

Policies that regulate Singapore's cultural landscape must also be reviewed for the extent to which they can obstruct various Singaporean voices from entering the public sphere. Restrictive policies also risk destroying citizens' 'capacity for cultural production' (da Cunha 1995: 290). We all grow up with cultural resources such as the languages we speak, the ways we interact with one another, the foods we eat, the ways that we celebrate and grieve, and the spaces in which our memories are created. These are materials and texts that we use to express our identities and to establish continuity between past, present, and future – in other words, to produce and regenerate our culture. By limiting the scope of cultural resources available to us (such as censoring cultural works containing Singlish) and by narrowly defining what constitutes legitimate participation in the public sphere (joining committees peopled by highly credentialed individuals), we in fact enjoin citizens to be embarrassed by our own cultural resources in favour of adopting cultural texts which present an ersatz picture of ourselves. One only has to listen to the highly artificial dialogue in almost any local television programme to see this at work.

Secondly, the assumption that citizens instantly become active when they are told to be must be deconstructed. Exhorting people to become active citizens is doomed to failure if substantive channels by which the populace can learn and exercise their citizenship continue to be disallowed. For example, the laws and practices enacted by the various arms that administer Singapore's public spheres must be reviewed and appropriately repealed. As Lee (6 January 2004) urges Singaporeans to emulate American citizens' willingness to organize themselves and 'solve their own problems', he should recognize that such organization does not occur overnight, but has been enabled by decades of protecting American citizens' rights such as the right to free speech, free assembly, and peaceful protest. The enjoinder for citizens to change rapidly also seems somewhat disingenuous when contrasted with the government's consistent warnings that liberalization must be allowed to evolve gradually and that the government should not be rushed in this process (Lee 6 January 2004). Indeed, the government bears the greater duty to act swiftly, as any delay in providing the conditions conducive to different forms of citizenship performances risks entrenching cynicism amongst the people.

Conclusion

When citizens have been denied self-designed forms of citizenship performance, when their own languages are excised from the public sphere, and when they have never experienced how their views can have an influence, they cannot justifiably be characterized as, in Lee's (6 January 2004) words, 'inarticulate'. They are, in fact, 'disenfranchised'. It is no wonder that the majority of Singaporeans are more concerned with the things that they are allowed to have a modicum of influence over – like the car, house, and plasma TV. And it is little wonder that all their grievances, observations, and joy find their expression less at committee hearings, than in humble talk cock sessions at the *kopi tiam* (Hokkien for coffee shop).

NOTES

1. The Substation describes itself as 'Singapore's first multicultural and multi-disciplinary arts centre'. Its website is available at <http://www.substation.org/> (accessed 1 October 2006).
2. MediaCorp describes itself as 'one of the region's most established broadcasters, ... play[ing] a key role in developing Singapore as a broadcasting and media production hub in Asia'. Its website is available at <http://www.corporate.mediacorp.sg/philosophy.htm> (accessed 1 October 2006).
3. Amongst many others, companies such as Infinite Frameworks and Yellow Box Studios were providing us with post-production services for nominal compensation. Northeast Community Development Council helped us with securing audition rooms and filming locations. And Lee Kwong Seng Studio in Sembawang lent us equipment and studio space. We are eternally indebted to them for their generosity.

REFERENCES

Arnot, M. and Dillabough, J. (eds.) (2000) *Challenging Democracy: international perspectives on gender, education and citizenship*, London: RoutledgeFarmer.

Balakrishnan, V. (2000) 'Singapore in 1999: a review', in S.L. Foo, Z. Ali, and C.T. Goh (eds.) *Singapore 2000*, Singapore: Ministry of Information and the Arts, pp. 3–10.

Buckingham, D. (2000) *The Making of Citizens: young people, news and politics*, London: Routledge.

Chua, M.H. (28 August 1999) 'Is there a gap between cosmos and locals?', *The Straits Times* (Singapore). Online. Available HTTP: <http://www. lexisnexis.com> (accessed 14 March 2004).

Chua, M.H., Ng, I., Long, S., Osman, A., Koh, L. and Andrianie, S. (24 August 1999) 'Out: Phua Chu Kang, in: proper English', *The Straits Times* (Singapore). Online. Available HTTP: <http://www.lexisnexis. com> (accessed 14 March 2004).

da Cunha, M.C. (1995) 'Children, politics and culture: the case of Brazilian Indians', in S. Stephens (ed.) *Children and the Politics of Culture*, Princeton, NJ: Princeton University Press, pp. 282–91.

Goh, C.T. (19 August 2001) 'New Singapore', Speech at the National Day Rally on 19 August 2001, Singapore. Online. Available HTTP: <http:// www.gov.sg/nd/ND01.htm> (accessed 22 December 2004).

Goh, C.T. (18 August 2002) 'Remaking Singapore – changing mindsets', Speech at the National Day Rally on 18 August 2002, Singapore. Online. Available HTTP: <http://www.gov.sg/nd/ND02.htm> (accessed 22 December 2004).

Goh, C.T. (17 August 2003) 'From the valley to the highlands', Speech at the National Day Rally on 17 August 2003, Singapore. Online. Available HTTP: <http://www.gov.sg/nd/ND03.htm> (accessed 22 December 2004).

Habermas, J. (1962/1989) *The Structural Transformation of the Public Sphere: an inquiry into a category of bourgeois society*, Cambridge, MA: MIT Press.

Habermas, J. (1987) (trans. T. McCarthy) *The Theory of Communicative Action, Volume 2*, Boston, MA: Beacon Press.

Josey, A. (1982) *David Marshall's Political Interlude*, Singapore: Eastern Universities Press.

Lee, H.L. (6 January 2004) 'Building a civic society', speech by the deputy prime minister at the Harvard Club of Singapore's 35th Anniversary Dinner, 6 January 2004, Singapore. Online. Available HTTP: <http:// www.newsintercom.org/index.php?itemid=34> (accessed 22 December 2004).

Lim, C. (20 November 1994) 'One government, two styles', *The Straits Times* (Singapore). Online. Available HTTP: <http://www.lexisnexis.com> (accessed 14 March 2004).

Lim, L., Vasoo, S., and Chia, S. (14 August 2001) 'MPs quiz minister on scope of bill', *The Straits Times* (Singapore). Online. Available HTTP:

<http://www.lexisnexis.com> (accessed 14 March 2004).

Lim, S.Y. and Leong, D. (Producers) and Cheah, C.K. (Director) (2000) *Chicken Rice War*, Motion picture, Singapore: Raintree Pictures.

Ministry of Information and the Arts (2000) *Renaissance City Report: culture and the arts in renaissance Singapore*, Singapore. Online. Available HTTP: <http://www.mita.gov.sg/renaissance/FinalRen.pdf> (accessed 22 December 2004).

Ng, I. (3 February 1995) 'PM Goh right in rebutting critics: SM Lee', *The Straits Times* (Singapore). Online. Available HTTP: <http://www.lexisnexis.com> (accessed 14 March 2004).

Pateman, C. (1989) *The Disorder of Women: democracy, feminism and political theory*, Cambridge, UK: Polity Press.

TalkingCock.com (n.d.) 'TalkingCock in parliament: so what's the big fuss about?', *TalkingCock.com*. Online. Available HTTP: <http://www.talkingcock.com/html/sections.php?op=viewarticle&artid=51> (accessed 22 December 2004).

TalkingCock.com (2002) *Coxford Singlish Dictionary*, Singapore: Angsana Press.

Tay, S. (2002) 'The future of civil society: what next?', in D. da Cunha (ed.) *Singapore in the New Millennium: challenges facing the city-state*, Singapore: Institute of Southeast Asian Studies, pp. 69–107.

Woo, Y.Y.J. and Goh, C. (Executive Producers) (2002) *TalkingCock SingingSong*, CD recording, Singapore: Auntie-Auntie Entertainment Pte Ltd.

Woo, Y.Y.J. and Goh, C. (Producers and Directors) (2002) *TalkingCock The Movie*, Motion picture, Singapore: Wu Liao Media.

Keeping vigil
Openness, diversity, and tolerance

KIRPAL SINGH

In Lee Hsien Loong's now well-known 'Harvard' speech, at least two important points became abundantly clear (Lee 6 January 2004). Firstly, Lee recognized that young Singaporeans are hungry for change – for greater liberalization – and that in order to keep apace with political developments at the global level, Singapore would have to transform itself and find ways and means of accommodating global pressures for change. Secondly, that no matter how the rest of the world changes, in Singapore certain things remain sacrosanct. For example, the kinds of freedom enjoyed by citizens of America and Europe are most definitely still foreign in Singapore.

Singaporeans – or more specifically perhaps, the 'heartlanders' – appear to agree with the overarching concern expressed in Lee's speech: that the time is not ripe for them to be given, or tested with, much greater freedoms of choice and expression. It will take a long time, these heartlanders often say, before the kind of democratic expression found in more advanced nations can firmly take root in Singapore. Lee's position would seem quite clear: those freedoms that open up greater access to political choice and decision-making on

'sensitive' issues – those freedoms that allow for the critical engagement of the non-state intelligentsia – will be subject to severe scrutiny
and, if needs be, censorship and curtailment. In 1994, then-Prime
Minister Goh Chok Tong reprimanded novelist Catherine Lim for
her political commentary in the local daily (Lim 20 November 1994)
and he introduced the notion of the OB markers – those 'out-of-
bound' themes and topics that would be plain folly for Singaporeans
to touch upon. Six years later at the Singapore 21 Forum, then-
Deputy Prime Minister Lee Hsien Loong described the OB markers
in a succinct way.

> As our society matures and grows more stable, and the population
> becomes better educated and more discerning, the limits for debate –
> the 'OB markers' – will widen ... As long as we are only arguing over
> policies, the limits are very wide ... However, if it is not just a debate
> over policies, but an attack on the Government or on its fitness to rule,
> then the Government's response has to go beyond the particular issue
> to address the broader question. (Lee 16 January 2000)

In the same speech, Lee suggested that the government's response would
be strong if the situation merited it. Naturally, many Singaporeans
wondered – whilst some were deeply concerned about – exactly how
strong the government's response could be.

The practice of censorship and curtailment are both familiar to
most Singaporeans. The government has regularly maintained that
Singapore is not ready for full democracy. When Singapore's version
of 'speakers' corner' was launched on 1 September 2000, Singaporeans
were, for the first time in a long while, free to express themselves, albeit
with proper controls in place. In his first National Day Rally speech as
Singapore's third prime minister, Lee explained how he was going to

> open up the Speakers' Corner where you can go and make any speech
> you like and we are going to say, 'Well, if you want to go there and have
> an exhibition, go ahead'. Once in a while, Think Centre [a very critical
> civil society organization] says they want to go to the Speakers' Corner
> and they want to plant 100 flowers there, let the 100 flowers bloom.
> Well, I think go ahead. They want to water the flowers, go ahead. They
> want to turn the flowers down, go ahead. I mean, free expression as
> long as you don't get into race and religion and don't start a riot. It's a
> signal – speak, speak your voice, be heard, take responsibility for your
> views and opinions. (Lee 6 January 2004)

The arguments against greater free speech have normally centred on national security and the maintenance of interethnic peace and harmony; and most Singaporeans – not only their heartlander caricatures – have tended to be in some agreement with these arguments. The aftermath and consequences of the crisis in Iraq have demonstrated how a nation not robust enough to withstand the consequences of global events will invariably be caught in an unpleasant drift and may even be swept away by the currents coming from all (and often unexpected) directions. Any nation that does not fully understand – or develop strong mechanisms to withstand – the tide of globalization in all its multi-dimensional intrusions is bound to suffer one way or another.

Negotiations between Singapore and the United States to sign a mutually beneficial free trade agreement (FTA) were delicate when it came to the very sticky issue of chewing gum. Singapore's long-standing ban on chewing gum – justified in terms of saving public money that would otherwise be spent on removing dried-up gum left all over 'clean and green' Singapore – had stalled discussions. However, in its eagerness to conclude the FTA, Singapore had to concede to US pressure to make chewing gum available in Singapore. The problem was resolved in a rather creative way; chewing gum is now available in Singapore, but only for medical use (Arshad 23 May 2004). However, the compromise underlined the fact that becoming globalized means surrendering some national autonomy to the big players in the competitive international fields of economics and politics.

Many of Singapore's problems have been a direct result of anxieties related to being a small nation. Singapore does not have that crucial space necessary for free debate and discussion. In a small country, hurt is so easy to give and receive, as is more serious harm. The practice of political lobbying, for instance, a practice that most developed democracies would take for granted as part and parcel of the daily business of government, is a very sensitive issue in tiny Singapore. Religious, ethnic, or cultural groups find it difficult to lobby the government openly for fear that such displays can easily turn public and lead to unwanted confrontation with a powerful state. When the Nature Society (Singapore) lobbied the government to prevent a section of the Lower Peirce reservoir from being turned into a golf-course, the civil society organization attracted media attention but met with a stone-faced government that warned the organization to stay out of 'sensitive' issues. Although this public mode of opposition may have, in this case, succeeded in getting the government to shelve developments that would have had significant environmental consequences, this has been regarded as an exception to the rule that advocacy work can only succeed in Singapore if conducted in a quiet and non-confrontational way (George 2000: 139–43). 'Lobbying' in Singapore is frequently conducted behind the scenes, a strategy that has proved far more successful than issuing public statements and openly pressuring the government.

A smaller nation is easier to manage, but it might be more difficult to govern. The perceived precariousness of a small nation can always be used by those in power to stay in power without granting citizens easy traffic in free speech. Managing a small nation can involve the simple task of ensuring its success as an essentially economic entity; governing it would imply giving its citizenry full rights of political participation. The US is easy to govern but very hard to manage, while Singapore seems easier to manage but harder to govern. In Singapore, the government has found it difficult to win the affection of its citizens. It has also been difficult to forge a happy working partnership between government and the governed.

The exact nature of the relationships and interconnectedness among small size, management, governance, and freedom will always be disputed because of the complex and subtle ways in which they interweave. A sustained study of these relationships will prove immensely useful and indicative of the ways in which small nations like Singapore have orchestrated their political scores.

Openness

Can Singapore be described as an open nation or an open society? Opinions vary. My friends in the business world tell me that for a country just coming out of third-world status, Singapore's is, indeed, a very open economy. It welcomes foreign businesses and foreign talent, and even provides numerous incentive schemes to encourage the inflow of foreign capital and skills. And yet, after some years of actually living here, many of these friends in the business world tend to say, 'I wish Singapore could be more open'. People wanting to live and

work in Singapore do wish for a more open and transparent society
in the sense of having easy access to information, critical debate, and
civil rights. Even if a nation-state acquires a worldwide reputation for
being economically robust, sooner or later the benchmarks will have
to include the question 'how do its citizens live?'
One has only to flip through the daily newspapers in the US,
the United Kingdom, or Australia to observe high levels of political
debate and discussion as well as citizens who take their authorities
to task in the very process of decision making. The freedoms enjoyed
by candidates campaigning during political elections in these countries contrast starkly with the notable occasions in Singapore when
political candidates are sued for making derogatory statements about
those in power. In the US, the UK, and Australia, political space is
much larger, and politics is conducted in the spirit of fair play.

Although the Singapore government is open to ideas and actions
that will give the country a distinct advantage in terms of real and
measurable material gains, it is not so open when it comes to a whole
host of other things, including the availability of certain kinds of
information. While there is a semblance of informational freedom
in Singapore, 'real' information, I am constantly told, is very hard to
come by. In 2003, the research findings of three economics professors
at Nanyang Technological University were publicly 'discredited' by the
Ministry of Manpower. Their interpretation of some labour statistics
available in the public domain was disputed using statistics that the
government had kept from the public domain (*Channel NewsAsia* 31
July 2003). The dispute merely underlines a much bigger and almost
endemic problem: the Singapore government is not very comfortable
about dispensing real information.

Researchers are often frustrated by their inability to obtain correct
or real information, even for legitimate projects. I was quite aghast
(but not entirely shocked) when a colleague doing research on the
relationship between ethnicity and academic achievement in specific
subjects told me that in spite of several attempts to obtain basic statistics on the percentage by ethnicity of undergraduates reading different
disciplines, the Ministry of Education simply refused to release the
figures. Most of the time, this bureaucratic practice of non-disclosure
has been justified or rationalized in the name of 'national security'.
How the release of such figures, especially for scholarly purposes,

can affect, hurt, or harm national security baffles me. But the fact remains that certain types of vital information remain deliberately obscured, while superficial information is handed out in a seemingly free and easy manner. There should, of course, be limits to national information that is shared openly. But in Singapore, these limits are too severe, and will stifle any attempts to develop a rich culture of research and its accompanying ethos of shared knowledge.

Singapore also lacks openness to new ideas, new people, and new visions. Unless and until an idea, for instance, has been tried and tested, Singaporeans generally do not want to adopt it. Singaporeans remain largely risk-averse. They are not prepared to experiment, even in the realm of pure theory. And so, for example, funding for workshops, seminars, or talks on experimental themes will not be forthcoming. Also, support for projects will depend on whether they fall in line with the political scene's 'flavour of the month'. Many years ago, I applied for funds to undertake a research project to compare how the different ethnic groups were represented in Singapore literature written in English, Chinese, Malay, and Tamil. I was gently advised that this might not be a suitable research area and that funds might not be available for it. I could not help but imagine that somewhere someone in charge did not want to have to deal with the 'sensitive' findings that might have emerged from such a research project.

Singaporeans believe in sticking to the so-called 'best practices' model without realizing that this will simply mean that nothing truly creative or innovative can come out of their culture – not, at any rate, in the foreseeable future. Singapore does have its small patents, and every now and then someone or something shows up which might reasonably be described as creative. But, in reality, nothing of moment has taken place in Singapore since the convoluted experience of Sim Wong Hoo and his Creative Technology. When Sim first realized the commercial value of marrying the 'mouth-organ' and the computer, no one in Singapore wanted to support his entrepreneurial hunch. And yet the Americans decided to support him, which led to the launch of SoundBlaster. On this product, Sim's fortune was made. More recently, Sim was quoted in *The Straits Times* (Fang 30 July 2003) as saying that one of the universities in Singapore was so slow in making a decision to fund his new ideas that he decided to take his latest innovation to a small private university in Malacca instead. Innovations cannot wait, said Sim. And he was right! If Singapore wants to be regarded as an open nation, then it must take risks and push on even when failure seems to be a very possible outcome. The university may have had good reasons for taking its time to process the funding, but the image projected to the world by that report in *The Straits Times* could not have done the university and Singapore's technopreneurial culture any good in the light of expressed plans to be more aggressively proactive in research collaboration with industry partners.

I have argued elsewhere why and how Singapore needs to change in order for creativity and innovation to become a feature of the Singaporean landscape (Singh 2004). It was therefore heartening for me to hear Prime Minister Lee Hsien Loong (2004) urge Singaporeans, in his first National Day Rally speech, to be less complacent and to think of better and more creative ways for change. He was basically promoting creativity and a culture brave enough to celebrate and adopt the ideas of its own people.

Singaporeans' attitude towards interethnic relations also lacks openness. If, by an open society, we mean a living and dynamic intercourse of people, places, and things, then Singapore can only superficially be thought of as open. An interesting comparison might be made with India. Following the Congress Party's victory in India's general election in May 2004, Manmohan Singh was eventually selected to be prime minister. India is a vast country of about 1.2 billion people. Singh belongs to the Sikh community, a minority ethnic group comprising no more than 20 million people in the whole of India, or less than 1 per cent of the total population. Even if one were to accept the argument that Singh was chosen as the 'compromise' candidate, it is still astonishing how the majorities have not seriously objected to him – not, at any rate, on ethnic or religious grounds.

In Singapore, by contrast, then-Prime Minister Lee Kuan Yew went on record in the late 1980s as saying that Singapore was not ready for an Indian prime minister (Mitton 2000). Indians form about 9 per cent of Singapore's population. Now if, in an open society, who becomes prime minister is determined purely on merit, then it would seem odd that an Indian – or anyone who is not Chinese (for I think that was Lee's real point) – should not be given serious consideration for this top political post. The kind of openness displayed by a vast

India has not been achieved in a small Singapore. But it ought to be if Singapore wants to be taken seriously as a meritocracy. Of course Lee, in historical context, was speaking at a time when ethnic and racial sensitivities were more pronounced than they are today. Still, it seems to have gone against the grain of efforts to integrate Singaporeans as Singaporeans first, and not Chinese, Malays, Indians, and so on.

Singaporeans are surprisingly chatty. However, the level of conversation often gives cause for some worry. Singaporeans are more than happy to engage over small and insignificant issues like shopping and eating rather than issues of politics, gender, business, and ethics. Shift the focus of the discussion to politics, especially domestic politics, and eyes begin to look around, ears prick, and lips generally go quiet. An atmosphere of anxiety pervades and, usually, the conversation comes to an end. Of course other Singaporeans – some taxi-drivers or 'coffee shop' patrons in particular – are ever-ready to criticize domestic politics (especially local politicians) in random fashion. But it is not loose and random diatribes that are important for our purposes here, but rather the question of whether the typical Singaporean is comfortable speaking openly about so-called sensitive issues. Here is yet another gauge of the nation's readiness to be more open.

As long as the element of fear prevails, as long as people feel they have to look over their shoulders, as long as people prefer to stay anonymous, I think the signals remain that an open Singapore is not yet in the making. At the centre of a more open Singapore would be public debate, and I firmly contend that Singaporeans ought to become more mature in public debates by elevating their standard of discussion from the humdrum concerns which now tend to dominate. While the established bread-and-butter issues (or 'roti-and-curry' issues) are certainly important, it is necessary for Singaporeans to move away from the trappings of fear and anxiety to the joys of openness and free expression. Of course there will be limitations – there are limitations everywhere! – but at least a modicum of maturity might be achieved in the next decade or so if Singapore starts now.

Diversity

In general, diversity in Singapore society has seldom been described as a cause for celebration. More often than not, diversity has been seen as a threat – if Singaporeans do not remain careful and watch what they say and do, they are going to be involved in endless conflict. With the official promotion of non-interference and superficial tolerance, is it any wonder that the genuine hallmarks of diversity seem to be missing in Singapore? I remember that when I was younger, Singaporeans seemed to mix more freely – more carelessly even – with members of different ethnic groups, at least compared to my children and my students today. Ethnicity, though only one obvious marker of diversity, is a significant one, and one with which Singapore has yet, I think, to make peace. My own sense that young Singaporeans today do not, for some inexplicable reason, mix easily – or perhaps do not even want to mix at all – has been strengthened by informal conversation with my students. Thus when I asked my non-Chinese students whether they visited their Chinese friends during the Chinese New Year celebrations, the answer was not at all encouraging. I received a similar response after the Muslim festival *Hari Raya Puasa* and the Hindu festival *Deepavali*. Today's young Singaporeans do mix professionally at the workplace, but rarely does this mixing extend to the more crucial areas of private and personal intercourse. But it is this 'non-institutional' mixing amongst peoples of various ethnic backgrounds that indicates real diversity. And this is lacking in Singapore.

As my former university professor used to say, if Singapore keeps the four main ethnic groups – Chinese, Malays, Indians, and 'others' – always consciously separate in most, if not all, official accounts and public communications, then the chances of real integration taking place are going to be slim. S. Rajaratnam, former foreign minister and for decades the People's Action Party's (PAP) ideologue, once publicly spoke about the possibility of a new ethnic type in Singapore that he labelled 'Chindians', the offspring of Chinese-Indian marriages that seemed to be increasing in number. The label was immediately excised from the public domain because, presumably, the social pressure to remain 'ethnically pure' – that is, to not belong to a mixed-race category – was high. The patrilineal system in Singapore has meant that children officially take on the racial category of their father. Singaporeans who choose to marry across ethnic, racial, or religious boundaries, though not openly ostracized or criticized, have always felt they were on the margins of society. This is an observation that a number of people have shared with me privately, but frequently enough. Parents who are intermarried find it hard, for example, to convince the Ministry of Education that the choice of their children's 'mother-tongue' – the second language that they learn in school – should not (ironically) always be the language of the father!

Special Assistance Plan (SAP) schools were introduced at the end of the 1970s to ensure that a certain section of the Chinese community would always keep their roots and traditions alive through an in-depth study of Chinese culture as manifested in its language and literature. These elite schools were said to retain a distinctively Chinese environment that was fast disappearing as more parents chose to send their children to English-medium schools. The non-Chinese communities in Singapore have lived with this exclusively Chinese component of the education system for many years now. And yet, public forums on this issue have usually been cautious and overly sensitive. However, it is important to stress that the SAP schools have been the source of much discontent among those who wish to see a truly diverse Singapore; the SAP system very noticeably privileges the large majority of Singaporeans who are Chinese.

Officially, non-Chinese students are not barred from enrolling in a SAP school; and some SAP schools will boast of having non-Chinese students even if the number of these students is two or three out of 1,000! Realistically speaking, it is extremely difficult for a non-Chinese student to get into a SAP school simply because the 'mother-tongue' policy would have made it administratively difficult for him or her to study Mandarin as a second language. Now a nation genuinely devoted to celebrating diversity would not continue with such an educational policy. In the long run, it only serves to create more problems than solutions. Surrounded, as Singapore is, by more than 200 million non-Chinese living in neighbouring Indonesia and Malaysia, Singaporeans should be wary of publicly upholding policies that can be perceived as discriminatory.

This debate was reignited with the announcement on 3 September 2004 of educational policies to nurture a 'bicultural elite' who will in the future be able to engage with China. These policies included the introduction of a new 4-year scholarship and 6-month immersion programme in China available to talented students in SAP schools (Ho 4 September 2004). Such an ethnically divided approach will inevitably lead to a polarization of scholars within ethnically specific elite groups. In this way, future leaders are less likely to be interested in working towards a truly multicultural society.

It is not just ethnic diversity that Singaporeans do not truly celebrate. Many Singaporeans articulate very negative views about homosexuals, the disadvantaged, the poor, and those who do not conform to the standards of beauty and good behaviour. Many Singaporeans are also very negative towards 'rebels' or those who fearlessly opt out of the obvious paths to success, choosing instead to pursue their own passions (many artists belong to this category). In Singapore, difference is not welcome unless it is fashionable and officially sanctioned! Many Singaporeans had treated HIV/AIDS patients with cold detachment before the authorities decided that it was time to be more charitable towards them (Ghosh 18 July 2004). Transsexuals, though, are still subjected to public ridicule (Ong 1 March 2003).

Singaporeans are afraid that if diversity were to be given free reign, then there will be anarchy; and the safe, secure, and clean environment which the Singapore government has sought so tremendously hard to provide will be threatened. I can well understand the misgivings here, but I am also confident that given the Singapore government's robust approach to solving any problem that has come its way, this kind of diversity could also be accommodated as long as there is sufficient political will.

If Singapore wants to be integrally plugged into the processes of globalization, then it must allow for more civic space and avenues of public expression for a wide range of cultural practices and habits. There are already signs of this happening, especially in the more cosmopolitan areas of Singapore, but it is a message which needs to be driven home at every level of societal interaction before the world can be convinced that Singapore has genuinely accommodated itself to the wider culture of globalization. The sooner the population gets educated about the virtues of real diversity, the better the long-term results. All over the world, the culture of diversity-celebration has set in. And Singapore needs to embrace this.

Tolerance

The near-elimination of traditional causes of strife and conflict relating to ethnicity, religion, and language must count amongst Singapore's many impressive achievements since gaining independence in 1965. Few nations can, after all, be proud of their track record of maintaining peace among ethnic, religious, and linguistic communities within their boundaries. But Singapore should move beyond tolerance and towards harmony. Tolerance is easy; it is simply the peaceful coexistence of people who are different, but who do not engage or interact at a deeper cultural level. Harmony, on the other hand, demands that all the different groups mix with one another, even taking pride in one another's diverse cultural practices and claiming them all to be a unique part of the Singaporean experience. For it is only when a nation is truly harmonious that its citizens can begin to realize the deep and powerful resonance of their cultural make-up.

A genuinely multicultural society is not easy to realize, but nations like Canada, Australia, and now South Africa are showing credible signs of a harmonious and diverse society that celebrates openness. These three nations have experimented boldly with the more fundamental problems of multiculturalism. They have moved away from the simple 'melting-pot' theories to the more subtle and sophisticated 'mosaic' and 'rainbow' analogies. Their experiences can serve as good examples of nations trying different mechanisms to realize what a globalized future demands: a true acceptance of diverse cultures in which individuals and groups of individuals live together without ever worrying about their different cultural practices, orientations, and histories.

In 2003, Singaporeans from all backgrounds participated in an event called the 'fabric of the nation'. They were invited to submit their personal messages sewn on pieces of cloth that were collected and patched into a large fabric for public display. Though its initial energies appear to have been drawn from the national fight against the outbreak of severe acute respiratory syndrome (SARS), its outcomes have gone beyond this. In the metaphor of 'fabric' – an open textile whose constituent parts hold together cohesively – Singapore may well have found an answer to its own preoccupations with diversity and perhaps even openness.

Conclusion

One of Singapore's pioneering artists, Liu Kang, passed away in 2004. Like so many others of his vintage, the late Liu Kang always maintained that it is vital for a society of people who see themselves as a community to allow the deeper passions to take root and find expression. For him, this was achieved or realized through his art. For many, such a realization remains remote because they live under the impression that Singapore is not an open, accepting, and creative society in which diversity can manifest itself without threat or compromise. Almost daily, Singaporeans read or hear about the kinds and degrees of freedom that Singapore can and ought to have. Because Singaporeans – particularly the more parochial versions of the heartlander – have been safe and comfortably ensconced in their little island, they have tended to forget the lessons of a wider history.

Venice was a glorious city-state that ruled the European shoreline and entire continent for some four centuries. Then the end came unannounced, and Venice was obliterated from the map of Europe's key provinces. Edward Gibbon famously argued that the Roman Empire fell because of the sheer decadence of luxury which permeated all sectors of Roman society in the closing years of its long and vast history. Of course, Singapore is not, and never will be, like Venice or Rome. But the impending threats – intense economic competition, terrorist activity, and so on – loom large. The government must pay heed to the demands for more openness, for diversity, and for tolerance to be translated into harmony.

A vigil is kept for the safe journey of the departed. It can also be viewed as a kind of blessing both from the departed to the vigil-keeper as well as from the vigil-keeper to the departed. But death is hardly a good metaphor with which to end this chapter. One other interpretation of 'keeping vigil' is of someone keeping active watch to ensure that nothing too extraordinary takes place. This is the sense that is referred to by the 'keeping vigil' in the title of my chapter. I believe Singaporeans are still at the stage of keeping vigil when it comes to questions of openness and diversity. The net result of this is tolerance, a sense of well-being comfortably adopted by people when they would rather not engage too seriously with sensitive issues.

However, if Singapore continues to exist at this level, it will face numerous challenges in the coming decades as more Singaporeans begin to desire more freedoms and the apprehension of the Other becomes more marked. In order to keep these challenges under control, Singaporeans will need to educate themselves towards acquiring a national identity that is geared towards the full acceptance and celebration of diversity in an environment proud of its freedom and protective of its independence.

REFERENCES

Arshad, A. (23 May 2004) 'Gum's still a sticky problem', *The Straits Times* (Singapore).

Channel NewsAsia (31 July 2003) 'NTU dons say disputed job data from MOM website', *Channel NewsAsia* (Singapore).

Fang, N. (30 July 2003) 'Creative campus tie-up', *The Straits Times* (Singapore).

George, C. (2000) *Singapore, the Air-Conditioned Nation: essays on the politics of comfort and control 1990-2000*, Singapore: Landmark Books.

Ghosh, N. (18 July 2004) 'Singapore's AIDS warriors', *The Straits Times* (Singapore).

Ho, A.L. (4 September 2004) '3 SAP schools in bicultural scheme', *The Straits Times* (Singapore).

Lee, H.L. (16 January 2000) Speech at the Singapore 21 Forum organized by Ang Mo Kio-Cheng San Community Development Council on 16 January 2000, Grassroots' Club Singapore.

Lee, H.L. (6 January 2004) 'Building a civic society', speech by the deputy prime minister at the Harvard Club of Singapore's 35th Anniversary Dinner, 6 January 2004, Singapore. Online. Available HTTP: <http://www.newsintercom.org/index.php?itemid=34> (accessed 22 December 2004).

Lim, C. (20 November 1994) 'One government, two styles', *The Straits Times* (Singapore).

Mitton, R. (10 March 2000) 'I had a job to do', interview with ex-Singapore president Ong Teng Cheong, *Asiaweek*. Online. Available HTTP: <http://www.asiaweek.com/asiaweek/magazine/2000/0310/nat.singapore.ongiv.html> (accessed 22 December 2004).

Ong, S.F. (1 March 2003) 'Sexual minorities here speak up', *The Straits Times* (Singapore).

Singh, K. (2004) *Thinking Hats and Coloured Turbans: creativity across cultures*, Singapore: Prentice-Hall.

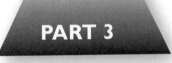

PART 3

NEW POLITICS IN CIVIL SOCIETY

Muslim politics, the state, and society

SUZAINA KADIR

On 4 January 2002, when four 7-year-old schoolgirls defied the Ministry of Education's warning and attended their public school wearing the Muslim headscarf or *tudung*, Singaporeans witnessed what *The New York Times* (Mydans 2 March 2002) described as 'the most potent act of civil disobedience this tightly controlled nation had seen in years'. Local and foreign media carried photographs of the four girls clutching their fathers' hands as they walked into the school compound in school uniforms modified by the modesty-preserving *tudung*. Fear and uncertainty registered on the girls' faces while school officials looked on uncomfortably. In interviews with the local media, one of the fathers admitted that his daughter was reluctant to attend school but he insisted that 'my religion is as important to me as education [so] why do I have to choose between them?' (Mydans 2 March 2002). The four girls were subsequently suspended from school.

The *tudung* controversy, as the incident has come to be called, sparked intense debate between representatives of the Muslim community and the government. The Islamic Religious Council of Singapore (MUIS) was forced to issue a public statement to defuse tensions, pointing out that Islam did not in fact require girls to cover their hair at such a young age (*The Straits Times* 3 February 2002). There were also heated debates on internet discussion groups and protests from international non-governmental organizations. The Association of Muslim Women Lawyers for Human Rights (KARAMAH) sent an official letter of protest to Singapore's ambassador to the United States, insisting that the Singapore government abide by its constitutional guarantee to uphold the religious freedoms of its minority communities (al-Hibri 2002). Since their political independence, Singaporeans have been both proud of and nervous about their ability to manage a multiethnic and multi-religious population. The *tudung* controversy uncovered a serious source of contention – previously downplayed – between a minority religious community and the state.

This chapter explores the contemporary relationship between the minority Muslim community and the state. How has this relationship evolved over time? Have new arenas of contestation emerged? Can the *tudung* incident be seen as an act of civil disobedience against an authoritarian state that infringed on the rights of its religious minorities? If there are new arenas of tension between the Muslim community and the state, what are their implications for a multi-religious and multiethnic Singapore?

These questions are situated within a larger debate surrounding the integration and adaptability of Muslims vis-à-vis the secular nation-state. This debate is not altogether new. Although Muslims comprise only a minority in Singapore, the city-state is not immune to the tensions that involve the larger Muslim world. The emergence in modern Europe of the nation-state, the Reformation, and the Enlightenment paved the way for the institutionalization of a secular public realm of government and a private realm for religion. However, the Muslim world, by and large not revolutionized by the European Enlightenment, propagated a holistic conceptualization of life that embraced politics, economics, and society. For some Muslim communities, this has led to the establishment of Muslim states in contrast to the secular nation-states. For others, it has meant the implementation of Muslim law and the establishment of a Muslim society within a modern state framework. Muslim scholars remain divided, however, on the position of Muslim minorities living within the territorial boundaries of a secular state.

The tensions between secularism and Islam have also been tied to the colonial experience and the nationalist struggles in the early twentieth century. In several parts of Southeast Asia – notably Indonesia and Malaya – Islam became an integral part of the anti-colonial struggle. Yet, the question of fusing Islam and the state was never settled in the post-independence era. The tensions between Islam, democracy, secularism, and the nation-state remain unresolved.

The arguments in this chapter are based predominantly on news reports, interviews with Muslim leaders, and participant observation at dialogue sessions variously involving Islamic organizations and the state. The chapter begins with a discussion of Islam and the Muslim community in Singapore, suggesting that modernization, Islamization, and globalization have produced new tensions within the Muslim community. The chapter then proceeds to explore the vertical linkages between the Muslim community in Singapore and the state, analyzing the public administration of Islam and the new arenas of tension in the evolving relationship between community and state. These horizontal and vertical contestations constitute the increasingly complex sets of linkages between the Muslim minority community and the secular state.

Malays and Muslims in Singapore

Muslims constitute a politically significant religious minority in Singapore, making up 14.9 per cent of a total population of 3.26 million (Singapore Department of Statistics 2001: 9). An overwhelming majority of Malays – some 99.6 per cent – are Muslims. The majority of Muslims in Singapore are Malays, leaving only about 1 per cent of non-Malay Muslims. This category consists of Singaporeans of Arab and Indian descent, as well as Chinese and Eurasian Muslim converts.

The conflation of ethnic and religious identities yields several implications. On one level, it means that the question of national integration or accommodation involves both a religious as well as ethnic dimension. On another level, this conflation has led to a perception of homogeneity when thinking about Muslims in Singapore. On a third level, it links Singapore's Muslims to an ethnic and religious majority in the region. Singapore's immediate neighbours – Indonesia and Malaysia – have populations that are overwhelmingly Malay and Muslim. Muslims make up some 87 per cent of Indonesia's 210 million people. In Malaysia, Malays and Muslims make up about 60 per cent of the population (Central Intelligence Agency 2004). Hence, while Muslims are a religious minority within Singapore's territorial boundaries, they constitute a majority within the region, a fact that the Singapore government has been acutely aware of. In 1987, then-Second Minister for Defence Lee Hsien Loong admitted that the government was uncertain about the loyalty of Singapore Malay-Muslims in the event of a war against fellow Malay-Muslims in the region (Leifer 2000: 94). This point was reiterated by then-Senior Minister Lee Kuan Yew in 1999 at a dialogue session with Malay-Muslim leaders (Ng and Lim 1999).

Much of the scholarship on ethnicity in Singapore focused on the issue of Malays rather than Muslims (Hanna 1966; Bedlington 1974; Li 1989; Rahim 1998). The socioeconomic status of Malays vis-à-vis the Chinese majority has been a matter of particular concern. For example, data shows that Malay-Muslims continue to lag behind the Chinese and Indian communities in education and income levels. Data from Gallup International shows that only 11 per cent of Malay-Muslims earn more than US$2,000 a month compared to 30.8 per cent of Chinese and 18.9 per cent of Indians (Kadir and Horiuchi 2003: 6–7). Also, only 28 per cent of Malays gained admission to post-secondary educational institutions and polytechnics compared to 68 per cent of Chinese and 37 per cent of Indians (Yayasan Mendaki 2002). At the tertiary level, only 4.2 per cent of Malay-Muslims were admitted to universities in 1999. These statistics have led to allegations that Malay-Muslims in Singapore are a marginalized community much like Muslim minorities elsewhere in Southeast Asia (Rahim 1998).

Singapore government officials have acknowledged the disparity and adopted a predominantly ethnic-linguistic lens when addressing the issue. For example, state policies have focused almost exclusively on helping the Malay community improve their economic status. In 1980, the government established Yayasan Mendaki, a self-help organization that provides free tuition classes for Malay students who cannot afford private tutors. Mendaki has also branched out to explore economic opportunities for Malays and to provide welfare services for poorer families. Other government-aided organizations such as the Association of Muslim Professionals (AMP) also focus on improving the educational standards and socioeconomic status of Malays. As a result of these collective efforts, the educational levels of Malays have improved over time. For example, according to data released by Mendaki, 1.3 per cent of the Malay community's Primary 1 cohort eventually gained admission to polytechnics and universities in 1980, but this figure rose to 13 per cent in 1990.

Islam arrived in Southeast Asia during the fourteenth century via Arab and Indian traders who plied the India-China trade routes. Mass conversions of indigenous communities, however, only occurred when sultans of the various coastal kingdoms began to embrace Islam (Roff 1967; Hooker 1984). The religion then spread inward, mixing with and adapting to the existing cultures and traditions in Southeast Asia. The emergence of a Malayo-Muslim community – the amalgamation of Islam and Malayness – occurred gradually (Roff 1967); but over time, Islam came to supersede the ethnic identity of the Malays.

At the beginning of the nineteenth century, Muslims in Singapore could be divided into two broad categories – those who migrated from within the region including Java, Sumatra, and Riau, and those who came from outside it, notably Indian and Arab Muslims (Siddique 1986). The migrant nature of Singapore society meant that there was no indigenous traditional authority which governed or represented Islam (Siddique 1986: 317). Hence,

> because of the ethnic heterogeneity of the Singapore Muslim population, one had, for at least a better part of the 19th Century, not a Muslim community but a number of Muslim communities … reinforced from within by the preservation of linguistic barriers, place-of-origin, occupational specializations, diverse economic and educational levels. (Siddique 1986: 318–19)

The situation began to change only at the end of the nineteenth century as British administration became more direct and urbanization started to break down existing barriers between the different Muslim communities. In 1877, representatives of the Muslim communities approached the British to improve on the administration of Muslim marriages, resulting three years later in the enactment of the Mohammedan Marriage Ordinance. These Muslim representatives also sought British help to coordinate *haj* (religious pilgrimages to

Mecca) activities and manage religious funds. In 1906, the Muslim Endowments Board was established, and in 1915 the Mohammedan Advisory Board was set up, providing an official avenue for Muslim representatives to negotiate with the British government.

These developments paved the way for Muslim representation in the colonial state. But more importantly, they began to centralize religious administration, allowing for the evolution of a specific religious consciousness among the different Muslim communities. The emerging Muslim elite emphasized the implementation and practice of Islamic *Shariah* law to anchor religious identity and transcend ethno-linguistic differences (Roff 1967). Influenced by modernist thinking from the Middle East that sought to purify Muslim communities from traditional non-Islamic practices, the Muslim elite turned to *Shariah* as the best way forward in the Islamization process.

The British, in turn, aided in the formation of a Malayo-Muslim identity among Singapore Muslims by recognizing Malays as the legitimate representatives of Islamic authority (Siddique 1986: 324–25). By the early 1900s, Muslim elites in Singapore had become intent on gaining representation in the legislative council. The British administrators promised that a seat would be created for a Muslim representative when a qualified person became available (Yegar 1979). In 1921, the Muslim Institute – a Muslim organization dominated by Arab and Indian Muslims – sought two seats for the legislative council, one for a Malay and the other for a non-Malay Muslim. The British eventually agreed to the appointment of a Malay – Mohd Eunos Abdullah – to the legislative council, but rejected the appointment of an Arab Muslim. Hence, when it came to Muslim representation, the British recognized only the Malays as legitimate representatives of Islam in Singapore.

The institutionalization of Islamic administration intensified and accelerated after the Japanese Occupation in the early 1940s, culminating in the Muslim Ordinance of 1957 and the setting up of the *Shariah* Court and the Registry of Muslim Marriages (ROMM) in 1958. After Singapore's independence, the Administration of Muslim Law Act (AMLA) was enacted, which allowed for the establishment of the Islamic Religious Council of Singapore (MUIS) in 1968. As sole legitimate representative of Islam in the eyes of the government, MUIS played a central role in shaping the Muslim community. The centralization of Malay-Muslim administration played a pivotal role in moulding a religious identity that sought to transcend the ethno-linguistic divide among Muslims in Singapore. The religious consciousness that emerged fused Malay and Islamic identities together and leaned heavily on the side of *Shariah* (Roff 1967). Malay-Muslim religious consciousness in Singapore continued to evolve in the later half of the twentieth century, impacted in large part by the global Islamic revivalism of the 1960s and 1970s. This movement pushed for Islam to be the dominant if not exclusive identity of its adherents. It propagated the notion of a transnational Islamic *ummah* (religious community) as an integral part of Muslim identity (Mutalib 1990: 878). The global Islamic revivalism of the 1970s also pushed for a comprehensive conceptualization of Islam as a way of life and an anchor for economics, politics, state, and society.

In Singapore, Islamic revivalism took the form of increasingly assertive manifestations of a stricter Muslim identity. For example, media images from the 1950s regularly portrayed Malay-Muslim women wearing *kebaya* that emphasized the female form. These *kebaya* were tight and often made of lacy, almost see-through material. The figure-enhancing corsets worn by many Muslim women underneath the *kebaya* were also visible in photographs and in film (Mutalib 1990; Fong 2000). By the 1990s, in contrast, a typical Malay-Muslim woman's dress code would include a headscarf that covered most of her head and a loose and baggy *baju kurung*. Similarly, Muslims were adhering more strictly to their Islamic obligations, particularly over stricter definitions of their *halal* dietary requirements (Fong 2000).

A growing Islamic consciousness is also evidenced by the increasing number of Muslim parents opting to enrol their children in *madrasah* (Islamic schools). Data from MUIS shows that the number of students applying to join *madrasah* jumped from 824 in 1994 to 1,354 in 2000. In 2000, a Gallup survey of 1,000 households asked respondents to rank their personal identification with race, religion, and neighbourhood (Kadir and Horiuchi 2003). The data showed that while the Chinese identified more strongly with their ethnicity and neighbourhood, Malays identified chiefly with religion. The data therefore supports the observation of a general trend among Malay-Muslims of increasing identification with religious symbols.

Growing pluralism

However, Islamic revivalism has not produced a homogeneous Islamic identity. Eicklemen and Piscatori (1996) show that a revivalist ideology, when coupled with modernization, urbanization, and globalization, in fact produced more sites for contestation of meaning and representation within Islam. While revivalist thought has reinforced the role of the *ulama* (Islamic scholar), greater access to education and exposure to different Muslim communities have produced newly emerging centres of religious authority. Cyber-*ulama* and younger western-educated Islamic scholars have become more vocal in their debates with the traditional *ulama*, especially over the latter's literal interpretations of the *Qur'an*. Even in Iran, there have been serious challenges to the dominant discourse of the traditional clerics.

In the increasingly globalized circumstances that characterize Singapore's 'renaissance' aspirations, the observation of a rising religious consciousness among Muslims should not lead to an erroneous assumption of homogeneity brought on by the global Islamic revivalism. Although historical developments in Singapore have conflated Islamic and ethnic identities, the Muslim 'community' is likely to become more heterogeneous and plural. For example, different levels of religiosity appear to be linked to different educational and income levels among Muslims, as inferred from the increasing trend among parents with post-secondary education to enrol their children in Islamic schools. As with other parts of the Muslim world, modernization and globalization are producing different understandings of Islam and its practices.

In Singapore, this can be observed especially among the *ulama*. The first generation of *ulama* from the 1940s to the 1960s were educated in Islamic schools in the region and were steeped in knowledge of the *Shariah*. Yet, they also embraced *Sufi* thought and retained an accommodating attitude towards local traditions and customs. *Sufi* mysticism is generally more tolerant of diversity in the teaching and practice of Islam. This can be contrasted with *Wahhabi* and *Salafi* thought that emphasize fundamentalist precepts in the interpretation of Islam.

The first generation of *ulama* taught in the various *madrasah* in Singapore and played an important role in making Singapore a regional hub for the teaching of Arabic languages in Southeast Asia (Mutalib 1996). Ustaz Burhanuddin Al-Helmy who taught at Madrasah Aljunied in the 1950s is an example of first-generation *ulama*.

By the end of the 1960s a few students from Madrasah Aljunied were able to gain entry to the prestigious Al-Azhar University in Cairo. Al-Azhar, the only Islamic university at the time to be recognized world-wide for its expertise and teaching methods, maintained strict admission criteria. The close connection between Al-Azhar and Madrasah Aljunied, however, allowed for a select few students to gain admission to the university. A second generation of Islamic scholars with wide exposure to the global revivalist thinking that was sweeping the Middle East in the 1970s emerged from this experience. Many of them were exposed to the teachings of the Muslim Brotherhood, whose members operated on the Al-Azhar campus in Cairo. Hence, this second generation of Islamic scholars developed a somewhat rigid interpretation of Islam and the *Shariah*. They sought to create an Islamic society in Singapore by focusing on raising religious consciousness among Muslims. For example, the Singapore Islamic Scholars and Religious Teachers Association (PERGAS) under the leadership of Ustaz Ali consciously chose not to engage the state on issues of morality or society (Murat 23 February 2004). Instead, PERGAS focused on educating the population to become better Muslims by eradicating their non-Islamic practices and beliefs.

The educational background of the third generation of Islamic scholars has been even more diverse. Haniff Hassan (2001) classifies these scholars into three groups – those who were educated entirely in local *madrasah*, those with a mixture of *madrasah* and secular (state-provided) education, and those who underwent the traditional method. The traditional method included some formal education in *madrasah* but consisted mainly of hands-on training under the first- and second-generation *ulama*. In addition to these three categories of third-generation *ulama*, an increasing number of *ulama* were coming back to Singapore after obtaining their degrees from universities in the Middle East, other than Al-Azhar. By the 1980s, *madrasah* graduates from Singapore were gaining entry to the University of Medina (Hassan 2001).

Islamic scholars returning from Medina displayed a staunchly *Shariah*-oriented mindset and were determined to push society towards the proper implementation of Islamic law in everyday life. Among the third-generation *ulama* in Singapore, there are several discernible groups with very different approaches towards Islamic teaching. For example, there is a recognizable difference between younger *ulama* trained in Al-Azhar and Medina. While both groups give a literal interpretation of the *Qur'an*, Medina graduates tend to be far stricter in their approach. The Medina-educated *ulama* also believe that engagement with society and state is necessary to protect the moral being of Muslims (Hasbi 2004). Interestingly, *ulama* with both secular and *madrasah* education – such as Ustaz Fatris and Ustaz Murat from PERGAS – display a reformist bent in their interpretation of Islam. In contrast to the Medina-trained *ulama*, this group, for example, insists on the need to understand the context of Islamic teaching, rejecting literal interpretations of the *Qur'an*.

Higher levels of education and technological advances have enabled ordinary Muslims to access and reinterpret their religion without the intermediary role of the *ulama*. In countries like Egypt, Iran, Malaysia, and Indonesia, for example, movements calling for a liberal or even secular interpretation of the *Qur'an* have emerged alongside more *Shariah*-minded approaches. Using new media of communication such as the internet, many western-educated Muslim scholars have challenged the traditional authority of the *ulama*. In Singapore, such movements are still in their infancy. Nevertheless, there has been greater openness on the part of the Islamic Religious Council of Singapore (MUIS) towards these liberal thinkers in recent years. In 2003, MUIS invited Muslim scholars like Asghar Ali Engineer, Tariq Ramadan, Abdullah An'Naim, and Ulil Abshor Abdillah to speak to the Muslim public. The response was very good, with high levels of interest from the younger, well-educated Muslims.

These developments suggest that, in addition to generational shifts among the *ulama* in Singapore, there may also be growing plurality among younger Muslims in their orientation towards Islam. Alami Musa, the president of MUIS, explained that Muslims in Singapore have gone through three phases of development to date. The first phase (1965–1979) – 'traditionalist Islam' – involved the fusion of religion with existing cultural traditions. Muslims then underwent a 'revivalist phase' – the second phase (1980–2000) – when they sought a return to a purified version of Islam as a way of life. Today, Muslims in Singapore are embarking on a 'progressive phase' – the third phase (2001–present) – exploring their position within a secular state (Alami 17 April 2004). These different phases have produced among Muslims a plurality of interpretations of and perspectives on their religion. Alami Musa added that the challenge for MUIS was to create an environment of tolerance for divergent views and ideas among Muslims (Alami 26 June 2004), an approach that seems to be in concord with the aims expressed in the *Renaissance City Report* (Ministry of Information and the Arts 2000).

To summarize, while there has been a conflation of ethnic and religious identity in Singapore, this conflation has not led to homogeneity within the Muslim community. Rather, modernization, Islamization, and globalization have produced a growing plurality of interpretations of and approaches to Islam in Singapore as well as in other parts of the world. This plurality of views can be seen through the generational shifts in Singapore's *ulama* community as well as the younger generation of 'progressive' Muslims.

Eickleman and Piscatori (1996) point out that the growing plurality of voices would inevitably result in a horizontal contestation for religious authority and representation among the Muslim communities around the world. They refer specifically to the emergence of a new religious elite who sought to challenge the traditional authority of the *ulama*. In Singapore, new tensions are emerging over a range of issues pertaining to Islamic identity within a secular nation-state. They include differences of opinion regarding the role of Islamic education, the wearing of Muslim headscarves in public schools, and secularism as a principle. More importantly, these horizontal contestations over meaning have spilled over into vertical tensions with the state over the legitimate representation of the Muslim community.

The administration of Islam

Singapore is a secular state. Its constitution upholds the right of groups to adhere to their religious faiths but enshrines a clear separation of church and state. A historical record of racial and religious riots, such as the 1964 riots that broke out during the Prophet

Muhammad's birthday celebrations, justifies strong controls on religious activities in Singapore. For example, while all religious groups are granted space to practise their faiths, open and aggressive proselytizing is not allowed. Additionally, following the involvement of church groups in an alleged Marxist conspiracy against the state in the late 1980s, a Maintenance of Religious Harmony Act (1992) was enacted, authorizing the state to 'take action against any religious group or institution that carried out subversive activities under the guise of practising religious belief'.

Yet, it is important to note that the state neither bans nor bars religious activities. In fact, it could be argued that the state actually encourages a moral code for its citizen-community, but insists that religious identity be kept out of politics. Singapore's version of secularism, as propagated by the state, is fairly complex and not simply a privatization of religion.

On Islam, the state's position is even more complex. The framework for the administration of Islam was laid out during the later part of the British colonial experience. The Muslim elite negotiated for state representation and pushed for greater coordination of Islamic practices. They also pushed for the implementation of *Shariah* as a customary code alongside civil law. In 1965, the Administration of Muslim Law Act (AMLA) was introduced in parliament. The bill was intended to reinforce the Muslim Ordinance of 1957 and synchronize the management of Muslim affairs such as the collection of *zakat* (tithe), administration of mosques, management of *wakaf* land (land bequeathed for religious purposes), and coordination of *haj* (pilgrimage) activities. Hence, AMLA reinforced the position of the *Shariah* courts and the Registry of Muslim Marriages (ROMM) established earlier under the Muslim Ordinance.

AMLA also called for the creation of a statutory board that could advise the government on matters pertaining to the Muslim community. The Islamic Religious Council of Singapore (MUIS) was set up in 1968 and was initially made up of an executive president who was appointed by the president of Singapore on the recommendation of the prime minister and a list of nominees from the different Muslim societies in Singapore. Additionally, the position of the *mufti* was also created. The *mufti* presided over the Fatwa Committee in MUIS with the responsibility of issuing religious rulings pertaining to Islamic law.

With the establishment of MUIS, Muslims in Singapore had a religious bureaucracy that sought to administer and manage the community. However, as Siddique points out, 'few foresaw the hegemonic role which MUIS would play in the development of the Muslim community in the 1970s and 1980s', and in particular its role in the collection of *zakat fitrah* (annual obligatory tax), the administration of all *wakaf* land by the Muslim Endowments Board, and the centralization of the *haj* pilgrimages (Siddique 1986: 326–27). From 1975 onward, all Singapore pilgrims had to register with MUIS before obtaining their travel visas. Also, they could only perform the *haj* through MUIS-approved vendors.

The centralization of religious administration was also evident in the role that MUIS came to play in mosque management. Before Singapore's independence, each mosque was constructed and maintained by Muslims living within its vicinity. However, in the post-independence period, the government embarked on a massive public housing development project, resulting in the repopulation of many Muslims into modern estates with high-rise apartments. As such, they were cut off from their village mosques. Although MUIS was originally given the responsibility for administering some 90 mosques (Siddique 1986: 327), it quickly became a key player in ensuring that the newly repopulated minority Muslim communities would not be deprived of their own neighbourhood mosques. In the 1970s, the decision was made to build large centralized mosques in each housing estate. To help in the building and maintenance of the mosques, MUIS pushed for the establishment of a Mosque Building Fund (MBF) which would utilize a small portion of the Central Provident Fund (CPF)[1] savings of Muslim citizens. The government finally agreed to the MBF in 1975.

The MBF is wholly administered by MUIS and has been crucial to the massive construction of 'new generation' mosques throughout Singapore. Between 1975 and 1980, six new mosques were built amounting to a cost of just under S$11 million. Each mosque was capable of accommodating between 1,000 and 2,000 people, and was equipped to house a wide range of activities. As a result, from the 1980s onwards, mosques flourished as centres of activity for Muslims. These new generation mosques have provided kindergartens, religious classes, pilgrimage classes, Arabic language courses, remedial tuition classes, and even family counselling services. Haji

Maarof Salleh, the former president of MUIS, proudly proclaimed that mosque building and management had been among the most successful responsibilities undertaken by MUIS. These projects were so successful that complaints were often heard from the government that Muslims were not making use of facilities provided by the community centres in the public housing estates (Maarof 21 April 2004).

The state's centralized administration of Muslims in Singapore, however, has not always been smooth. While the administration of *Shariah* courts and the Registry of Muslim Marriages were made possible with the Administration of Muslim Law Act, and while tasks like mosque building and maintenance were being handled by MUIS, obtaining centralized control over autonomous Islamic institutions – such as the *ulama* and PERGAS – was more difficult to achieve. Many of these institutions had been in existence before the establishment of MUIS. Even though nominating people for the mosque management committees required MUIS' approval, the *ulama*'s authority within the mosques cannot be easily challenged (Razak 15 January 2004). Individual *ulama* can still deliver their own sermons over and above the texts provided by MUIS, although most would read the MUIS-prescribed texts first.

More recently, the question of Islamic education in Singapore has highlighted the difficulties of administering Islam through a centralized bureaucracy. In 1999, then-Prime Minister Goh Chok Tong voiced his concerns over the number of *madrasah* students who were dropping out of school without completing their 'O' level examinations (*The Straits Times* 23 August 1999). The speech and subsequent announcement that the Ministry of Education would make elementary school education compulsory for all Singaporeans sparked a storm of discussion within the Muslim community on the future of Islamic education in Singapore. In the process, it became clear that MUIS had been unable to extend its administration over the *madrasah* in Singapore. MUIS officials I interviewed admitted that they had very little power and authority over these schools that had been in existence since the late-nineteenth and early-twentieth centuries (Razak 15 January 2004). Additionally, the *madrasah* have come under the purview of the Ministry of Education as 'private schools' whose authority supersedes that of MUIS. Therefore, the *madrasah* and their *asatizah* (religious teachers) enjoyed substantial autonomy in administration, curriculum, and teaching. There are in fact a number of religious organizations and bodies that operate with relative autonomy from MUIS, including PERGAS, the Young Muslim Women's Association (PPIS), and Jami'yah. Many of these organizations existed before Singapore's independence. Although MUIS oversees them, these organizations retain their institutional independence. Disagreements between MUIS and these associations have occurred in the past but, more often than not, behind closed doors. For example, there were disagreements between MUIS and Indian-Muslim associations over the use of the Muslim endowment fund in the 1970s. In the past few years, disagreements between MUIS and Islamic bodies have become rather more public. For example, in the run-up to the war on Iraq, four Islamic organizations in Singapore issued a statement objecting to the US move. MUIS registered discomfort but stopped short of making a statement against the US-led war.

Emerging arenas of contestation

Islam in Singapore has seen both horizontal and vertical contestations of meaning and representation. Globalization, Islamization, and modernization have enabled a growing pluralism of meaning in the theology and practice of Islam among Muslims in Singapore. Evidence of this can be seen most clearly in the emergence of a new generation of Islamic scholars, including a growing number who are returning with university degrees from the Middle East. There are also secular-educated Malay-Muslim professionals who are embracing different perspectives on Islam as a way of life. These emerging pluralities of meaning are, however, confronted by a push for the centralization of religious administration by the state, a process that started during the later half of the British colonial period. In other words, while new ideas and interpretations continue to evolve from within the Muslim communities in Singapore, the space for these contestations to play out appears to be shrinking. This paradox is producing new arenas of tension between the state (often represented by MUIS) and groups within the Muslim community. I highlight here four issue areas that reflect the growing tensions over legitimate representation of Islamic authority in Singapore. The *tudung* controversy mentioned at the beginning of this chapter must be understood in the context of these other areas of contestation.

The madrasah issue

There are six full-time Islamic schools or *madrasah* in Singapore: Madrasah Aljunied, Madrasah Alsagoff, Madrasah Wak Tanjung, Madrasah Al-Maarif, Madrasah Al-Irsyad, and Madrasah Al-Arabiah. They all predate Singapore's independence. After independence, however, *madrasah* education grew increasingly less popular as Malay-Muslim parents opted to send their children to national schools. This was understandable since the government embarked on an extensive programme to standardize and upgrade education in Singapore. For example, the primary school leaving examination (PSLE) and the GCE 'O' Level certification examinations were introduced in the early 1970s. These examinations determined students' access to the next level of education. It soon became clear to many Muslim parents that the national schools were more equipped to administer and prepare students for these examinations. As a result, more parents chose to enrol their children in national secular schools as opposed to the *madrasah*.

Enrolment figures changed in the mid-1980s, with a growing number of parents opting to send their children, in particular young girls, to Islamic schools. Like their counterparts in other parts of the world, Singaporean Muslims were exposed to the ideational flows from Islamization in the 1970s. Many of these Muslims had become parents with school-going children by the middle of the 1980s. With a new understanding of Islam, these parents opted for *madrasah* education since it was perceived to be the best all-round education for their children (Razak 17 July 2003).

Parents were also choosing to send their daughters, more than their sons, for an Islamic education. The gendered nature of Islamist thought that emerged in the 1970s can perhaps explain this. Maududi, an influential Islamic thinker at the centre of Islamization in the 1970s, advocated a clear division between the roles accorded to women and men in an Islamic society. The need to protect the 'weak', of which women were a core component, served as a justification for many parents to enrol their daughters in an Islamic school. Many of these parents had also come to believe that wearing the headscarf was a religious obligation for Muslim women. The *madrasah* were the only educational institutions that allowed this practice.

By the 1990s, there was a discernible increase in the number of students enrolled in the *madrasah*. In August 1999, government officials expressed concern about increased enrolment in such schools, sparking off heated discussions within the Muslim community and between the representatives of the *madrasah* and the government. Much of this debate occurred within the now inactive PERGAS website – *CyberUmmah* – with accusations that the state intended to eliminate the last bastion of autonomous Islamic activity in Singapore.

When the government subsequently announced its intention to make education compulsory for all children from ages 6 to 10, PERGAS issued a stern warning against any effort to undermine or shut down Islamic education in Singapore (*The Straits Times* 1 April 2000). PERGAS' statement caught many by surprise. For the first time, it indicated a willingness to confront the state openly. PERGAS officials explained that they had little choice but to express their views on the issue in this direct and uncompromising way (Hasbi 15 October 2003; Murat 15 October 2003; Zul 15 October 2003). Meanwhile, those from outside the *ulama* community argued that if public schools could allow Muslims to adhere to Islamic practices, including the wearing of headscarves for women and scheduled prayer times, *madrasah* education would not be so attractive to Malay-Muslim Singaporeans. Yet, others agreed with the government's position that the *madrasah* were not performing up to the mark. They called for greater coordination of *madrasah* curriculum and teacher training by MUIS.

The *madrasah* debate appeared to have opened a pandora's box in the struggle for meaning and representation within the Muslim community and in the relationship between the Muslim community and the state. Government officials appeared to be surprised at the emotional response from the *ulama* community, while the debates clearly showed that Muslims themselves were quite divided on the issues. Finally, the government backed off and decided to exempt students enrolled in the six full-time *madrasah* from compulsory education in the public school system. The state insisted however that the six *madrasah* would have to prepare their students for the nationally standardized primary school leaving examination and that it had the right to review the performance of these students at the end of their six years of primary school.

The tudung *issue*

The controversy over the wearing of Muslim headscarves in public schools did not suddenly emerge in 2002. Since the beginning of the 1990s, parents had been asking public school authorities to allow their daughters to wear the headscarf (Murat 17 March 2004; Razak 25 May 2004). Some schools did in fact allow their female Muslim students to cover their heads and wear school uniforms with longer sleeves and skirts. The issue had been frequently raised at dialogue sessions between Muslim groups and the government as well as during the government Feedback Unit's dialogue sessions with the Malay community. In 2000, the issue was raised once again in a dialogue with then-Prime Minister Goh who was told that allowing Muslim students to wear the headscarf would help to control the rising number of parents who were sending their children to *madrasah*. On 4 January 2002, disagreement over the official policy was displayed publicly and civil disobedience led to the suspension of four young girls from school.

Following the incident, MUIS issued a public statement asserting that Islam did not actually require young girls to cover their heads (British Broadcasting Corporation 6 February 2002). MUIS went on to state that, if a choice had to be made, Islam prized education over *aurat* (what is allowed to be displayed in public). This position was, however, not accepted by the *ulama* community. PERGAS issued a statement the next day maintaining that the *tudung* was compulsory and that 'it is the responsibility of every individual Muslim to strive as best he/she can to remove whatever causes which obstruct the fulfilment of one's religious duties'. The scholars implored the Muslim community to play a part in 'finding a way such that our children can be permitted to don the modest attire as required by Islam when they are in school' (PERGAS 2002).

Today, the *tudung* issue has not disappeared completely. Muslims were merely placated when then-Prime Minister Goh announced that he might consider the possibility of female students being allowed to wear the Muslim headscarf in the future. Muslim leaders whom I interviewed, including the scholars in PERGAS, were confident that if dialogue with the state on the issue was kept open and consistent, the government would ultimately allow the Muslim dress code to become institutionalized. In their refusal to refute the claims of the *ulama* on the issue, MUIS officials put themselves in an awkward position. The *tudung* issue could have been an opportunity for MUIS to discuss the fundamental question of women's rights in Islam, including the issue of attire for Muslim women as mandated by the religion. However, the discussions did not focus on the validity of the *ulama*'s claim. They instead focused on strategies of negotiating with the state. In so doing, MUIS reinforced the belief that the *tudung* is mandated by the religion and suggested patience on the part of the Muslim community. As a result, MUIS ended up looking powerless as the representative of the Muslim community since all they could do was suggest patience in negotiations with the state. It reduced the legitimacy of MUIS vis-à-vis the *ulama* community, who argued eloquently on religious grounds. At the same time, it kept alive the hopes of many within the Muslim community that the state would come to understand that a Muslim woman must be adequately attired in public.

Islam and secularism

Alami Musa acknowledged an emerging perception that tensions had been developing between Islam and secularism in Singapore (Alami 26 June 2004). An emerging segment of progressive Muslims has been trying to make sense of their position vis-à-vis a secular nation-state, coming to grips with what it means to live as a Muslim minority in a secular state. This may involve maintaining an autonomous sphere for Islamic beliefs and practices without contradicting the basis of a secular state. Muslims would reject secularism if it were an ideology that negated the position of religion. But Muslims would have no argument with a secular state that respected the basic religious beliefs of its citizens. Alami Musa felt that Singapore already guaranteed this in its constitution.

Alami Musa's comments came after a statement on secularism and Islam was issued in 2003 by an *ulama* congress organized by

PERGAS. At this congress that was closed to the public, the *ulama* deliberated on a range of issues including the labelling of Muslims as moderates and radicals, as well as future challenges facing Muslim communities around the world. In a strongly worded response to a local Malay newspaper's report stating that the PERGAS *ulama* had endorsed the need for Singaporean Muslims to adapt themselves to a secular environment, PERGAS denied that such a position was taken at the congress (*Berita Harian* 16 September 2003). The president of PERGAS, Ustaz Hasbi, explained that Muslims could only accept a secular state if it meant that the state would remain neutral towards religious groups in society. He reiterated that Islam was a comprehensive way of life and did not distinguish between the public and private spheres.

The issue of how Muslims should adjust to a secular environment was actively discussed at the 2003 *ulama* congress. It was clear that the *ulama* were cognizant of the tensions inherent in accommodating Islam and a secular environment. For example, the younger, university-trained *ulama* were concerned with addressing the temptations facing Muslim youth, including basic questions on the drinking of alcohol, abortion, and pre-marital sex. There was a clear recognition that the globalized and westernized nature of Singapore society would seriously challenge Muslims and their faith. The newer generation of *ulama* felt it was their responsibility to serve as the moral anchor for Muslim society since, as an *ulama* explained, 'MUIS could not do it'. When asked why, he explained that since 'MUIS is a statutory board, they must serve the interests of the state. It is our responsibility to serve the interest of the Muslim community' (Hasbi 2004).

In the published proceedings of the 2003 convention of *ulama*, entitled *Moderation in Islam in the Context of the Muslim Community in Singapore*, the opening statement of the advisory council of PERGAS stated that they 'endorsed the documents [in the book] as PERGAS's guiding principles for the community' (PERGAS 2004a: xvii). The book reiterated the position of PERGAS on secularism by pointing out that, fundamentally,

> Islam differs from secularism ... [since] secularism segregates the role of religion from matters of society and state, limiting it only to individuals and places of worship [while] Islam has guidelines for

all aspects of life and demand[s] its believers' commitment to *all* its teachings. (PERGAS 2004a: 108–9, emphasis mine)

The tensions between Islam and secularism are likely to persist in the near future. In 2004, PERGAS (2004b) issued a press statement declaring their objections to government plans to turn Sentosa island into a Las Vegas-like casino strip on grounds that gambling is immoral and encourages other immoral activities. Sentosa, a small island off the southern tip of Singapore, has been a tourist and recreational destination for many years. However, dwindling visitor arrivals prompted discussions to locate a casino there to generate economic activities and attract the tourist dollar. The statement by PERGAS was part of a heated public debate over the casino issue, which ended with a government decision to build not one, but two of them in Singapore. It is clear, though, that a new generation of *ulama* is taking a proactive role in protecting the community from what they perceive as the onslaught of secularism.

Publication of the book by PERGAS also reiterated the intention of the association to be proactive in clearly representing the *ulama* and Muslim community to the secular state. The articles contained in the book provide carefully thought out positions on a range of issues that would confront a Muslim minority including Islamic law, militancy, fundamentalism, democracy, and political space. Immediately after the publication of the book, *The Straits Times* reviewed it with a specific focus on the issue of secularism (Simon 2 October 2004). Subsequent reactions in the forum pages included a letter that voiced concern about the possible tensions between secularism and the PERGAS position (Rosle 7 October 2004). A few days later, Ustaz Murat from PERGAS responded with a call for Singaporeans to read the book so that they could better understand how Muslims should behave while living in a secular environment. He emphasized that Muslims could adapt to a secular environment for as long as it did not require them to reject Islamic law and practice (Murat 11 October 2004).

Alternative Muslim leadership

The Association of Muslim Professionals (AMP) was formed in 1991 as an alternative voice to the government self-help group Mendaki. In its early years, the AMP concentrated its activities on the educational and economic advancement of the Malay-Muslim community. Like Mendaki, the AMP conducted remedial classes, provided social welfare services for poor Malay families, and ran enrichment classes for Malay children. However, in 2000 – its tenth anniversary – the AMP proposed a multi-pronged approach towards the betterment of the Malay-Muslim community. It stated an interest in managing the growing Islamic consciousness among Malay-Muslims in Singapore. The organization proposed to develop mosques and argued in favour of harnessing the leadership potential of religious leaders in helping the community move forward. They sought a public role for Islam (Association of Muslim Professionals 2000).

The state's reaction was to reject outright the proposals for alternative Muslim leadership, regarding them as efforts to undermine the legitimacy of the Malay members of parliament. The Prime Minister's Office issued a press statement declaring that if AMP wanted to propose alternative leadership for Malays, they should form a political party and contest the general elections (Osman 10 November 2000). The AMP's proposal for an alternative Muslim leadership marked a rejection of the ethnic and religious conflation of identity that has shaped the way Malay MPs have been taken to be the exclusive representatives of Malay-Muslim interests in parliament and through MUIS. The AMP acknowledged the role that the Muslim elite – clearly the *ulama* – could play as a real bridge between the state and Muslim society in Singapore.

The proposal died a quick death, but not before pointing to an important tension that resulted from the growing plurality among Muslims in Singapore and the diminishing space from the state administration of Islam. Horizontal contestations of meaning and representation have led to questions about who best represents the Muslim community in their negotiations with the state. The colonial period had paved the way for a Muslim elite to administer Islam. In the post-independence period, the state established MUIS as a kind of religious bureaucracy that could advise it on matters pertaining to Islam. This religious bureaucracy has been in the hands of the Malay politicians and not the *ulama*. However, there has been growing contestation over who should legitimately represent religious authority in negotiations with the state. Growing plurality within Islam makes this an even harder question to answer.

Debates over the proposed amendments to the Administration of Muslim Law Act (AMLA) in the late 1990s, for example, testify to this emerging tension between the *ulama* and the Malay elite. In 1995, a review of AMLA was carried out by a select committee consisting of officials from MUIS and Muslim professionals. No *ulama* were specifically consulted during the review. MUIS officials explained that involving the *ulama* at that stage was not necessary since many within MUIS were also Islamic scholars (Maarof 27 March 2004). MUIS then met with several Islamic organizations including PERGAS to discuss the proposed amendments to AMLA. PERGAS objected to the proposal that would give Muslims a choice in going to either the *Shariah* or civil courts to sort out ancillary matters such as custody, maintenance claims, and division of matrimonial property. PERGAS interpreted these moves as undermining the jurisdiction of the *Shariah* court. The exchanges between representatives from PERGAS and MUIS were heated, but the amendments to AMLA were finally enacted in 1998 without incorporating PERGAS' objections. The committee explained that Singapore citizens had to be accorded the right of equal access to civil courts in the event of an irreconcilable dispute at the *Shariah* court (Select Committee 1999).

Conclusion

I have tried to show that Islamic society in Singapore is an evolving entity. While there has been a substantial fusion of localized ethnic identities and religious consciousness, society – and particularly one that aims to be a renaissance society – remains open to external influences and ideational flows. Modernization and globalization have brought dynamic shifts within the Muslim community. Hence, Islamic society in Singapore has not only evolved through different phases, but has become increasingly more pluralistic and complex. At the same time, the relationship between state and society can be characterized by careful attempts to centralize religious authority. The incongruence of growing pluralisms within the society and a centralizing tendency on the part of the state is producing new arenas of contestation. This has led to tensions between the state-sanctioned Muslim elite and the *ulama* community, who are themselves becoming more diverse.

Muslim politics in Singapore can therefore be characterized by these horizontal contestations of meaning and a vertical contest for legitimate representation of Islamic society. To put it another way, emerging tensions between the state and Islam may not, as it is often thought, be about the infringement of religious rights of a minority Muslim community or about a marginalized Malay community. Rather, they are consequences of the growing complexities within Muslim society itself.

The question, therefore, turns to whether the state should allow a new Muslim elite to emerge. This may be problematic since not every Muslim agrees with PERGAS' brand of Islam. The tone that PERGAS has taken, namely in stepping forward as the defenders of the religion, suggests an intolerant attitude to reformist elements within Islam. For example, on the issue of the Muslim headscarf, PERGAS insisted that any ruling on the matter could only be undertaken by 'those qualified in the field so as to avoid confusing the masses'. Muslim politics requires a careful balance between the public administration of Islam and the opening of space for Islamic society to reform itself from within. This may entail less centralization and more space for greater pluralism within Islam in Singapore.

In the aftermath of the 'September 11' terrorist attacks in the United States and the arrest in 2001 of 34 Singaporean Muslim men for planning terrorist attacks in Singapore, this balance will be much harder to achieve in spite of the assertions of the *Renaissance City Report*.

NOTES

1. CPF is a comprehensive social security savings plan originally aimed at providing all Singaporeans with sufficient funds for retirement and medical expenses.

REFERENCES

al-Hibri, A.Y. (2002) 'Letter to Heng Chee Chan', KARAMAH website. Online. Available HTTP: <http://www.karamah.org/press_letterto_ singapore.htm> (accessed 2 October 2004).

Alami, M. (17 April 2004) Discussion between the President of MUIS and Suzaina Kadir, Singapore.

Alami, M. (26 June 2004) Discussion between the President of MUIS and Suzaina Kadir, Singapore.

Association of Muslim Professionals (2000) 'Vision 2010: setting the community agenda in 21st century Singapore', Second National Convention of Singapore Malay-Muslim Professionals, 4–5 November 2000, Singapore Expo Hall, Singapore.

Bedlington, S. (1974) *The Singapore Malay Community: the politics of state integration*, Ithaca: Cornell University Press Southeast Asia Program.

Berita Harian (16 September 2003) 'Pergas tidak seru masyarakat Islam bersifat secular', *Berita Harian* (Singapore).

British Broadcasting Corporation (6 February 2002) '*Mufti* puts schools over scarves'. Online. Available HTTP: <http://news.bbc.co.uk/1/hi/world/asia-pacific/1804470.stm> (accessed 10 November 2004).

Central Intelligence Agency (2004) *The World Factbook*. Online. Available HTTP: <http://www.cia.gov/cia/publications/factbook/> (accessed 9 November 2004).

Eickleman, D. and Piscatori, J. (1996) *Muslim Politics*, New Jersey: Princeton University Press.

Fong, M.-L. (2000) *Modelling Islamization in Southeast Asia: Brunei and Singapore*, Taipei: Program for Southeast Asian Studies.

Hanna, W. (1966) *The Malays' Singapore*, New York: American Universities Field Staff.

Hasbi, b.H. (15 October 2003) President of PERGAS interviewed by Suzaina Kadir, Singapore.

Hasbi, b.H. (23 February 2004) President of PERGAS interviewed by Suzaina Kadir, Singapore.

Hassan, H. (2001) 'Asatizah: siapa dan bagaimana', *At-Takwin*, July–September 2001.

Hooker, M.B. (1984) *Islamic Law in Southeast Asia*, Singapore: Oxford University Press.

Kadir, S. and Horiuchi, Y. (2003) 'Political culture and the Singapore puzzle', IOC Discussion Papers no.8, Institute of Oriental Culture, University of Tokyo, March 2003.

Leifer, M. (2000) *Singapore's Foreign Policy: coping with vulnerability*, London: Routledge.

Li, Tania (1989) *Malays in Singapore: culture, economy and ideology*, Singapore: Oxford University Press.

Maarof, S. (27 March 2004) Former president of MUIS and research fellow at the Institute of Southeast Asian Studies (ISEAS) interviewed by Suzaina Kadir, Singapore.

Maarof, S. (21 April 2004) Former president of MUIS and research fellow at ISEAS interviewed by Suzaina Kadir, Singapore.

Maintenance of Religious Harmony Act, Cap 167A (1992). Online. Available HTTP: <http://statutes.agc.gov.sg/non_version/cgi-bin/cgi_retrieve.

pl?&actno=Reved-167A&date=latest&method=part> (accessed 9 November 2004).

Ministry of Information and the Arts (2000) *Renaissance City Report: culture and the arts in renaissance Singapore*, Singapore. Online. Available HTTP: <http://www.mita.gov.sg/renaissance/FinalRen.pdf> (accessed 22 December 2004).

Murat, M.b.M.A. (15 October 2003) Scholar at PERGAS interviewed by Suzaina Kadir, Singapore.

Murat, M.b.M.A. (23 February 2004) Scholar at PERGAS interviewed by Suzaina Kadir, Singapore.

Murat, M.b.M.A. (17 March 2004) Scholar at PERGAS interviewed by Suzaina Kadir, Singapore.

Murat, M.b.M.A. (11 October 2004) 'Law that governs Muslims lives dynamic and realistic', *The Straits Times* (Singapore).

Mutalib, H. (1990) 'Islamic revivalism in ASEAN states: political implications', *Asian Survey*, 30(9): 877–91.

Mutalib, H. (1996) 'Islamic education in Singapore: present trends and challenges for the future', *Journal of Muslim Minority Affairs*, 16(2): 233–40.

Mydans, S. (2 March 2002) 'By barring religious garb, Singapore school dress code alienates Muslims', *The New York Times*.

Ng, I. and Lim, L. (19 September 1999) 'Reality is race bonds exist', *The Straits Times* (Singapore).

Osman, A. (10 November 2000) 'Malay MPs to reach out more to community', *The Straits Times* (Singapore).

PERGAS (2002) 'English translation of PERGAS stand on hijab issue', PERGAS website. Online. Available HTTP: <http://www.pergas.org. sg/hijab-press2eng.html> (accessed 8 November 2004).

PERGAS (2004a) *Moderation in Islam in the Context of the Muslim Community in Singapore*, Singapore: PERGAS.

PERGAS (2004b) 'PERGAS' response to the proposal to build a casino in Sentosa', PERGAS website. Online. Available HTTP: <http://www. pergas.org.sg/casinoeng.htm> (accessed 8 November 2004).

Rahim, L.Z. (1998) *The Singapore Dilemma: the political and educational marginality of the Malay community*, Singapore: Oxford University Press.

Razak, M.L. (17 July 2003) Director (Mosque Division) of MUIS interviewed by Suzaina Kadir, Singapore.

Razak, M.L. (15 January 2004) Director (Mosque Division) of MUIS interviewed by Suzaina Kadir, Singapore.

Razak, M.L. (25 May 2004) Director (Mosque Division) of MUIS interviewed by Suzaina Kadir, Singapore.

Roff, W. (1967) *The Origins of Malay Nationalism*, Singapore: University of Malaya Press.

Rosle, M.A. (7 October 2004) 'Muslims can benefit from secular governance', *The Straits Times* (Singapore).

Select Committee on the Administration of Muslim Law (Amendment) Bill, Report, Singapore, 1999.

Siddique, S. (1986) 'Administration of Islam in Singapore' in T. Abdullah and S. Siddique (eds.) *Islam and Society in Southeast Asia*, Singapore: ISEAS.

Simon, M. (2 October 2004) 'Soul-searching continues for Muslims in S'pore', *The Straits Times* (Singapore).

Singapore Department of Statistics (2001) *Census of Population 2000*, Singapore: Singapore Department of Statistics.

The Straits Times (23 August 1999) 'Study on fate of madrasah students', *The Straits Times* (Singapore).

The Straits Times (1 April 2000) 'Schooling for all "threatens madrasahs"', *The Straits Times* (Singapore).

The Straits Times (3 February 2002) 'Take practical approach to tudung issue', *The Straits Times* (Singapore).

Yayasan Mendaki (2002) 'Progress of the Malay community since 1990'. Online. Available HTTP: <http://www.mendaki.org.sg/content. jsp?cont_cat_id=12&cont_id=92> (accessed 2 October 2004).

Yegar, M. (1979) *Islam and Islamic Institutions in British Malaya (1875–1941): politics and implementation*, Jerusalem: Magnes.

Zulkifli, b.O. (15 October 2003) Scholar at PERGAS interviewed by Suzaina Kadir, Singapore.

The canary and the crow
Sintercom and the state tolerability index

TAN CHONG KEE

The canary is a popular caged bird that has been bred in captivity for centuries. It is considered a pretty little bird that is pleasant to listen to. Since the fifteenth century, canaries have also been accompanying miners underground to detect poisonous gases that can accumulate in the shafts. As long as the canary remains alive and continues to sing, all is well. Its pleasant song connotes safety. In 1995, after the sarin gas attack, canaries were also used for a similar purpose in the Tokyo subway system. The canary started its relationship with humans as a decorative pet, and evolved to take on the additional function of an early warning system. It is a caged bird that humans have found to be both pretty and useful. The canary represents the pretty bringer of good news.

The crow, on the other hand, is an unpopular wild bird with a harsh voice. Farmers consider these birds to be pests. The Chinese consider their black plumage to be ugly, and they have a saying 天下烏鴉一般黑 ('all crows under the heavens are just as black'). The English sometimes say 'a crow on the thatch, soon death lifts the latch'. Since 1973 in Singapore, crows have been routinely shot in a long-term plan to reduce their numbers (ABC 13 December 2001; Kaur 11 December 2001). But crows are among the most intelligent and adaptable of birds (Microsoft Encarta 2004). In contrast to the canary, the crow represents the ugly speaker of unpleasant truths.

In 1990, Goh Chok Tong became Singapore's second prime minister, promising a 'gentler, kinder society'. Under his administration, there were national consultation exercises like Singapore 21 and Remaking Singapore, as well as policies that pointed towards a flowering of culture and the arts as reflected in the *Renaissance City Report* (Ministry of Information and the Arts 2000). But since 1990, I have been struggling with a certain cognitive dissonance, unable to reconcile official rhetoric with official actions.

In this chapter, I attempt to grapple with this cognitive dissonance by reflecting upon my experience of managing a website called *Singapore Internet Community* (more commonly known as *Sintercom*), and working towards a model to explain what observers have called the paradox (Ignatius 29 September 2002) or puzzle (Haas 1999) that is Singapore. I will first discuss my reasons for founding and then closing down *Sintercom*, and then generalize the experience into an abstract model that might be able to explain the cyclical 'opening up' and 'clamping down' pattern of politics and the similarly cyclical 'rise and fall' pattern of civil society in Singapore. Finally, I will use the model to explain the lack of enthusiasm among the arts community for the articulation of the renaissance city vision.

The insight from the interplay between the two avian metaphors of the canary and the crow lies at the heart of this model.

Reining in the net

The story of the internet in Singapore began in 1990 when Singapore Telecom, then a state-owned monopoly, launched Teleview. While the rest of the world was adopting the internet, the Singapore government chose not to allow public access, but instead established Teleview as the national network.

I remember visiting an information technology exposition in Singapore in the early 1990s and asking the sales manager at the Singapore Telecom booth if he knew when Teleview subscribers would gain access to the internet. I received a strange look from the man. He knew what the internet was. He just did not think my question was appropriate since the sites I wanted to access, such as soc.culture.singapore, contained 'anti-government materials'. Subsequently, Teleview decided to offer limited access to the internet but this concession proved no match for the real thing. Full internet access was, at the time, only available through a separate provider, Technet, and only a limited number of Singaporeans such as government officials, some staff and students at the National University of Singapore, and certain businesses had access to it. Even reporters from the well-established local newspaper, *The Straits Times*, once had to share one email account on a terminal located in their library at the now demolished Times House. Fortunately, such a rear-guard approach was doomed to be a commercial failure. By 1994, SingNet, a subsidiary of Singapore Telecom, started offering internet accounts to Singaporeans (Rodan 1996).

The Teleview experience showed that the internet could not be controlled by *denying* access because this not only incurred huge costs of building an alternative and inferior network, but locked Singapore out of the information technology boom. However, the internet could still be controlled by *restricting* access. The question then was how to restrict access without losing the internet's commercial benefits. The state came up with two groups of strategies to achieve this goal.

The first of these took aim at the 'demand side' of the equation, making access to 'undesirable' content more difficult for users (thus dampening demand) while encouraging more commercial uses of the internet (thus stimulating demand for other kinds of content). The state required that all internet service providers operate proxy servers through which all individual users had to connect. Proxy servers did not just cache copies of websites visited, they denied access to sites banned by the state. In effect, a firewall was erected around Singapore, not to prevent the net-based commercial world from coming in but to stop Singaporeans from going out to 'undesirable' parts of the net. The proxy server strategy was quietly abandoned, to be replaced by parental advisory groups teaching parents the IT skills necessary for installing 'surf guard' software, and prompting them to take personal responsibility in guiding their children's surfing activities. Ang and Nadarajan (1996) discuss other demand-side controls including the deliberate crippling of the Unix shell, the refusal to carry certain usenet newsgroups, the introduction of conditions for usage, the revoking of certain services from users' accounts, and the total denial of log-in access. Also, various attempts have been made to scan users' emails and computers. The second group of strategies to restrict access took aim at the 'supply side'. A poster to soc.culture.singapore, whose messages were critical of government policies, wrote to say that his phone was being tapped (Rodan 2004). While it is certainly true that members of the Young PAP used to lurk in soc.culture.singapore to read and argue against critics of the PAP, it is difficult to find any evidence to prove that phone tapping really happens. Nevertheless, Rodan (2004) argues that 'what matters, however, is the impact these messages have on other users. It is even possible that some claims are fabricated by, or on behalf of the authorities with the aim of creating apprehension and promoting self-censorship'. Self-censorship affects the supply of 'undesirable' content in two ways: it reduces the quantity and quality of such content as fewer people are willing to produce it and those who are willing do not dare to tell the full story.

Since the 1990s, the government has been taking many measures to bring a range of media under surveillance and prohibition. In 1998, the Undesirable Publications Act (UPA) was amended 'to include CD-ROMS, sound recordings, pictures and computer-generated drawings'. In the same year, the Films Act was amended to ban political parties from making or distributing political films or videos (Rodan 2004: 95). In 1996, the government announced the Broadcasting (Class Licence) Act requiring websites to register with the authorities and refrain from producing content deemed undesirable.

A simple registration would appear to be innocuous at first glance until one realizes what else is involved. Firstly, the webmaster is required to sign a contract agreeing to take full personal responsibility for all content that appears on the website. In effect, this means that if an anonymous user posts a libellous message on an unmoderated online forum, the webmaster can be sued for libel. Secondly, registration requires the webmaster and all associated with the running of the website to supply the authorities with information on their salaries and their employers' contacts. Whatever the rationale for requiring this information, the very act of demanding it was sufficient to inspire fear for one's livelihood. To further tighten control over the supply of internet content, the Singapore Broadcasting Authority (Amendment) Bill of April 2001 outlawed engagement in domestic politics through broadcasting, thereby bringing broadcasting in line with printed media (Rodan 2004: 94). The government also passed amendments to the Parliamentary Elections Act to bar any non-political party websites from promoting or campaigning in the name of any candidate or party.

The search for breathable air

Sintercom was a labour of love. Even though my name has been most strongly identified with *Sintercom*, the site grew through the efforts of many people. It would have only been a fraction of what it was at its height had I been the only person directing and developing it. Through email voting, all its members were involved in making major decisions that affected the whole group. Everyone had an equally weighted vote. Through this voting system, for example, it was decided that *Sintercom* would not be turned into a money-making enterprise. Individual editors enjoyed tremendous autonomy in deciding what content to publish. For example, not all editors agreed to launch a black ribbon campaign against internet censorship, but those who felt strongly about it could still go ahead, as long as it was made clear who were responsible by appending names to documents.

Sintercom went through three main stages in its history. The early expansion phase from 1994 to 1997, when *Sintercom* was based overseas, saw increasing numbers of people joining to start new content sections. The second phase from 1998 to 1999 saw a decline in the number of volunteers who were graduating and returning to join the Singapore civil service. In the final two years of existence from 2000 to 2001, *Sintercom* became almost a one-man show again.

In 1994, the first web browser – called Mosaic – was published. That was a time when there were no internet regulations anywhere in the world, a time of the great internet free-for-all. It was when the early state-funded research networks such as ARPANET (Advanced Research Projects Agency Network) had expanded enough to reach a critical mass, but before state agencies realized the need to regulate (Hauben n.d.). As a graduate student at Stanford University – and thus right in the heart of Silicon Valley – I realized that this technology would revolutionize how information is stored and accessed. I decided to use this nascent web technology to make an impact on what I felt was a gaping need in Singapore: honest public debate on current issues.

My first project was to make a selection of pertinent discussions on Singaporean issues permanently and easily accessible by archiving them in web space. These discussions were drawn mainly from the usenet newsgroup called soc.culture.singapore. Usenet was instrumental in opening up space for public debate on almost any subject imaginable. However, its main drawback was that most internet service providers did not keep usenet postings for more than a few weeks, thus rendering them ephemeral. Systematically archiving usenet debates using a web interface allowed the ideas to persist and be easily accessible (Tan 1996). I believed that the web would finally give Singaporeans access to a medium that was not unduly constrained by the state, and this would help Singaporeans to think more deeply about national issues.

Very soon, Singaporeans from all over the world found out about this website and many volunteered to help. They came from the National University of Singapore and the Nanyang Technological University, as well as overseas universities and colleges such as Yale, Oxford, Cambridge, London, Oberlin, etc. Each new volunteer brought their own vision and unique talents, and very quickly, the website became a hot bed of innovations. It produced the first Singlish dictionary, the first online Singapore food guide, the first comprehensive online report on the Singapore general elections, and the first mailing list distributing news about Singapore from foreign media. It managed to clinch first online interviews with many well-known Singaporeans such as diplomat Tommy Koh and banker Wee Cho Yaw. As the de facto champion of internet freedom, it organized in 1996 a very successful online campaign to persuade the Singapore government to review its internet content guidelines, with more than 250 people making very cogent arguments and signing the online campaign using their real names.

In 1994, the founding members of *Sintercom* understood how public debates were made extremely difficult by the prevailing habit of labelling any opinion contrary to the People's Action Party (PAP) orthodoxy as 'anti-government', or worse, as 'disloyal to Singapore'.

The result was either the silencing of critics, or worse, the degeneration of public discourse into emotional name calling, known in internet parlance as a 'flame war'. In soc.culture.singapore, flame wars erupted all the time. However, when the most cogent arguments were extracted from this space and archived on the web, a completely different view of the newsgroup emerged. Opinions ranging from those that staunchly supported the status quo to those that argued passionately for change were all represented. Their inclusion and exclusion were based not on any specific ideology, but on the quality of argument. This first *Sintercom* project, called the Singapore Electronic Forum, was a demonstration of how easy it was to have in Singapore a rational, non-partisan debate. Each member of the *Sintercom* team had their own political stance ranging from conservative to left-leaning liberal, but all felt comfortable being a *Sintercom* member because it was a group that embraced all these persuasions in a spirit of democracy and mutual respect.

A strategy of deliberate naiveté

Many readers believed that the open discussion and bold action they observed on *Sintercom* were possible because the website was not based in Singapore but housed in various university web servers overseas. However, every *Sintercom* editor put his or her identity on public record, and many of us planned to return to Singapore after completing our studies. As editors, we felt that we could act more boldly than others imagined possible because we were merely heeding the Singapore government's call for youths to be more politically engaged. Then-Prime Minister Goh's call for youths to take an active interest in politics was met only with questions about 'jobs, homes and studies' (Ng 18 July 1993). Although the obsession with 'youth apathy' has been a complex ideological phenomenon in Singapore, and one that Kenneth Paul Tan attempts to critique in Chapter 12, the young *Sintercom* editors strategically adopted it as an explicit justification for acting boldly. Two years earlier, then Minister for Information and the Arts George Yeo had used the analogy of 'pruning the banyan tree' to describe the need to reduce the state and allow civil society to grow (Teo 21 June 1991). We acted 'bravely' in *Sintercom* in the reasoned belief that the government surely could not punish those who were merely heeding its call.

In 1997, we accepted an invitation from Philip Yeo, then chairman of Singapore's Economic Development Board, to consolidate all *Sintercom* content onto one server located in Singapore. We felt that moving to Singapore would make our Singaporean readers feel safer about speaking up on issues close to their hearts, in much the same way that a singing canary in a coal pit makes the miners feel safer about descending into the depths of the mine. With hindsight, I can say that we intuitively knew that being hosted on a Singapore server was akin to accepting a gilded cage. But we were on a quest for breathable air for everyone; and thus, willingly became canaries.

The core *Sintercom* team were not interested in scoring points with the PAP by acting as self-appointed champions of government policies – although when we felt a new policy had merit, we would say so. Neither were we interested in scoring points with foreign journalists and observers by styling ourselves as dissidents – although when we felt something was amiss, we would say so too. This insistence on being non-partisan was something hard for casual observers to understand or accept. For example, I was informed on several occasions that someone in the government ministry had counted up all posts and found that those that opposed the government out-numbered those that supported it. Instead of being interpreted as a possible indicator that more and more people were becoming dissatisfied with the government and could make cogent arguments in support of their positions, the observation was taken as an indicator that *Sintercom* was getting more 'anti-government'. Ironically, Australian journalist Eric Ellis (2001) found that '[a]s far as "dissident" websites go, Sintercom.org is pretty tame. In fact it's so underwhelming most days that some of the Singaporeans who visit the site wonder if it's not some cunning plot by their government'. Throughout *Sintercom's* existence from 1994 to 2001, the website was constantly accused of being both an anti-government rant site and a government stooge at the same time. This shows that although what we did touched many nerves, it was never really understood outside of a simplistic pro- or anti-government frame of reference.

The *Sintercom* project revolved around one central question: could ordinary Singaporeans have a stake in their country if they operated only within the bounds of what the PAP had publicly said it would tolerate? One very important thing to realize about *Sintercom* is that the whole project was an attempt to take the Singapore government's words at their face value. At the simplest level, this was a strategy of justifying our entry into civil society as heeding the government's call and obediently doing what we were told to do. At another more important level, it was a strategy to experiment and find out just how feasible it would be to operate within the playing field that the state had delineated for us. If one refrained from contesting the PAP government for political power, gave constructive criticism always, avoided engaging in libel or disrespectful language, stayed resolute on matters of principle, and avoided criticizing personalities – in short, if one did everything in one's power to obey the rules of public discourse as they were laid down by the state – could one, in any meaningful sense, thus speak? (Tan 2001).

Sintercom's stance was circumspect because we were uncertain about what to make of the widely perceived social pact in Singapore that exchanged freedom for prosperity. Was there an inevitable trade-off between freedom and prosperity, or was this trade-off simply a myth? Were Singaporeans really hungry for greater freedom? Or were they – as the 'heartlanders' have often been described – perfectly happy with authoritarian rule as long as they were prosperous? Although, as members of *Sintercom*, we had our own values and beliefs, we did not want to impose these beliefs onto others. Otherwise, we would become a mirror image of the authoritarian state. That is why our mission was not to promote free speech or liberalism in Singapore, but to find ways for ordinary Singaporeans to have a stake in the country, in accordance with what the state said it would allow. If that meant working completely within the publicly declared bounds of state tolerability – because the racial and religious fissures in Singapore were really so deep and powerful that only the state could play the arbitrator role through tight control of free speech, or because most Singaporeans did not want free speech and believed that excessively free speech could lead to the collapse of the economy – then so be it.

After moving the *Sintercom* server to Singapore, we quickly became aware that there was more to being a canary than we had earlier thought. The outburst at the publication of novelist Catherine Lim's two critical commentaries in *The Straits Times* (3 September 1994; 20 November 1994) made it obvious that the Singapore government welcomed certain kinds of political engagement and not others. If Lim's articles had, instead, analyzed and praised the PAP government's success in governing Singapore, would Lim have been told so unceremoniously not to engage in 'politics'? To believe absolutely that the Singapore government welcomed independent and critical engagement was to be naïve. But to continue behaving as if it did, steering clear of issues that had angered the government in the past in order to define a space – no matter how circumscribed – for some kind of open debate, was a strategy of deliberate naiveté.

Realpolitik meets deliberate naiveté

From 1998, as we completed our studies and returned to Singapore, some of us had to stop editing *Sintercom* because of career demands, but others among us became more plugged in to Singapore society and launched new projects on *Sintercom*. One of these projects was to publish original letters sent to *The Straits Times'* forum pages that had either been rejected or substantially modified. It was hoped that by bringing *The Straits Times'* editing decisions into public knowledge, *Sintercom* could induce the newspaper to practise greater editorial circumspection. Another project was to monitor the local news and comment on how it was reported in an attempt to raise people's awareness about journalistic standards and integrity. A third project was intimately tied up with an initiative to promote mutual trust and collaboration among local non-governmental organizations (NGOs), especially between advocacy groups and social service groups. Under the PAP administration, NGOs in Singapore had become increasingly disempowered and isolated from one another. In 1998, a ground-up initiative called The Working Committee (TWC) heeded the Singapore 21 call for active citizenship and tried to revitalize civil society space mainly through capacity building (Singam et al. 2002). Leveraging on the success of these initiatives, the *Sintercom* editors, together with many other activists whom I had met through TWC, even tried to form a media watchdog NGO.

However, things came to a screeching halt in July 2001 when we were told that the Singapore government had decided to classify *Sintercom* as a 'political website', and as such, it had to register. Accepting full responsibility for everything that appeared on the site – including unmoderated postings by readers on the online forums – meant that, as webmaster, I would have had to consult the Singapore Broadcasting Authority (SBA, the predecessor of the Media Development Authority) on the suitability of a great deal of content, in accordance with its Code of Practice (Media Development Authority 1997: paragraph 4[4]).

In theory, if every webmaster of 'political websites' in Singapore had to seek the SBA's judgement on specific web content that was likely to be prohibited, the illusive 'out-of-bound' (OB) markers would over time become more clearly defined. For a brief moment, I believed that as the government tightened its grip, the silhouette of its iron glove would at least begin to show. Once the OB markers became more visible, they could be contested more strategically. This might have led to greater transparency and political accountability. Instead, when the SBA received my inquiries, its officers refused to answer directly, saying that it was up to the webmaster to 'exercise best judgment' on such matters. In order to keep the OB markers undefined, the SBA was willing to disregard its own regulations. This was a seminal moment because it revealed much about the way the Singapore system works. The insight gained from this moment has enabled me to explain why the authorities require that OB markers remain illusive, an explanation that I will offer in the later part of this essay.

After registration, the sword of Damocles hung precariously over our heads. The invitation to 'exercise best judgement' was in effect an invitation to self-censorship. Media researcher and former journalist Cherian George (2003) explains that 'the licensing rule was an administrative procedure to impose accountability, and not a means of preventing anyone from setting up a website'. Concluding that there is really little difference between the regulatory regimes of Singapore and Malaysia, George effectively absolves the government of responsibility for the dearth of internet activism in Singapore, a situation that stands in stark contrast with Malaysia. But George's argument is deeply flawed. For one, regulatory frameworks rarely tell the whole story – what actually happens in practice is often more important. Mahathir Mohamad, then prime minister of Malaysia, made a public commitment not to censor the internet in his bid to attract high-tech companies to the country's Multimedia Super

Corridor. Malaysian activists capitalized on this commitment to launch many alternative websites, especially after the arrest of then-Deputy Prime Minister Anwar Ibrahim. In Singapore, there were no such public commitments or political developments on the internet. Media regulation that presents the threat of being punished under deliberately unclear content guidelines is considerably more insidious and draconian than a mere 'administrative procedure to impose accountability'. The meaning of 'accountability' in this instance is in fact self-censorship.

To continue in self-censorship mode would have been completely against the purpose for which *Sintercom* was founded. But proceeding in the manner that it had done before registration would have risked being interpreted by the state as ignoring a clear official warning. As webmaster, I made one last attempt at finding a solution. Assuming that the decision to make *Sintercom* register as a political website had been a result of some misunderstanding, I requested a meeting with any decision-maker in the SBA or the Ministry of Information and the Arts to discuss the *Sintercom* case in greater detail. Both organizations refused the request.

Having exhausted all possibilities, I reluctantly concluded that the project of fostering open and honest debate on national issues was, in the political climate, premature. After being in existence for eight calendar years and gaining a large loyal following, the website closed down in August 2001. Deliberate naiveté as a strategy had failed. The canary died, illustrating *Sintercom*'s inability to expand the space for debate even by operating completely within the bounds of tolerability that were publicly declared by the PAP government. This can only be due to some undeclared bounds of tolerability, or – to use a term that the state has made popular – the presence of a hidden agenda.

The tale of *Sintercom* has a cautionary happy ending. After it was closed down, many readers missed it so much that various 'new *Sintercom*' sites began to mushroom in cyberspace. These sites, completely anonymous and hosted on overseas servers, do not respect any OB markers. While *Sintercom* was online, it dominated the alternative discourse to such a degree that only a handful of similar sites could be found in cyberspace. The moment *Sintercom* died, cyberspace became much more diverse and even more critical of the PAP government. Ironically, these new sites cannot be forced to register as 'political' sites, since MDA cannot even determine the identity or location of their webmasters. The choking of the canary woke the crows.

The state tolerability index (STI)

From the state's point of view, *Sintercom*'s 'space' was tolerated as long as the annoyance it caused as a crow voicing the occasional criticism of the state was less than its value as a canary that served to deflect charges of state suppression of free speech. When the annoyance caused was eventually judged to be higher than *Sintercom*'s usefulness in this respect, that space shrank and eventually vanished. Conversely, from *Sintercom*'s point of view, its space was only worth maintaining if there were a positive difference between the value of occasionally influencing people into thinking more deeply about the 'freedom versus prosperity' trade-off and the price of being used by the state as evidence to disprove criticisms directed at the lack of free speech in Singapore. When the costs of being used in such a manner became greater than the value of making a critical impact on society, *Sintercom* would have no more reason to continue its operations. Thus, vis-à-vis the state, social activism has two values. The canary value measures how much the state welcomes it, while the crow value measures how much the state dislikes it. The canary value is not merely the reverse of the crow value because the state can simultaneously welcome particular activists for one reason – for example, to serve as poster boy to deflect 'free speech' critics – and yet dislike them for another reason – for example, for using free speech to advocate for change.

The difference between the canary and crow values can therefore measure the state's net tolerance for any particular civil society activism in an environment where the state publicly declares support for such a project yet maintains a hidden agenda to suppress its critical dimension. Let us call this difference the 'state tolerability index' (STI). For example, Remaking Singapore was a state-directed, nationwide consultation exercise that served to demonstrate the government's keenness to listen to the people. It welcomed people like me pushing for reform of the Societies Act because I was evidence that the 'remaking' framework was able to surface tough issues. But at the same time, the Societies Act was being redrafted, seemingly in response to the demands of the Singaporean majority, to make

TABLE 9-1 Sample STI score table (on a 0–10 scale)

Activities	Canary score	Crow score	STI
Challenge PAP rule at general elections	0	10	−10
Criticize a minister's decision and judgment in public	0	8	−8
Be a non-contesting member of an opposition party	1	7	−6
Engage in public debate over government policies	2	6	−4
Take part in civil society	3	5	−2
Non-partisan apathy	0	0	0
Help in voluntary welfare organizations	5	3	2
Join government-linked volunteer groups (for example, through the National Volunteers and Philanthropy Centre)	6	2	4
Be a grassroots leader (for example, join a Citizens' Consultative Committee)	7	1	6
Join the PAP youth wing	8	0–1	7–8
Join the ruling party	10	0–1	9–10

it even more difficult for advocacy groups to be registered (Lim 17 July 2004). In such an environment, civil society activities have a canary value because they are the examples that the state can offer as evidence against accusations of state suppression of civil society. When the canary value is high enough, these activities may even attract state support. However, if these civil society activities go beyond what the state can tolerate – for example, if they are overly critical of the state, or if they advocate for fundamental policy changes – then they will also have a crow value. When the crow value gets too high, the state will act to reduce it, first through warnings, then through direct action.

The canary and crow values shown in Table 9-1 are hypothetical indications of the intuitive sense that individual Singaporeans might have about the state's attitude towards a range of 11 politically related activities. They are presented here for illustrative purposes only. It is important to note that the state probably will not want the crow value of each activity to be too close to zero because it knows that its

FIGURE 9-1 STI curve in 2007

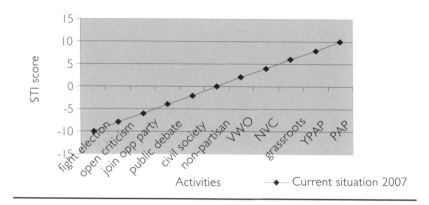

grip on power will be less secure if all it hears are obsequious praises shielding it from the hard truths on the ground. Nor do civil society activists want their canary value to be too close to zero because they understand that a cordial relationship with the state – a body that not only regulates but controls vast resources – is a prerequisite to their own survival.

Shifts in the STI curve

If we draw a 45-degree line with the STI scale on the Y-axis, we can plot out the position of various activities on the X-axis using their respective hypothetical STI scores. Once the X-axis is thus fixed, we can plot out the STI curves at different times and use the STI curve for year 2007 (Figure 9-1) as a basis for comparison.

After Goh Chok Tong took office as prime minister, there was a short interval between 1990 and 1994 when people generally believed that the rhetoric of 'a kinder, gentler society' would herald considerable change, especially a relaxation of authoritarian rule. In Figure 9-2, this perception of a new, more tolerant government is represented by an upward shift of the left part of the curve. The shift indicates a perception of change – what the state had considered intolerable (for example, public debate and an active civil society) became more tolerated with Goh's administration.

FIGURE 9-2 STI curve in 1990 compared with STI curve in 2007

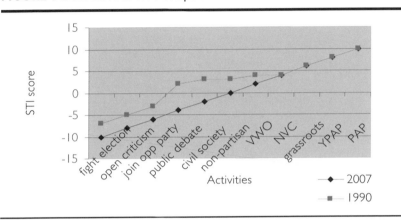

In 1994 though, Catherine Lim wrote her two newspaper articles that were critical of the PAP government, believing perhaps that the Goh administration would be more tolerant of critical discourse. When Goh firmly reprimanded Lim for these articles, warning that critics of the government should join a political party, the public realized that things had not changed significantly (Han 17 December 1994) and the curve shifted down to pre-1990 levels (Figure 9-3). In the remaining years of the Goh administration, much effort went into portraying Singapore as a liberalizing country bolstered by some real examples of liberalization in the field of public entertainment like the relaxation of film censorship and the lifting of the ban on bar-top dancing in nightclubs. The progress in liberalizing public entertainment masked the lack of progress in political liberalization and the STI curve gradually shifted up to the 2007 position illustrated in Figure 9-1. I will examine the discrepancy between public perception and reality as reflected in the STI curve in more detail later.

When Lee Kuan Yew was at the height of power as prime minister in 1980, the STI curve showed a uniform −10 score on all activities that could be remotely conceived as 'anti-government' (Figure 9-4). Lee's attitude towards any kind of opposition was to 'nip it in the bud', and the people were expected to regard as forbidden anything that was not explicitly allowed by the state. Many political activities

FIGURE 9-3 STI curve after the Catherine Lim affair

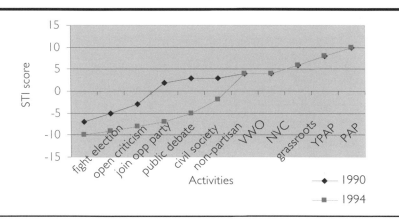

were, in fact, suppressed; and the forcefulness with which they were suppressed is well-expressed by Lee himself even after he handed over the office of prime minister to Goh.

> Supposing Catherine Lim was writing about me and not the prime minister ... she would not dare, right? Because my posture, my response has been such that nobody doubts that if you take me on, I will put on knuckle-dusters and catch you in a cul de sac ... Anybody who decides to take me on needs to put on knuckle-dusters. If you think you can hurt me more than I can hurt you, try. There is no other way you can govern a Chinese society. (Han, Fernandez, and Tan 1998: 126)

When the STI scores of civil society activities are −10 (that is to say, when the state is thought to regard these activities as absolutely intolerable), they will be suppressed at all cost. But where activities are more tolerable, the state will have to think about the cost of suppression. In general, 'suppression costs' consist of administrative costs (policing, public prosecution, etc.), institutional costs (damage to the integrity of institutions such as the constitution, the judicial system, etc.), public relations costs (loss of legitimacy and domestic good will, damage to international image, etc.), and economic costs (loss to gross domestic product due to capital flight, immigration, and so on). If suppression costs are relatively higher than the tolerance for an activity, then that activity can continue to take place.

FIGURE 9-4 STI curve in 1980

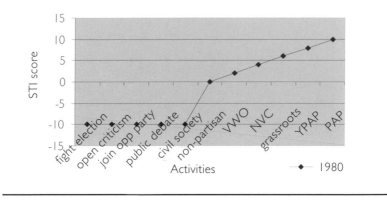

However, even if the tolerance for that activity remains unchanged, a lowering of suppression costs could well lead to it being suppressed. This is why it is possible to argue that there has been an 'opening up' in Singapore since what used to be suppressed has now been allowed. But it is also possible to argue the reverse – that there has not been an opening up – since what used to be suppressed can still be suppressed if suppression costs fall. Thus, in this case, what has changed is merely the suppression cost.

The editors of *Sintercom* believed in the beginning that it was possible to collaborate with the Singapore state and took the deliberately naïve stance of believing the state's public declaration in support of civil society. As a result, *Sintercom* was perceived by the state as having a high STI, let's say 4. Over the years as *Sintercom* championed issues such as the redrafting of internet content regulation, civil society alliance building, media watch, etc., its crow value started to rise, eventually resulting in a STI of say −2. The state stepped in to address that imbalance by requiring *Sintercom* to register as a political website. If, after registration, *Sintercom* had continued to operate under self-censorship mode, the STI balance would have been restored to perhaps +2. However, since that would mean *Sintercom* going back on its founding mission – or to put it another way, since it represented to us a lower crow value than what we were prepared to accept – we chose to close down instead.

FIGURE 9-5 How S21 and Remaking Singapore shifted the STI curve

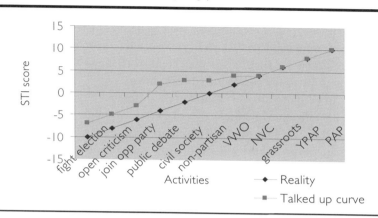

The people's trust and mistrust

When the STI curve for civil society activities shifts upward – that is, when the public perceives that the state is more tolerant of open criticism and civil society activism – this upward shift releases tension and generates hope for change. Citizens become more willing to participate in public life and, through such participation, feel they have an emotional stake in the country. On the other hand, when the STI curve shifts downward, the public perceives that the state is clamping down on them and this generates disappointment and fear. Citizens then become less willing to participate in public life and they lose their emotional stake in the country.

If the state wants to maximize the people's emotional stake in their country without the corresponding opening up, it could attempt to 'talk up' the curve. To a certain extent, this talking up the curve can be seen in initiatives such as Singapore 21 and Remaking Singapore. Through these high-profile 'public consultation' initiatives, the state espoused the core idea that 'everyone matters'; nevertheless it continued to deny gay and lesbian Singaporeans the constitutional right of assembly (Au 13 April 2004). While espousing the core value of 'active citizenship', the state continued to place advocacy groups in the 'red zone' for additional scrutiny when they apply for registration as societies (Lim 17 July 2004). After promising to 'slaughter sacred cows', the Remaking Singapore report had nothing to say about sacred cows such as state control of the mass media or gerrymandering. Its recommendation to amend the Societies Act in effect made it harder for advocacy groups to register as a society. Before the results of these initiatives were publicized, the STI curve could remain high; but once the public saw for themselves the extent of change that was really being permitted, the curve shifted back down.

It can be quite difficult to discern a difference between official talk of liberalization and the reality of continued suppression, mainly because the state has, especially in more recent times, avoided the use of such overt security instruments as detention without trial. The state now prefers more subtle and invisible techniques such as the threat to withdraw favour or funding, and the encouragement of self-censorship (Tan and Ng 2004: ix–xvi). Talking up the curve, in this regard, has become an increasingly available option. One is, however, reminded of Abraham Lincoln's famous aphorism, 'You can fool some of the people all the time, and all of the people some of the time, but you can't fool all of the people all the time'. If practice never lives up to the talk, the day will come when most of the people no longer believe the talk. What can happen then is a general voluntary shift of the STI curve downwards. It shifts downwards not because the people think that the state is now less tolerant per se, but because they have lost faith in the state.

Each voluntary downward shift would generate distrust towards the state – perceived as the boy who cried wolf – and make it much harder to talk up the curve the next time. After a downward shift – whether voluntary or state-induced – the state will have a strong demand for people who are not identified as part of the state to speak well of it so as to minimize damage and to model acceptance and loyalty. More often than not, these people are the first step towards restoring the STI curve. To put it more bluntly, cronyism is a natural by-product of a state that tries to talk up the STI curve. This is because opportunists quickly realize that they can supply the state's demand for public enthusiasm and support after a downward shift. In a general climate of fear and/or distrust – more commonly described as 'cynicism' in the local mass media – these people would stand out as loyal supporters of the state, demonstrating that they truly understand the state's difficulty in maintaining a balance between the demand for control and stability by 'heartlanders' and the demand for openness and freedom by 'cosmopolitans'. In this way, they offer themselves for co-optation by the ruling elites.

OB markers, self-censorship, and elections

I will now apply the STI curve to several prominent features of the Singapore political landscape to generate explanations and inferences that go beyond the *Sintercom* experience.

Firstly, the STI curve gives a visual representation of where people think the OB markers might be – the part of the curve below the horizontal axis. Secondly, the curve gives an indication of how firm these OB markers are – activities with large negative scores are much more likely to be suppressed than those with smaller negative scores. Thirdly, remembering that the STI curve is in fact the people's perception of the state's tolerability for their activities, when trying to talk up the curve, it is in the state's interest to hide what its true levels of tolerability are. Since OB markers define the limit of state tolerability, making them clear would render talking up the curve impossible as the talk can be easily compared with a well-defined reality. Thus, as long as the state wishes to talk up the curve, the OB markers must necessarily remain vague and undefined.

Fourthly, remembering Lincoln's dictum, open debate enables a large number of people to discover the discrepancies between talk and reality, and such discoveries can lead to voluntary downward shifts of the curve. Thus, as long as the state intends to pursue a continued strategy of talking up the curve, it will always be intolerant of open criticism and debate. Although the government has recently removed the need to obtain a public entertainment licence for organizing closed door forums, this is barely significant for open criticism and debate since such forums typically involve small audiences and make a limited impact. More important would be the removal of the Newspaper and Printing Presses Act whose provisions make it extremely difficult for Singaporeans to start an alternative new media. Through this piece of legislation also, the government can restrict the circulation of foreign publications that it deems to have 'interfered' in Singapore's domestic affairs. These arrangements have severely limited the capacity to report and analyze local news in Singapore.

Fifthly, self-censorship is the key to making the system work. If there is no self-censorship, then public debate and sharing of information will quickly reveal the discrepancies between reality and the talked-up curve. If the state tries to suppress free speech to prevent the public from discovering the discrepancies, it would just lead to a state-induced down-shift of the STI curve. The only way for a talked-up curve to stay up is when self-censorship prevents complete sharing of information in public debates, so that it becomes difficult to uncover discrepancies.

Sixthly, the reason why clamping down tends to occur around election time is because that is when the attention of the nation is focused on those with alternative ideas. Thus, the campaign period must be as short as possible; and indeed in Singapore, this can be as short as nine days. Furthermore, if there is any danger that open criticism during the campaign period may trigger a voluntary down-shift – which can translate to a massive vote swing – then such criticism will be stopped at all cost. The government also makes a lot of promises during election time, and hands out 'goodies' such as the new Singapore Shares. This heavily publicized handout of money from the state creates the impression that the state has delivered and will continue to deliver on its other promises.

Drawing these threads together, we can use the STI model to explain the mechanics behind Singapore's opening up and clamping down. It is basically an arbitraging of the effects of state-induced and voluntary down-shifts of the STI curve. A talked-up curve cannot remain up forever, and will eventually result in a voluntary down-shift. To prevent the voluntary down-shift, the state can clamp down and trigger a less costly state-induced down-shift instead. The fear generated from a state-induced down-shift will then fuel self-censorship. With self-censorship in place, the state can again begin the process of talking up the curve. At the same time, undefined OB markers are used to maximize self-censorship while more heavy-handed instruments of coercion can be positioned to silence those who refuse to censor themselves. Finally, cronies step in to sing praises and minimize the significance of the clamping down. In effect, they signal to the state that the state-induced down-shift is relatively cost free. Such price-distortion signals from opportunistic cronyism persuade the state that it can repeat this cycle with another state-induced downward shift for great political profit and at minimal cost. Thus, the cycle repeats itself.

The renaissance city meets STI

The renaissance city rhetoric is an example of talk that probably did not result in an upward shift of the STI curve as there was little euphoria over the report among artists and academics in Singapore. I would argue that this was because artists and academics did not believe that talk and reality would coincide. The issue was not whether Singapore was a renaissance city, since that is just a label. Are Paris, New York, London, Sydney, or San Francisco renaissance cities? Does it matter how these cities are labelled? More tellingly, do these cities need to engage in such incessant talk about themselves? The real question was: can the Singapore government ever allow real passion, adventure, and creativity to break out?

'Creativity', 'adventurous spirit', 'inquiring and creative mind', and 'strong passion for life' are in fact the traits explicitly valued in the report. But these traits inherently do not respect limitations. As Terence Lee argues in Chapter 4, creativity must challenge the status quo, and so the government's favoured version of creativity – depoliticized and industrialized – belongs only to the politics of gestures. Any person who takes pains to stay on the government's good side by operating well within the OB markers cannot by any stretch of the imagination be described as 'creative', 'adventurous', 'inquisitive', or 'passionate'. Do Singaporeans possess these traits? I believe such human traits are universal, and thus it is a priori that Singaporeans also possess them, at least at birth. The question is what happens when their creativity and sense of adventure lead them into the negative portion of the STI? History has shown that the state very decisively extinguishes any perceived or projected threats to its power, rationalized in terms of 'stability', 'prosperity', and 'harmony'. State censorship of the arts is ever present and insistent. Any artist who was recently censored would find it hard to believe the state truly wants an 'adventurous spirit' in the arts.

I have described activities on the left side of Singapore's STI curve. Many activities on the right side of the curve face no government restrictions; for example, joining the Young PAP or volunteering for PAP grassroots activities. People who pursue these activities can exercise their passion, adventurous spirit, and creativity as much as they like, as long as they stay on the right side. They will be able to create a semblance of vibrancy, but it would be one that is strangely lop-sided, lacking in diversity, and devoid of depth. And what is vibrancy without depth? Kitsch. If a passionate, adventurous, and inquisitive person mounts a challenge to the PAP government, will he or she get a fair fight on a level playing field? If not, then it is clear that the state has marked out places where passion, adventure, and creativity cannot go.

Conclusion

In this chapter, I have shown that opening up and clamping down in Singapore can be represented by shifts in the STI curve. I have argued that the STI curve is continuously shifting, either through real change or through a process of 'talking up'. A talked-up STI curve will easily shift downwards the moment politicians' talk turns hard-line. If an up-shift of the STI curve unleashes hope and enthusiasm, a down-shift induces disappointment and fear. Even more damaging is when people see that the status quo-supporting actions of the government do not square with its rhetoric of change, and the STI curve down-shifts voluntarily. A voluntary down-shift induces apathy and distrust. The more the STI curve shifts up, the more enthusiasm it unleashes. Similarly, the more the STI curve shifts down, the more fear or distrust it induces. When the STI curve is too frequently talked up only to suffer a downward shift, it will become much harder to talk it up again the next time. The *Renaissance City Report* (Ministry of Information and the Arts 2000) is perhaps a good illustration of this. More importantly, if the STI curve voluntarily shifts down too many times, not only does it induce apathy and distrust, the state will eventually lose credibility and find it very hard to rally the people.

A key assumption in my argument is that a curve that shifts up unleashes hope and enthusiasm and a curve that shifts down induces fear or distrust. It is quite possible to invert this assumption. For a people who truly prefer stability to freedom, an up-shift will unleash apprehension and bewilderment – apprehension about having to take care of themselves instead of relying on a cradle-to-grave nanny state, and bewilderment over how to do it. For such people, a down-shift will induce comfort and calm – comfort that the government is again taking charge decisively and so they can return to the old routine of obeying those who are more qualified and rest assured that everything will turn out alright.

When I started *Sintercom*, I might have believed that there was some truth in this second assumption about the hopes and fears of Singaporeans. I am less convinced now that this assumption holds, especially given the state's more recent refusal to be the all-providing nanny (Lee 22 August 2004). The Singapore government, however, still refers to 'the silent majority' (variously mapped onto ideological notions of the 'conservative majority' and 'heartlanders' discussed elsewhere in this book), invoking their silent consent on many occasions when calls for liberalization are heard in public. But how long can the state sustain this construct of a 'silent majority' who wants it to have near-absolute control and needs nothing to fuel their enthusiasm for a common future other than the occasional talking-up of the STI curve?

REFERENCES

ABC (13 December 2001) 'Singapore home to 100,000 crows', *ABC Science*. Online. Available HTTP: <http://www.abc.net.au/science/news/enviro/EnviroRepublish_438509.htm> (accessed 30 July 2004).

Ang, P.H. and Nadarajan, B. (1996) 'Censorship and the internet: a Singapore perspective', *Communications of the ACM*, 39(6): 72–78.

Au, A. (13 April 2004) 'What's so subversive about People Like Us?', *Today* (Singapore).

Ellis, E. (17 July 2001) 'Hot potato: the Singapore government should leave Sintercom alone', *Time*. Online. Available HTTP: <http://www.singapore-window.org/sw01/010717ti.htm> (accessed 20 July 2004).

George, C. (2003) 'The Internet's political impact and the penetration /participation paradox in Malaysia and Singapore', Asia Research Institute Working Paper Series 2003, No. 14, November.

Haas, M. (ed.) (1999) *The Singapore Puzzle*, Connecticut: Praeger Publishers.

Han, F.K. (17 December 1994) 'PM's remarks show that on fundamental issues, nothing has changed', *The Straits Times* (Singapore).

Han, F.K., Fernandez, W., and Tan, S. (1998) *Lee Kuan Yew: the man and his ideas*, Singapore: Singapore Press Holdings.

Hauben, M. (n.d.) *History of ARPANET: Behind the Net – The untold history of the ARPANET, Or – The 'Open' History of the ARPANET/Internet*. Online. Available HTTP: <http://www.dei.isep.ipp.pt/docs/arpa.html> (accessed 20 July 2004).

Ignatius, D. (29 September 2002) 'Singapore's paradox of freedom and order', *The International Herald Tribune*.

Kaur, S. (11 December 2001) 'Battle plan to cut crow menace', *The Straits*

Times (Singapore). Online. Available HTTP: <http://www.ecologyasia.
com/NewsArchives/Dec_2001/straitstimes.asia1.com.sg_primenews_
story_0,1870,89950,00.html> (accessed 30 July 2004).

Lee, H.L. (22 August 2004) Speech at the National Day Rally on 22 August
2004, Singapore.

Lim, C. (3 September 1994) 'The PAP and the people – a great affective
divide', *The Straits Times* (Singapore).

Lim, C. (20 November 1994) 'One government, two styles', *The Straits Times*
(Singapore).

Lim, L. (17 July 2004) 'Scoping out societies', *The Straits Times*
(Singapore).

Media Development Authority (1997) 'Internet code of practice'. Online.
Available HTTP: <http://www.mda.gov.sg/medium/internet/i_coden-
practice.html> (accessed 8 September 2004).

Microsoft Encarta (2004) 'Crow (bird)', *Microsoft Encarta Online Encyclopedia*.
Online. Available HTTP: <http://ca.encarta.msn.com/encyclopedia_
761570987/Crow_(bird).html> (accessed 30 July 2004).

Ministry of Information and the Arts (2000) *Renaissance City Report: culture
and the arts in renaissance Singapore*, Singapore. Online. Available
HTTP: <http://www.mita.gov.sg/renaissance/FinalRen.pdf> (accessed
22 December 2004).

Ng, W.J. (18 July 1993) 'Political awareness does not come about overnight',
The Straits Times (Singapore).

Rodan, G. (1996) 'Information technology and political control in Singapore',
Japan Policy Research Institute Working Paper no. 26, November.
Online. Available HTTP: <http://www.jpri.org/publications/working-
papers/wp26.html> (accessed 30 July 2004).

Rodan, G. (2004) *Transparency and Authoritarian Rule in Southeast Asia:
Singapore and Malaysia*, London: RoutledgeCurzon.

Singam, C., Tan, C.K., Ng, T., and Perera, L. (eds.) (2002) *Building Social
Space in Singapore: The Working Committee's initiative in civil society
activism*, Singapore: Select Publishing.

Tan, C.K. (1996) *soc.culture.singapore: an unauthorized version*,
self-published.

Tan, C.K. (2001) 'Can the co-opted speak? a brief history of one theatre
company's negotiation with the Singaporean state', *Focas: Forum on
Contemporary Art & Society*, 3: 306–29.

Tan, C.K. and Ng, T. (eds.) (2004) *Ask Not: The Necessary Stage in Singapore
theatre*, Singapore: Times Editions.

Teo, A. (21 June 1991) 'How to make Singapore a home, not a hotel', *The
Business Times* (Singapore).

Theatre and cultures
Globalizing strategies

ALVIN TAN[1]

Singapore theatre: General directions

To a great extent, overtly political theatre in Singapore ended in 1987 when 22 people were arrested for taking part in an alleged 'Marxist conspiracy'. Two of them were members of radical theatre company The Third Stage. With the demise of political theatre, social theatre gained prominence in the early 1990s. The world was fast changing and Singapore increasingly had to open up and reach out. By the mid-1990s, original, intracultural, indigenous, and social theatre began to move into the margins, while plays that were influenced by postmodern traits and tendencies gained prominence. The new millennium has seen a rise in both avant-garde as well as commercial theatre, with a large volume of foreign plays imported, adapted, and produced by local theatre companies. This development has been mainly spearheaded by theatre practitioners returning to Singapore from overseas.

Political theatre challenges the dominant ideology that sustains the way things are. It is theatre that attempts to change the audience's point of view about the way things should be. Often, political theatre directly challenges the policies of the government and the ruling class. Through its themes, plots, characters, symbols, and ironies, political theatre lobbies the audience directly to resist the policies of those in power and to question the rationale behind the worldview of the ruling party or class. For instance, 'agitational propaganda' is a genre of political theatre that works by directly confronting the policies of those in power through protest, satire, and ridicule.

Unlike political theatre, social theatre does not necessarily challenge the political status quo or the values propagated by those in positions of power, although it very often critiques the unequal relations of power within society. Social theatre or socially engaged theatre refers to theatre that deals with social issues, often in everyday-life contexts. These issues may include problems of inter-racial relationships and the discrimination of minority communities in society. Social theatre often looks into the subcultural concerns of people who lead alternative lifestyles or who live on the fringes or in the underbelly of society. Gay, bisexual, lesbian, and transgendered (GBLT) people, for example, belong to this group, as do drug addicts. Subcultural theatre deals with a level of cultural reality that escapes – or perhaps is exiled from – the simple binaries of dominant and subordinate classes.

Broadly speaking, avant-garde and postmodern forms of theatre belong to the same category: both refer to theatre ahead of its time. Such theatre pieces challenge traditional theatre precepts in many different ways. They give much more importance and attention to interpretation and performance than to the written text on which performance is based. They position the audience – and not the playwright or director – as the 'author' or meaning-maker. They are opposed to giving the literary author, playwright, or director of a theatre piece the controlling perspective for an audience to discover; instead, the audience's perspective is just as, if not more, important. Inevitably, avant-garde and postmodern forms of theatre are opposed quite profoundly to authoritarianism.

Interdisciplinary theatre involves conversations that cross the traditional domains of art, science, and technology, often dealing with new forms of media. It can also refer to the interaction between different artistic disciplines – like literary text and music – but in new or innovative ways. For example, a conventional musical like

Cats uses music to support psychological realism whereas interdisciplinary theatre may elevate music to the same level of importance as the literary text or the psychological scoring of a character on stage. Music and multimedia, as artistic disciplines, are employed in primary rather than supportive or decorative ways.

In Singapore, the state is everywhere. There are various reasons why artists in Singapore would wish to escape the state. One major reason is to attain some form of autonomy in which art can be a space or beacon for free expression. Art should not be circumscribed by external or institutionalized forces since it is essential for artists – and indeed citizens – to reflect on and grapple with issues and themes of cultural expression in complex ways. For art to be effective in challenging established or reductive perceptions and mindsets, it often must transgress social mores or conventional forms. In Chapter 5, Kenneth Paul Tan argues that the Singapore government very strategically censors art of this kind in the name of a mythical heartlander class that makes up an even more mythical conservative majority. In effect, censorship creates an atmosphere of fear that limits the people's capacity to think outside of the box. To escape the state, artists often look for new ways of creating art. Since 'realistic' theatre is highly accessible, and therefore highly susceptible to censorship, artists have turned to avant-garde, postmodern, and interdisciplinary theatre. For professional theatre company The Necessary Stage (TNS), founded in 1987, the strategy has involved harnessing the possibilities of globalization.

Indigenous theatre in a global city

Whilst countries like Australia have enjoyed a substantial phase searching for and establishing their national identity through the arts and popular culture (Turner 1994), Singapore's efforts were somewhat interrupted by the impact of globalization. Increasingly, Singaporeans passionate about local plays were accused of being parochial or insular. Increasingly, at the same time, local plays faced fierce competition from foreign works, and practitioners focusing on local plays needed to improve their marketing strategies to remain sustainable. And increasingly, employing foreign talent to raise local production value has become the way forward for many practitioners. Why nurture talent when one can simply acquire it from overseas? Creating indigenous work, especially from scratch, would seem to be unproductive. A focus on production quality and market demand would seem to require an international pool of cultural capital. The 'exotic' foreign element adds value to productions, easily justifying higher ticket prices while ensuring full houses. Internationality ensures quality and clout, drawing recognition and economic capital which then ensures the sustainability of a theatre company.

This follows the logic of the culture industry. In a globalized, cosmopolitan, and capitalistic environment saturated with cable television, cyberspace, and international arts and film festivals, the local space is a contestation of influences from all sorts of cultures and arts practices. Whilst the audience enjoys a diverse palette of cultural productions, Singaporean artists focusing on the indigenous, and faced with censorship and funding limitations, can feel quite overwhelmed.

Overcoming censorship limitations

In 1999, *Completely With/Out Character*, a mono-drama that featured the late AIDS patient Paddy Chew, was – somewhat surprisingly – staged without any censorship. The performance included a 'live' interactive question-and-answer session that extended to Singaporeans from other parts of the world who communicated with Chew via a real-time chat room. The performance was described in an article 'Singapore lightens up' in *Time Magazine* – with the caption 'Singapore swings!' on the front cover (McCarthy and Ellis 19 July 1999) – and was offered as evidence that the Singapore government was loosening its control over a country that was becoming livelier.

A few years later, the National Arts Council (NAC) expressed deep reservations about two other TNS productions, *ABUSE SUXXX!!!* (2001) and *Mardi Gras* (2003). Although the NAC continued to fund both productions, it nevertheless recommended that its logo be withdrawn from publicity materials. Furthermore, TNS had to negotiate with the Media Development Authority (MDA) on the censorship of *Mardi Gras*, in the knowledge that the MDA could refuse to grant a licence for the play to be performed. MDA objected to the man-to-man kissing that it felt went on for too long, but interestingly it left the lesbian kissing scene intact. MDA was also opposed to the vulgar language and allusions to incest. After negotiations that ran over three meetings and a preview, the play was left mostly intact, although its final scene – when homosexual volunteers had been scheduled to 'come out' on stage – was removed. MDA considered this scene to be an instance of 'social action' rather than art.

Mardi Gras was a harmless comedy fundraiser whose tickets were already selling very well. In arguing its case, TNS made reference to then-Prime Minister Goh Chok Tong's relatively liberal comments, made overseas, that his civil service would hire openly gay Singaporeans even to hold sensitive appointments (Elegant 7 July 2003). As artistic director of TNS, I also explained to MDA how I had, in a BBC interview, expressed hope that things were opening up in Singapore. So it would be an embarrassment if MDA did not grant the licence for something as harmless as Mardi Gras. At the final meeting, MDA questioned TNS' motivation for staging Mardi Gras. The reply was: to raise funds by reaching out to the gay and lesbian community. TNS got its licence. Mardi Gras filled 92 per cent of the house even though tickets were steeply priced at S$31, S$51, and S$71.

In the same month, two gay-themed performances – Bent and The Wedding Banquet – were staged by Toy Factory and a touring American theatre company respectively. Why were licences issued for these two performances, but funding refused for Drama Box's Vaginalogue? Could it be that the former were foreign works and handsomely packaged? The decision to describe a work as offensive to the public or as being more 'social action' than art cannot be anything more than arbitrary. In fact, as Kenneth Paul Tan argues in Chapter 5, all censorship is fundamentally arbitrary.

Plays by Singaporean playwrights Kuo Pao Kun, Haresh Sharma, and Eleanor Wong are taught at universities in Singapore. For example, the Theatre Studies programme at the National University of Singapore includes Sharma's This Chord and Others (1999) in its reading list. The O- and N-level curricula for English literature include Sharma's Off Centre (2000). But for the longest time, schools and pre-university institutions in Singapore have not exposed Singapore students to locally authored plays. One reason is simply that many schools had opted to remove English Literature from their subject offering because – it is reasonable to conjecture – the subject does not guarantee the high grades that schools need to produce in order to stay within a respectable range in the national ranking tables. Another reason may be the official hostility towards Singlish, the vernacular form of English in Singapore. But this is a policy mistake. The mastery of a language cannot be attained without an appreciation of its historical-cultural context. Students can appreciate Singlish without compromising their ability to improve their own command of standard English. More importantly, Singlish is valuable indigenous cultural capital. In Chapter 6, filmmakers Woo Yen Yen and Colin Goh, lamenting that the government had censored the use of Singlish in the local media, argue that the so-called 'heartlander' Singaporeans are at their creative best when expressing themselves in Singlish. A playwright like Arthur Miller draws large audiences because many Americans – and in fact people all over the world – have grown up reading *The Crucible*, a play that is easily identified as 'American'. But Singapore theatre companies, in the absence of a rich vernacular palette, must resort to casting television celebrities in their local theatre productions in order to fill the house.

Overcoming funding limitations

The NAC provides subsidy funding to 'major arts companies' like TNS. With up to 30 per cent of its operating costs financed by the NAC, TNS must secure the other 70 per cent on its own. Besides looking for partners such as corporate sponsors and the state-sponsored Community Development Councils,[2] TNS also does its own fundraising to support its full-time artistic and administrative staff. A funding cut of 10 per cent in 2002 – the result of an economic recession – adversely affected plans for artistic and administrative development, especially in the areas of research, process, and experimentation.

Local artists have come a long way with government support. And yet, local artists are themselves 'subsidizing' the arts, as a considerable part of their efforts and resources is dedicated to developing both local practitioners and audience. If the arts are believed to be a merit good, intrinsically beneficial for the wider society, then the collective cost burden of ensuring a vibrant arts scene needs to be shared out more evenly. Some arts companies choose of their own accord to bear the cost of developing local practitioners and audience. Alternatively, they can hire foreign talent (which may come cheaper) or produce established and tested foreign works (riding on the good reviews of past performances), and in this way lower costs and increase revenue. Arts companies need to make a profit – or at least not suffer unsustainable losses – whilst they develop the local industry. To remain sustainable, TNS opted to 'globalize' its theatre.

In the past, it was much more possible for TNS to produce experimental and socially challenging works in 'poor theatre' form that places emphasis on actors rather than lavish sets. Today, a theatre company with a full-time staff or a professional team cannot be supported by mounting productions on the fringe. The question of funding has had to be addressed more strategically. Towards this end, TNS tries to ensure that there is at least one big 'money-making' project every year. Unlike TNS' more exploratory and therefore challenging works, these commercial projects will tend to be more accessible with the potential to reach out to a mass audience. Smaller fundraising performances and gala nights such as *Mardi Gras* (which played to a 92 per cent house in 2003) and *Starlight!* (which raised S$150,000 in 2003) have also been quite profitable ventures. As part of the company's annual output, TNS includes a number of external projects that are commissioned but not listed in its own artistic calendar. The play *Not Guilty!* (2004), commissioned by local television station TV12, was a mono-performance that starred Kumar, a well-known cross-dressing performer. With guaranteed television publicity, all 10 shows were sold out even though tickets were priced at a relatively high average of S$60 each. These money-making projects serve to fund TNS' more difficult and exploratory works. Pointing to TNS' unconventional plays that have over the years defied the traditional rules of theatre, critic David Chew (22 February 2006) observes that 'it is hard to imagine a theatre scene without the alternative influence of TNS, which remains in the forefront of efforts to offer theatre-goers here an alternative to the mainstream'.

Every year in March, since 1997, TNS organizes its own arts festival sponsored by telecommunications company M1. Named Youth Explosion! in 1997, M1 Youth Connection in 1998, M1 Theatre Connect in 2004, and M1 Singapore Fringe Festival in 2005, the festival has become 'one of Asia's largest international fringe festivals' featuring theatre, performance arts, film, dance, visual arts, mixed media, music and forum created and presented by Singaporean and international artists. Themed differently each year, the Festival aims to bring the best of contemporary, cutting-edge and socially-engaged works to the Singapore audience. First held with great success in 2005, the M1 Singapore Fringe Festival is set to be a creative centre, with a twin-purpose of innovation and discussion; a platform for meaningful and provocative art to engage our increasingly connected and complex world. (Singapore Fringe 2006)

The 2006 festival was supported by the NAC. Performances were held in major venues like the Esplanade – Theatres on the Bay, The Substation, and Cathay Cineplexes. Various embassies and cultural attachés helped to bring in foreign art works – photography exhibitions, film, installation work, and short plays – that were relevant to the festival's annual themes: Art and War in 2005, Art and Healing in 2006, and Art and Disability in 2007. An important festival goal is to attract both the Singaporean and the expatriate audiences. With more embassies coming onboard as partners, TNS is able to disseminate its fringe festival collaterals via the embassies' enormous databases. In the M1 Singapore Fringe Festival in 2007, expatriates made up approximately 30 per cent of the 153,000 people who attended both ticketed and non-ticketed events.

At the same time, TNS has been exploring the development of marketing strategies and networks for exploratory works and to educate audiences about such works in order to achieve full houses. This is a strategy that will be pitched to local, regional, and international audiences. TNS reaches out to co-producers or venue presenters in the region, creating works that are socially engaged, innovative, and yet accessible – rather than esoteric – at the regional and international levels. This helps co-presenters to market and publicize these works in their respective countries. TNS also connects with sources of funding and supporters who are sympathetic to contemporary exploratory works, including overseas foundations that offer collaboration grants. The challenge is to give due regard to the interests of these foundations without compromising the methods and outcomes of the works themselves. TNS is also exploring different fundraising strategies, some of which involve inviting potential fundraisers to participate in the creative process by offering their inputs to themes and issues to be explored in future works.

Having worked for over two decades with Singapore actors from different ethnic backgrounds, TNS has developed a working methodology that integrates multiple languages and cultures using different artistic disciplines. With *Mobile* (2006), this methodology was extended beyond the Singapore context. The play revolved around the theme of human mobility, focusing specifically on migrant workers and urban professionals who cross borders for work, business, and leisure. In the process of devising the play, TNS was determined to overcome the limitations of a singular Singaporean perspective on this complex theme. By conducting extensive workshops, TNS researchers and artists sought inputs from people affected by this 'mobility' in Japan, Thailand, and the Philippines. (Large numbers of Thais and Filipinos are employed in Singapore and Japan.) The result was a contemporary, collaborative, intercultural, multi-language, and socially challenging work that captured the sensibilities and perspectives of four different Asian countries. It premiered at the Singapore Arts Festival in 2006 and toured to Kuala Lumpur (Actors Studio, 2006) and Tokyo (Setagaya Public Theatre, 2007). The cost of devising the work, putting it up as a production, and touring it amounted to S$200,000. Funding support from Saison Foundation, Asahi Beer Arts Foundation, Tokyo Metropolitan Council, Setagaya Public Theatre, Actors Studio, NTUC Income, Singapore International Foundation, Singapore Arts Festival, and the National Arts Council was therefore quite crucial.

Resident playwright at TNS Haresh Sharma's *Eclipse*, commissioned by Scottish theatre company 7:84, was staged at the Traverse Theatre in Edinburgh in 2007 before touring to other venues in Scotland. Another work by Sharma, *godeatgod*, played in Glasgow and has toured to Romania, Hungary, Hong Kong, and Manila. The process of developing these international-intercultural projects is shared and in that way escapes the conventions of theatre-making that are derived from just one country. Similarly, resources are drawn from multiple funding sources in different countries, an approach that requires administrative stamina and alertness to funding opportunities and schemes. TNS is exploring the possibility of three other international collaborations with partners from Japan, Australia, and Scotland. With so many international collaborations in the pipeline, TNS has finally broken out of the local in terms of funding while gaining opportunities for rich intercultural dialogue with partners around the world.

Developing a work to full maturity

For years, it has been the practice of organizers of the annual Singapore Arts Festival to commission works from local companies just eight months before the start of the festival. The organizers want only new works from participating local theatre companies. These new works are showcased together with foreign works that are at least two years old. But for a work to reach full maturity, there must be heavy initial investment and time to develop. Tony Kushner's *Angels in America* (now a television movie) was first read and premiered at the Mark Taper Forum in Los Angeles in 1991 before it hit Broadway in 1993. The musical *Rent* was first staged at off-Broadway New York Theatre Workshop. In the United Kingdom, similarly, new works tour regional theatres before opening in London's West End. In the US and the UK, this development mechanism is well established. Not so in Singapore.

Mobile is a good example of how TNS has dealt with this problem: enriching the artistic process through international collaboration. The Setagaya project was essentially a collective of 16 theatre practitioners from six Asian countries that met for workshops from 2003 to 2005. Sharma's participation in this collective gave TNS access to artists from around the region who were also socially aware. A play like *Mobile* needed to be built on culturally-grounded perspectives since the issues and questions were very complex. Thai and Filipino women are employed as foreign domestic workers ('maids') and prostitutes in both Japan and Singapore. What are the social and cultural implications of this, and what happens to them when they return home? Some are able to get married, but many others are unable to do so. The cultural displacement, the need to support families back home, and the discrimination they face due to economic disparity go mainly unnoticed. To find some answers to these questions, TNS organized a one-week fieldwork session in Bangkok and Chiang Mai in 2005 that included visiting a shelter and interviewing traumatized Thai sex workers who had returned from Japan. Also interviewed were Thai workers who were leaving to find work in other countries and Thai

NGOs involved in empowering migrant sex workers in Bangkok. The second phase was a 14-day workshop and presentation at the Morishita Studio in Tokyo in January 2006. During this phase, the artists heard and recorded the stories of (Japanese-speaking) Filipinos working in Tokyo, a Filipino man and his Japanese wife, children of mixed parentage, and Japanese NGOs involved in migrant issues. Some of the artists visited the Japanese courts to witness a Filipina appealing for her child to be legally recognized. The third phase was a workshop and presentation called *Something in the Way She Moves* held during the M1 Singapore Fringe Festival in March 2006. Artists from each country presented a 30-minute work followed by a discussion. The team also interviewed Thai, Indonesian, and Filipino foreign workers in Singapore.

On 8 May 2006, everyone re-assembled in Singapore for the final phase which involved composing and rehearsing the play until mid-June. This was a very challenging phase that demanded intense levels of intercultural dialogue and negotiation. Writing, composing, and editing the scenes depended firmly on everyone's receptiveness to opinions, mutual respect, and professional integrity. A scene that has come to be known as 'Elena's Nightmare' was probably one of the best examples of the kind of intense intercultural exchange during the writing phase. It began when I read an article about a Filipina domestic worker who discovered she was pregnant when she arrived in Singapore and was told by her agent to go for an abortion or else she would be sent home. But she was a staunch Catholic. I sent the story to Rody Vera, the Filipino playwright, who scripted a mono-logue entitled 'Elena's Nightmare' and forwarded it to Sharma, the head playwright. Sharma then added two parts to this monologue: a Singaporean 'maid agent' and an Indonesian maid who became Elena's friend. A monologue evolved into a three-person episode. The team then decided to adopt a 'conference on migrant workers' as a context for the various narrative strands in the play. 'Elena's Nightmare' evolved yet again into a seven-actor ensemble piece, this time framed as a performance by an advocacy theatre group that was participating in the conference.

Mobile eventually comprised a prologue, an epilogue, four episodes, and a conference strand that threaded the play. Tatsuo Kaneshita directed two of these episodes and the epilogue. I directed one episode, the prologue, and the conference strand. Both directors and the entire cast worked on 'Elena's Nightmare'. When we started composing the work as a whole, we made various proposals to one another. The work had a first run, after which the playwrights and directors edited the text, shaving off extraneous text. Towards the tail-end of the rehearsal stage, the process became more traditional, with the co-directors making final decisions. *Mobile* premiered at the Singapore Arts Festival on 17 June 2006, and then toured to Malaysia and Japan.

Mobile presented the team with two main challenges. One involved language. Throughout the whole process, we relied on translators for the Japanese actors: we did not have direct communication with them during rehearsals. As for the Thais, although a translator could have enabled them to communicate more comfortably in their mother-tongue, their ability to speak and understand some English prompted us to do without one. Translators definitely help to speed up communication but the translation process itself can take up time and so actors shy away from elaborating their points. The second challenge was the need to be sensitive to the fact that *Mobile* was a project helmed and funded by the richer countries, Japan and Singapore; the co-directors were Japanese and Singaporean; and the head playwright was Singaporean. By being sensitive to these relationships, we could focus on being Asian practitioners in dialogue with one another about how our contemporary realities are so interconnected. In this way, we actively engaged with our diversities to bring 'multiple Asias' onto the world stage.

Transcultural works, composed through intercultural dialogue and collaboration, encourage cultural empathy and multiple ways of reading. By shifting their positions, audience members can experience the different perspectives on a single issue or gain insight into how apparently disparate issues are actually interconnected, which makes for a complex life or art experience. When artists work cross-culturally, the intercultural challenges and discoveries they experience in the process can become material for their work. The polyvocal and multiple sensibilities of transcultural works challenge the conventional unities of character, narrative, and worldviews. They welcome multiple perspectives, a character's fluid change in opinion or position, and equal weightage accorded to contradictory discourses without giving any one perspective a dominant position.

Globalization of indigenous work

Globalization has often been regarded as a threat to indigenous cultures. The global dominance of Anglo-American and even Euro-American cultures makes it difficult for 'non-western' indigenous works to tour, unless they are deliberately exotic, highly visual, or physical (and less 'text-based'). The more 'western' model of theatre in Singapore produces works that are just too close to what the west itself can do (and perhaps do better), and are therefore much more difficult for presenters to market. In the light of current trends, though, it has become impractical to resist the notion that one's value as an artist rises with greater internationalization, at least in the estimation of the Singaporean audience.

As there is no way to arrest globalization, the next best thing is to work with it, at least in ways that allow artists to do the work that they want to do. That reality can be embraced, though, without compromising integrity. There is, after all, a positive side to globalization. Sornarajah (n.d.) describes one 'current' of globalization as rising 'like hot air from the grassroots'. Non-governmental organizations – at the grassroots – are gaining influence in the larger moral and ethical issues that confront the world. Theatre companies – it could be argued – can also be influential in this way.

Independent cultural institutions and artists can ride on globalization to encourage the global appreciation of local cultures. Globalization has opened up sites where imperialistic forces and local cultures contest one another. Artists who become internationalized find opportunities to meet with overseas 'allies' who, for example, may organize festivals that respect cultural difference and stage works with a local flavour, not productions that only employ dominant languages. Globalization has given cultural workers the opportunity to explore theatre-making in larger arenas, bringing together varied forms of cultural expressions of the universal human condition. Theatre practitioners now have the opportunity to come face to face with their counterparts overseas and to confront in profoundly personal ways how people relate to one another as human beings and not just as political and economic animals. Culture should be the basis of human relationships across national boundaries and it should transcend political and economic concerns.

In renaissance Singapore, art can engage the creative industries whose development is propelled by the forces of globalization. Experimenting with new media and even the life sciences provides artists with new vocabularies that can bridge indigenous material to audiences from other cultures via global trends and humanitarian themes. TNS intends to invest in a research and development arm of the company that will think through and operationalize the creative intersections between art and technology. Besides looking into new artistic forms and media, TNS also conducts content research. For example, *Mobile* was constructed out of research projects and workshops that spanned the Philippines, Thailand, Japan, and Singapore. Alongside civil society efforts to look after the welfare of foreign domestic workers, described by Chng Nai Rui in Chapter 11 of this book, TNS has also played its part in bringing their voices to the stage.

TNS has, over the years, been developing a methodology that involves both research and theatre 'devising'. Research begins with library work to understand the themes, issues, and contexts (social, cultural, economic, and political) surrounding a topic on which a theatre work is based. This is followed by fieldwork, a more experiential approach that allows playwrights, directors, and actors to encounter the human subject by visiting locations, conducting interviews, and facilitating focus group discussions. The second part of this methodology – devising theatre – involves improvisations, games, and other drama exercises that help to 'create' characters, their personalities, and their relationships. Through these exercises, actors are able to find, clarify, and take ownership of the characters that they create. TNS is confident of being able to explore this methodology with interested overseas partners.

For TNS, the international audience is still a new and untapped constituency. Collaborating with foreign performers or merely playing to a foreign audience can redefine its theatre-making. It can provide refreshing and multiple opportunities for artists to focus on indigenous works, challenging them to hold on to their cultural mission while revising their artistic devices and strategies. Artists can raise awareness of how people affect one another in this globalized world by digging deep into their respective intracultural realities. For example, artists can explore the effects of trade agreements on the quality of everyday life in developed and developing countries in the Asian region, and uncover the stories of ordinary people and cultures that have been silenced by official accounts. Through interviews, role-playing improvisation, and methods of devising theatre with actors and non-actors, artists can track the development of humanity. How do parallel worlds resonate with one another? How do we give voice to ordinary people's stories? Cultural engagement through the collaboration of theatre companies in Asia can open up more spaces to let these voices emerge.

The TNS play *koan* communicates, via a mono-performance, the parallel journeys of two women. In the metaphorical journey, one woman (performed by a 'live' actress) discovers at the end of her spiritual journey that she should stop searching and start finding. The second journey is recounted through a multimedia presentation of segments from an interview with a 68-year-old widow who talks about her marriage, the deaths of her mother and husband, and coming to terms with her son's homosexuality. Presented in Mandarin and Singlish with Korean subtitles, *koan* premiered at the Asian Festival in Busan (2003) and was subsequently performed at The Next Wave Festival in Seoul (2003). It has yet to play in Singapore. This marks a new artistic strategy for The Necessary Stage.

Working with regional and international cultural workers opens up access to artistic talents that can contribute to developmental, experimental, and exploratory theatre, of the kind that is in line with Singapore's renaissance city vision. With access to a larger talent pool, TNS will be able to develop its capacity to be more innovative and visionary. TNS needs to persuade its regional partners that its devising and collaborative methodology is an effective tool for bringing contemporary Asia to the west. Once companies and artists in the region are persuaded that working together to combine one another's strengths can be an effective way to combat the common prejudice that each nation's artists face, interesting and challenging works can be created. Only then will TNS be able to succeed in creating exploratory works that can live up to the renaissance city vision without being destroyed by the commercial imperative.

This vision of a globalized theatre moves away from some of the ideals of political theatre. For example, TNS theatre pieces now try to avoid directly commenting on party politics. Instead, through ingenuity and creativity, a more globalized theatre can deal indirectly, though no less effectively, with issues that are potentially confrontational or controversial. Internationally collaborating artists will face constraints working within each artist's own country and culture. But working together will help artists to invent new devices to communicate or transmit sensitive issues and taboo subjects. Also, collaboration of this kind can enable suppressed voices to escape censorship by staging such works in partner countries, away from the violence of local censors.

Working regionally and internationally opens up possibilities to address sensitive topics. Instead of continuing to (re)construct tired images, artists can find more opportunities to create works that encourage critical reflection at a more complex cross-cultural level, challenging themselves to look for or create new and fresh metaphors with universal application and appeal. New media and an interdisciplinary approach provide new resources for creating visual and auditory metaphors that are relevant and at the same time challenging.

NOTES

1. I am grateful to Kenneth Paul Tan for helping to clarify and firm up some of the ideas in this chapter.
2. CDCs are district-level administrative units that often develop projects with welfare, civic, and arts groups.

REFERENCES

Chew, D. (22 February 2006) 'A necessary revolution', *Today* (Singapore), 42–43.

Elegant, R. (7 July 2003) 'The lion in winter', *Time Asia*, 161(26). Online. Available HTTP: <http://www.time.com/time/asia> (accessed 4 September 2003).

McCarthy, T. and Ellis, E. (19 July 1999) 'Singapore lightens up', *Time Magazine*.

Sharma, H. (1999) *This Chord and Others: a collection of plays*, London: Minerva Press.

Sharma, H. (2000) *Off Centre*, Singapore: Ethos Books.

Singapore Fringe (2006) *M1 Singapore Fringe Festival 2006: art and healing*. Online. Available HTTP: <http://www.singaporefringe.com> (accessed 21 February 2006).

Sornarajah, M. (n.d.) 'The clash of two globalisations', National University of Singapore Research Gallery. Online. Available HTTP: <http://www.nus.edu.sg/corporate/research/gallery/research21.htm> (accessed 28 July 2004).

Turner, G. (1994) *Making it National: nationalism and Australian popular culture*, St. Leonards, NSW: Allen & Unwin.

The Working Committees
From 'fear' to creative activism

CHNG NAI RUI[1]

If civil society can be said to exist in Singapore, then its extent depends largely on what the state permits. This has been the dominant way of thinking about Singapore's civil society, a cynical way of thinking that is perhaps not entirely mistaken. The 'developmental state' in Singapore's post-independence history has played a dominant role in national development. An economically oriented civil bureaucracy – at the centre of this developmental state and insulated from political pressures – has denied civil society any space to grow (Leftwich 1995). Politically, the cooption and intimidation of civic energies necessary for the growth of civil society (Tan 2000) have resulted in a state of affairs described by a leading local academic and long-time civil society practitioner as 'pathetic' (Kwok 2003). Much of this condition has been attributed to what many local civil society activists and opposition party members have called 'a culture of fear' (Gomez 2000).

This culture of fear has been described as irrational because of its intangibility – no one can put a finger on what it is that Singaporeans really fear. Sometimes, the image of a 'knock on the door at 3 am' is offered to signify something of a police state. However, for the vast majority of Singaporeans who do not engage in terrorist activities, this threat of arrest is quite implausible. Yet, the mere uncertainty related to this prospect brings out a 'rational' fear in risk-averse Singaporeans. Even though the state often attempts to convince its citizens that the use of coercive instruments of law and order has been guided by maturity and fairness, as evidenced particularly by its absence in recent years, the true basis of fear is not what the eye can see – like 'shells falling in Bosnia on newsreels' (Chan 2000) – but what the mind can imagine. Uncertainty among citizens about what kind of political role the state will tolerate has led to widespread reluctance to participate in public life. In this sense, civil society would not exist if its citizens were completely rational.

This chapter, related from the personal experiences of a civil society activist, attempts some preliminary analysis of a new development in Singapore's civil society, one that has not only defied the culture of fear but that has also, ironically, been made possible by the 'enabling' effect of a fear that has forced civil society actors to think more creatively about their methods, strategies, and solutions. The total erosion of civic solidarity – so feared by Furedi (2002) in his *Culture of Fear* – has not happened in Singapore. This chapter argues that fear and other barriers to activism can explain the unique and creative form of civil society engagement and political risk-taking developed by The Working Committee (TWC) and The Working Committee 2 (TWC2) in Singapore. A more creative mode of activism within Singapore's civil society would, after all, appear to be an unintended contribution to the creative aspirations of the *Renaissance City Report* (Ministry of Information and the Arts 2000: 5).

In my account, I take the existence of civil society in Singapore as a given and base my arguments on the premise that discourses on civil society must be situated within local political and cultural contexts (Glasius et al. 2004). Singapore's civil society must be understood on its own terms through an analysis of what it is, rather than what it is not as determined by the prejudiced standpoint of liberal democracy. I believe that civil society has the potential to be one of the most important means of empowering citizens, and I make no apologies for an explicitly functional employment of the concept. This essay thus seeks to understand the empowering and emancipatory potential of civil society in Singapore.

The Working Committee

The Working Committee (TWC) was formed in late 1998 as a network of individuals and civil society organizations. Its chief aim was to build up networks in civil society 'so as to contribute to its development' (Singam et al. 2002: x). The main 'issue' for TWC was the state of civil society itself and how it might be nurtured. In the one year of its existence, TWC organized a series of public forums and 'open houses' at the premises of various non-governmental organizations (NGOs) where members of the public and other members of the network were invited to acquaint themselves with these NGOs. These activities culminated in a conference and a public exhibition by some 23 civil society organizations. At the end of 1999, save for a few partnership projects that had spun-off from the process, TWC unilaterally disbanded.

Although TWC has ceased to exist, its network of individuals and organizations has lasted informally until today. Through this network – and frequently via emails – information is disseminated, assistance is requested for, and invitations to events are extended. The concept of civil society refers not only to the activists and organizations that constitute it, but also to civic mores and norms. Social capital – the institutionalized social norms and networks that encourage cooperation among groups and individuals (Putnam 2000) – is perhaps the most useful way of understanding the impact of TWC.

In the interest of expanding and enriching the network to increase social capital, TWC's membership structure was kept 'open'. Anyone and any organization could theoretically sign up to be a member. To encourage the formation of partnerships within the network in a short space of time, a non-hierarchical structure was maintained. Although essentially anarchic in the implementation and monitoring of projects, the non-hierarchical structure allowed numerous initiatives to germinate, a number of which continued to grow beyond TWC's own lifespan.

Singaporeans are under Article 14 constitutionally guaranteed the freedom to associate and assemble, but this right has been restricted by the state through the Societies Act (Chapter 311) that requires any association of more than ten persons to register with the Registry of Societies, a process that has not been straightforwardly administrative for associations perceived to have a political complexion. TWC never registered as a society because its pioneer members never saw themselves as founding a new association. They felt that formalizing a loose network of individuals and organizations into an institution would have taken too much effort and resources that could be better channelled elsewhere. The founding members were also implicitly making a political point. Contrary to government statements that citizens who want to participate in politics should join a formal political party, TWC was trying to make the point that citizens could participate in politics as citizens, without needing formal affiliation to more traditional political machinery.

Fully aware that the larger question of its legitimacy would be problematized by its legal status, TWC's founding members went as far as they could to maintain transparency, frequently through the use of information technology and the internet (Tan 2002). They believed that doing so would demonstrate that TWC had 'nothing to hide' and was above board in its conduct. Differences within TWC were expressed rather than suppressed. Even very personal and controversial disagreements were communicated in the public domain. However, the limitations of an over-reliance on information technology for internal communication (and the email medium in particular) were revealed as some discussions quickly degenerated into personal attacks, leading to the departure of several members from the group (Gomez 2002; Ng 2002).

The Working Committee 2

While TWC had put civil society and social capital on the agenda, with the entire range of civil society issues as its context, The Working Committee 2 (TWC2) in contrast was a 'single issue group'. One clearly inspired the other – several members of TWC2 (including myself) had also been members of TWC. But in reality, TWC and TWC2 were altogether separate creatures.

Civil society and foreign workers

Today, there are more than 150,000 female domestic workers in Singapore. Coming from less developed countries like Indonesia, the Philippines, Sri Lanka, Thailand, Myanmar, and India, these workers are viewed by Singaporeans as 'fortunate' people who have escaped the conditions of unemployment and poverty in their own countries, to do a job that Singaporeans do not want to do themselves (Gee and Ho 2006: 8–9). But the issue of foreign workers has been a problematic one throughout the history of civil society in Singapore (Lyons 2004: 6–7). In May 1987, some members of the Geylang Catholic Centre for Foreign Workers who campaigned to improve the working conditions of foreign workers were detained under the draconian Internal Security Act (Chapter 143). This episode has come to be known as 'the Marxist conspiracy' because the detainees were accused by the state of conspiring to turn Singapore into a Marxist state. The memory of the events of May 1987 has since festered in the minds of civil society activists, as a chief source of the 'culture of fear'.

Local feminist groups, it can be argued, have neglected the issue of foreign domestic workers (who are entirely female and popularly known as 'maids' in Singapore) because of this fear generated from the 1987 incident (Lyons 2004: 7). However, this gives too much explanatory value to the culture of fear, and perhaps too much credit to the feminist groups. Some feminists were known to be reluctant to take up the cause of foreign domestic workers because they wanted to avoid pitting Singaporean women against one another, a position that is not difficult to understand. Flanagan (2004), for instance, argues controversially that middle-class women in the west have been able to achieve career success even while having a family, but their emancipation has been won by the exploitation of other women who are lower on the socioeconomic scale. They deny these mostly foreign women the very rights and benefits that they themselves have long demanded from the state and society. Hence, the cause of foreign domestic workers in Singapore depended not only on being able to reinterpret the events of May 1987 and the fear that has come to be associated with them, but also on the ability to break free of the need to identify their cause only with traditional feminist politics in Singapore. This opportunity was to be provided by the highly emotive and unfortunate case of Muawanatul Chasanah.

The founding members of the group that would eventually be called TWC2 came together in the wake of an outpouring of national soul-searching sparked by what has been described as the worst case of maid abuse in Singapore's history. Muawanatul Chasanah, a 19-year-old Indonesian domestic worker, was subjected to a period of extensive physical and emotional abuse by her Singaporean employer.

She was starved and had 'more than 200 injuries on her body as a result of whipping, kicks, punches, burns and scalding', a series of torture that ended only when she died from her injuries on 2 December 2001 (Chong 20 July 2002). What motivated the founding members of TWC2 was not only the cruelty of such a crime against a young girl eking out a living far away from home, but the sheer apathy of the culprit's neighbours who witnessed the abuse. 'It is not my business, he can do what he wants, that's his problem [a]nd anyway, God can see' was the quoted response of one neighbour (The Working Committee 2 2003a).

Chasanah's horrifying death was evidence of just how much Singaporeans had become alienated from foreigners and from one another. Relatives and neighbours who had witnessed the abuse and doctors who had given Chasanah her regular medical check-ups all failed to raise the alarm. A society where there is almost one case of maid abuse reported every nine days is a society that has failed to protect its weakest members. Furthermore, there is inadequate regulation to govern an industry that profits from the supply of 150,000 foreign domestic workers to households (Ibrahim 2004). Responding to this unacceptable situation, the founding members of TWC2 met regularly on an informal basis in 2002. On 14 February 2003, TWC2 held a press conference to announce its establishment as a civil society organization (though it had not been registered as a society as required by law).

It should be noted that the death of Muawanatul Chasanah did not only provoke the formation of TWC2 in civil society. *The Business Times* also organized a fundraising campaign for the family of Chasanah (*The Business Times* 13 February 2003). The local broadsheet had earlier received a deluge of sympathetic letters in response to a column written by Lee Han Shih (27 July 2002) who argued that the government should step in more aggressively to address the failure of ordinary Singaporeans to act as a proper check against domestic worker abuse.

Organizational structure

TWC2 came into being in a way that was unlike any other civil society organization in Singapore. Firstly, it did not have any formal status, which meant that it was a legally questionable entity. Secondly, the organization was chaired by a nominated member of parliament (NMP), Braema Mathiaparanam, and was structured in a clearly defined and hierarchical fashion. Thirdly, TWC2 had a clear sense of its own lifespan, and communicated this fact to the public. Members of TWC2 envisioned a one-year deadline beyond which they would cease to work, a genuine intention that was perhaps a little naïve – the members, in fact, continued to work well beyond the deadline and then successfully registered TWC2 as 'Transient Workers Count Too' in May 2004. Nevertheless, the combination of these three features in the early phase of TWC2's existence was unprecedented in Singapore's civil society.

In designing the organizational structure of TWC2, the founding members clearly had TWC in mind, even if they had not intentionally set out to create a second TWC. In the early discussions, it was felt that the principles of transparency and accountability – to its members, the public, and even agents of the state – were important for keeping the organization 'open'. While focused on the issue of foreign domestic workers, members were also cognizant of the need to empower civil society, and hence develop a workable model of activism that could deal with some of the more controversial issues of governance in Singapore. The founding members were therefore eager to create a model that was also open and fluid in an organizational sense, welcoming volunteers from (almost) all walks of life to take part in activities and to initiate and take responsibility for various projects. Surrounding a core group of members was a fluid belt of individuals who regularly joined and left TWC2.

Such a loose membership structure supporting numerous concurrent projects depended unavoidably on effective means of communication round the clock. Cyberspace proved crucial and its ubiquitous presence in the work of TWC2 supports Tan Chong Kee's claim that information technology has grown to become a very important feature of civil society activity in Singapore (Tan 2002). Significantly, some foreign domestic workers were also members of TWC2 on an informal basis. This was perhaps the first time in many years – certainly since the events of May 1987 – that foreign domestic workers could indirectly take part in Singapore's civil society. However, the extensive use of information technology and asymmetrical accessibility to this technology did not help communication between TWC2 and members who were domestic workers. The organization had to depend on a few individuals who were personally in contact with them.

Membership of TWC2 did not consist only of individuals who had a natural affiliation with the cause of foreign domestic workers. At least one owner of a maid agency has also been a supportive member. Other members have included academics, students, working professionals, and civil servants. Nevertheless, TWC2 faced chronic shortages of funding and manpower, and was in this respect no different from other civil society organizations in Singapore. The open nature of membership (no membership fees were collected prior to its eventual registration) posed a number of other problems. For example, no one was really sure about the exact identities of 'volunteers' who had signed up on the mailing list. On a few occasions, TWC2 was approached by individuals with more than the interests of the community in mind. High membership turnover also inevitably affected the quality of some projects. The need to balance accountability and openness in membership led to the maintenance of a 'clumsy' and ever-changing mailing list.

Strongly aware of the complexity and controversy surrounding the issues related to foreign domestic workers in Singapore, the members of TWC2 set a specific time limit on their activities and organizational life in order to provide focus and also a more realistic sense of what could be accomplished. One year – also the lifespan of TWC – was as long as TWC2 members felt they could test the patience of the state. Since the 'time limit' principle had also informed the formation of TWC in 1998, the suggestion by a key member of TWC to call the new organization TWC2 was readily accepted by members.

While TWC had an informal and network-based structure, TWC2 operated in terms of a division of labour marked out in an organizational hierarchy. TWC2's chairperson Mathiaparanam, then a nominated parliamentarian, had already been an established public figure and vocal critic of the state since her days as a journalist in *The Straits Times*. Popular among civil society activists and Singaporeans from many segments of society, she was well-known for her no-nonsense and hard-hitting approach and was much respected for it. It was perhaps a good strategy to capitalize on her popularity and clout as a parliamentarian to gain access to policy makers and other stakeholders that would otherwise have been denied. The public profile of the chairperson also meant that she was sometimes positioned as TWC2's 'lightning rod' for criticism when problems occurred or controversy cropped up. This had the effect of limiting how far TWC2 could push for change and also circumventing what its members could say publicly and what TWC2 could actually do. In 2004, Mathiaparanam was not selected to serve a second term as NMP. It remains to be seen what impact this will have on TWC2. For instance, this presents an opportunity to develop new organizational structures that will be less dependent on the profile of the chairperson, with smaller project groups formalized and led by their own project heads.

TWC2's non-legal status, limited lifespan, and open membership raised much suspicion, especially from public officials, towards its agenda. It was often difficult to explain 'civil society' to civil servants, and much less account for features that were novel in the context of Singapore.

Activities: Stakeholder engagement

A complex set of questions surrounds the foreign domestic worker industry in Singapore (Yeoh, Huang, and Gonzalez 1999; Rahman, Yeoh, and Huang 2005). TWC2 (2003a) had, from the onset, identified some of the main issues, including:

1. The processes by which domestic workers are brought into Singapore and sent home.
2. The availability of support structures for domestic workers in distress.
3. Regulation and/or legislation needed to protect foreign domestic workers from ill-treatment and to govern the foreign domestic worker industry as a whole.
4. The strategies and structures needed to reduce Singapore's over-reliance on domestic workers.
5. The economic and cultural environment of abuse and the impact of this abuse on Singapore's culture and economy.

TWC2 launched itself publicly in 2003 with the tag line 'dignity overdue' to address what it saw as the negative regard among

Singaporeans for foreign domestic workers. It hoped to address this problem through public education by organizing forums, seminars, exhibitions, and community events. Between March and November 2003, TWC2 aggressively participated in the public discourse on foreign domestic worker issues mainly by getting press coverage of its activities and writing letters to *The Straits Times* forum pages. On 5 July 2003, for example, TWC2 held a public forum to discuss the difficult conditions that foreign domestic workers find themselves in. To raise awareness among youths, a Saturday morning was spent with students (aged 16 to 18) from a junior college discussing these issues. An essay-writing competition for upper primary school children (aged 10 to 12) was also organized in August 2003, with a member of the government attending as guest-of-honour. Art and photographic exhibitions were staged at community venues like bus interchanges and libraries throughout the country.

Employers of foreign domestic workers were also engaged directly. The 'Sundays off campaign' (later renamed 'days off campaign') was launched to encourage employers to provide regular days off for their foreign domestic workers. TWC2 members went door-to-door posting flyers and inviting employers to attend a 'song and dance session'. Employers were encouraged to attend the event with their foreign domestic workers. Through the simple event held in the local community, TWC2 was communicating a somewhat controversial message that employers can interact with their foreign domestic workers as they would with any other Singaporean in their own neighbourhood. As its profile increased, TWC2 quickly became seen as the 'maid NGO', perceived by the public and the state as taking a strong human rights approach to the issue of foreign domestic workers. TWC2 was aware of this and made no apologies for it. It had to intervene in a highly asymmetrical power relationship between foreign domestic workers, maid agencies, and employers. This was however always going to be a temporary strategy. Human rights causes have not generally enjoyed a positive record of drawing support from the Singaporean public. Moreover, to engage fully with the complexities of the industry, TWC2 had to look beyond foreign domestic workers and consider the other stakeholders in the industry. Later in the year, TWC2 started to lay more emphasis on the need to improve working relations between employers and their foreign domestic workers to correct the misperception that it was merely a champion for the rights of foreign domestic workers.

TWC2 astutely recognized that the key to improving the situation for foreign domestic workers lay in constructively engaging other more powerful stakeholders. Numerous private dialogues and meetings have taken place with representatives from the Bangladeshi, Indonesian, and Filipino communities (especially embassy officials), the Ministry of Manpower, employment agencies, and other NGOs and voluntary welfare organizations (VWOs). The aim of these dialogues was to establish more channels of communication among the stakeholders with a view to improving the welfare of foreign domestic workers and the industry as a whole. Discussions also involved attempts to initiate projects like the introduction of 'reporting templates' for foreign domestic workers in distress and improvements to the regulatory framework through better contracts and legislation. A strategy for improving the working conditions of foreign domestic workers that increases costs to stakeholders and employers will not find widespread support. Letters have been written lambasting TWC2 for not considering the plight of employers. Even if the long-term solution to the problem is for a mindset change among Singaporeans, tackling the deeply entrenched culture of reliance on domestic workers has been viewed by some stakeholders as political suicide. TWC2's most important contribution, it might therefore be argued, has been its ability to secure dialogue among stakeholders.

In their illuminating discussion of 'regulatory spaces', Hancher and Moran (1989) argue that regulation can be conceptualized as 'spaces' occupied by actors who contest one another for power. 'Regulatory politics' is a contestation over the power to determine the rules of regulation as its ultimate prize. Since it is extremely difficult for small non-traditional actors like NGOs to claim the regulatory prize, the only value NGOs can add to the regulatory process is through the projection of its 'voice' to articulate the interests of citizens. With a moral claim on these citizens, NGOs can influence the key stakeholders in regulation. In positioning itself as a disinterested stakeholder, TWC2 has repeatedly offered itself as 'the bad guy' to push for issues that other stakeholders may be unable or unwilling to take up. But in this way, TWC2 benefits the overall regulatory process. To do that effectively in the context of Singapore's regulatory politics, however, TWC2 needed to become a formal (legal) stakeholder.

This explains why TWC2 tried in early 2004 to register itself as a formal society in compliance with the law, even though it had promised to stop its activities after November 2003. Its members felt that it had become 'too involved' in the issue to let go so prematurely. They and others in civil society believed that TWC2 could still make a significant contribution to the regulatory process of the foreign domestic worker industry. A legal status would signal to the public and the state that TWC2 was a formal stakeholder. But the application was only approved in mid-May 2004, after a relatively long time, suggesting that the state did not fully welcome TWC2, whose role and intentions it was never really sure about. Generally inexperienced in dealing with civil society groups, the state needed to be persuaded via several discussions before it would give its blessings. It is perhaps significant that such discussions even took place, demonstrating that TWC2 was able to exercise some influence in shaping regulatory politics in Singapore.

Some preliminary conclusions

As a new organization, TWC2 was not considered by many stakeholders in the foreign domestic worker industry to be a bona fide stakeholder. And yet, it was surprisingly successful at gaining access to stakeholders and effecting a limited degree of influence in policy making. Tay (2000) argues that civil society can play a role in law making in Singapore, a perspective borne out by TWC2's experience. Although no laws were actually made or changed, TWC2 maintained legitimacy in the eyes of the public and the state by willingly revisiting its own assumptions and premises, even abandoning the transitional model of citizen participation first demonstrated by TWC. It showed itself to be a sincere and pragmatic actor, winning the trust of the state and thereby encouraging greater engagement with the state.

At the end of the day, though, it is extremely difficult to identify who should be given credit for any positive developments in the foreign domestic worker industry. In the political context of Singapore, it remains extremely difficult for civil society practitioners to take credit for work that they have done, especially if such work receives positive public attention. It is often observed, too, that the state tends to monopolize civic energies and also claim credit obtrusively for any successful outcomes. It is, in any case, an extremely complicated task to draw causal linkages between the actions of an NGO, policy changes, and consequences (expected and unexpected). Morale is easily weakened by members' inability to see clearly the results of their hard work. Not surprisingly, membership attrition is high. Yet, for TWC and TWC2, there has always been a hopeful and stubborn persistence among members who expect neither reward nor recognition. The culture of fear that was supposed to be so crippling turned out instead to have been the enabling factor that led to the unique experiments of the two 'Working Committees'.

TWC and TWC2 engaged other citizens and the state using a diverse range of instruments. Although engaging the state 'behind closed doors' has continued as a dominant strategy, attempts have been made to augment this with public engagement and awareness-raising activities. Both organizations were able to sustain consistent engagement in the public sphere to effect policy change without being punished by the state (an outcome suggested by the 'culture of fear' thinking). In the case of TWC, it was important not to take too partisan a stand on the many complex issues within civil society as this 'open policy' would help to widen the space for activism. TWC2 was then able to benefit from this widened space, and it took strong positions on many issues concerning foreign domestic workers. At the same time, by astutely engaging in regulatory politics, it was able to present itself as a neutral and disinterested party that was willing to advocate for issues and policies that were in the overall interest of the industry.

In TWC, the subject of fear was an occasional topic of conversation and the motif of not a few nervous jokes. While it cannot be said that TWC members were gung-ho cowboys testing how far they could go before they were arrested by the sheriff, it can be said that the members constantly tried to create organizational structures and undertake projects that would minimize risk, and hence the fear associated with it. Always pragmatic – and sometimes to a fault – the main objective of TWC was to build up networks of civil society by occupying the space that had been abandoned by risk-averse Singaporean. Occupying the space to realize the potential for empowerment was more important than engaging in more confrontational and controversial issues that might give the state an excuse to colonize the space once again. Since TWC2 stood firmly on secure foundations set up by TWC, it did not find itself treading on ground that was entirely unfamiliar. Therefore, the element of fear was somewhat reduced. In spite of the difficulties faced by civil society actors in Singapore, activists have never stopped trying. The culture of fear has been offered as one of the main reasons for the overall lack of activism and its general ineffectiveness. But instead of stifling ground energies of civil society altogether, fear can promote the development of alternative and novel ways for activists to engage citizens and the state, and avoid punishment from the latter. The experience of the two Working Committees represents an interesting chapter in the history of civil society in Singapore. Before TWC and TWC2, civil society was limited by the requirement to register itself as a society and submit itself to regulations. The transitional model of the TWCs showed a different approach to activism in Singapore.

In its creative interpretation of the law and political status quo, TWC and TWC2 (in its unregistered form) took certain liberties to achieve its political goals, but checked itself constantly to forestall any reprisal from the state. This dynamic process of testing boundaries and then quickly checking oneself is also demonstrated in TWC2's decision to register itself in 2004, an act that did not render the transitional model of TWC obsolete but instead demonstrated to Singaporeans a wider range of options for activism than is conventionally thought possible. The experience of TWC and TWC2 shows how the culture of fear can be transformed into a culture of creativity, quite in line – ironically – with the state-sponsored renaissance city aspiration.

NOTES

1. The opinions expressed here are the author's own and should not be taken as indicative or representative of the views of any organizations and individuals that he mentions. Most of the materials in this chapter are drawn from personal knowledge and experience as a member of TWC from June 1999, and more actively as TWC2's 'temporary' secretary from September 2003 to August 2004.

REFERENCES

Chan, S.S. (2000) 'The Singapore government and civil society' in Koh, G. and Ooi, G.L. (eds.) *State-Society Relations in Singapore*, Singapore:

Oxford University Press, pp. 122–38.

Chong, E. (20 July 2002) '18 ½ years, caning for man who abused maid', *The Straits Times* (Singapore).

Flanagan, C. (2004) 'How serfdom saved the women's movement: dispatches from the nanny wars', *The Atlantic Monthly*, March.

Furedi, F. (2002) *The Culture of Fear: risk taking and the morality of low expectation*, Revised edn, London and New York: Continuum.

Gee, J. and Ho, E. (2006) *Dignity Overdue*, Singapore: Select.

Glasius, M., Lewis, D. and Seckinelgin, H. (eds.) (2004) *International Civil Society: exploring political and cultural contexts*, London: Routledge.

Gomez, J. (2000) *Self-Censorship: Singapore's shame*, Singapore: Think Centre.

Gomez, J. (2002) 'Internal competition and interaction', in Singam, C., Tan, C.K., Ng, T., and Perera, L. (eds.) *Building Social Space in Singapore: The Working Committee's initiative in civil society activism*, Singapore: Select Publishing, pp. 97–105.

Hancher, L. and Moran, M. (1989) 'Organizing regulatory space', in Hancher, L. and Moran, M. (eds.) *Capitalism, Culture and Economic Regulation*, Oxford: Clarendon Press.

Ibrahim, Z. (27 July 2004) 'Who's looking out for maids here?', *The Straits Times* (Singapore).

Kwok, K.-W. (13 December 2003) 'Public space and new politics', paper presented at Singapore Forum on Politics 2003 organized by the Political Science Department, National University of Singapore on 13 December 2003, Singapore.

Lee, H.S. (27 July 2002) 'Silence on maid abuse must end', *The Business Times* (Singapore).

Leftwich, A. (1995) 'Bringing politics back in: towards a model of the developmental state', *Journal of Development Studies*, 31(3): 400–27.

Lyons, L. 'Organizing for domestic worker rights in Southeast Asia: feminist responses to globalisation', paper presented at the 15th Biennial Conference of the Asian Studies Association of Australia on 29 June–2 July 2004, Canberra, Australia.

Ministry of Information and the Arts (2000) *Renaissance City Report: culture and the arts in renaissance Singapore*, Singapore. Online. Available HTTP: <http://www.mita.gov.sg/renaissance/FinalRen.pdf> (accessed 22 December 2004).

Ng, T. (2002) 'Party politics: dealing with disagreement', in Singam, C., Tan, C.K., Ng, T., and Perera, L. (eds.) *Building Social Space in Singapore: The Working Committee's initiative in civil society activism*, Singapore: Select Publishing, pp. 119–32.

Putnam, R.D. (2000) *Bowling Alone: the collapse and revival of American community*, New York: Simon & Schuster.

Rahman, N.A., Yeoh, B.S.A., and Huang, S. (2005) 'Dignity over due: transnational domestic workers in Singapore', in Huang, S., Yeoh, B.S.A., and Rahman, N.A. (eds.) *Contemporary Perspectives on Transnational Domestic Workers in Asia*, Singapore: Marshall Cavendish.

Singam, C., Tan, C.K., Ng, T., and Perera, L. (eds.) (2002) *Building Social Space in Singapore: The Working Committee's initiative in civil society activism*, Singapore: Select Publishing.

Tan, C.K. (2002) 'Impact of technology in discussion and interaction', in Singam, C., Tan, C.K., Ng, T., and Perera, L. (eds.) *Building Social Space in Singapore: The Working Committee's initiative in civil society activism*, Singapore: Select Publishing, pp. 107–18.

Tan, K.Y.L. (2000) 'Understanding and harnessing ground energies in civil society', in Koh, G. and Ooi, G.L. (eds.) *State-Society Relations in Singapore*, Singapore: Oxford University Press, pp. 99–105.

Tay, S.S.C. (2000) 'Civil society and the law in Singapore: three dimensions for change in the 21st century', in Koh, G. and Ooi, G.L. (eds.) *State-Society Relations in Singapore*, Singapore: Oxford University Press, pp. 170–89.

Teng, Q.X. (5 July 2003) 'Dignity for maids – forum to highlight the plight of foreign domestic workers', *Today* (Singapore).

The Business Times (13 February 2003) 'BT fund for maid raises $47,000', *The Business Times* (Singapore).

The Working Committee 2 (2003a) 'Our programme', TWC2 website. Online. Available HTTP: <http://www.twc2.org.sg/programme.shtml> (accessed 4 January 2005).

The Working Committee 2 (2003b) 'Who we are', TWC2 website. Online. Available HTTP: <http://www.twc2.org.sg/who.shtml> (accessed 4 January 2005).

Yeoh, B.S.A., Huang, S., and Gonzalez, J. (1999) 'Migrant domestic female workers: debating the economic, social and political impacts in Singapore', *International Migration Review*, 33 (1): 114–36.

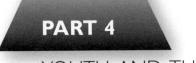

PART 4

YOUTH AND THE FUTURE

Youth

Every generation's moral panic

KENNETH PAUL TAN

In his first speech as Singapore's third prime minister, Lee Hsien Loong (12 August 2004) called upon Singapore's youths – the so-called 'post-65' generation[1] – to come forward with new ideas and contributions as citizens and perhaps even future political leaders. Over mumbled undertones of scepticism from those who had heard this kind of rhetoric many times before, a series of stylized initiatives followed. These included an invitation to young Singaporeans to send their ideas (mainly on the monumental question of how to build a better nation) through mobile telephone text messages or SMS (Balakrishnan 4 September 2004). Expecting youths to contain their vision of a monumental nation within the tiny screen of a mobile phone (that great signifier of contemporary Asian youth culture) has the unfortunate effect of making these attempts to engage with the youth seem patronizing and trivializing. The worldview of Singapore's youth, it might unfortunately be suggested, is as small as the screen of a mobile phone, and should therefore be taken just as seriously.

In the early 1990s, then-Prime Minister Goh Chok Tong memorably launched one of the annual street parties on Orchard Road with

the cheeky exhortation to 'keep the Party going!' Since the release of
the *Renaissance City Report* (Ministry of Information and the Arts
2000) a decade later, young Singaporeans have been reverse bungee
jumped into a cultural renaissance, where the enlightened dance
seductively on lucrative bar table-tops. In his first National Day Rally
speech, Prime Minister Lee Hsien Loong told Singaporeans that one
of the country's most progressive dance clubs – Zouk – had a branch
in Kuala Lumpur that was, in his own words, 'quite funky' (Lee 22
August 2004). Less than a month later, Singaporeans witnessed
on television news a 45-second clip of a cabinet minister dancing
along with a group of overseas-bound Singapore students at another
trendy dance venue, the Chinablack Club. The same minister had,
only in the previous year, cautioned Singaporeans against the life-
threatening risks of late-night dancing on bar table-tops (*The Straits
Times* 3 October 2002). On 23 September 2004, the People's Action
Party celebrated its fiftieth anniversary at Zouk. The media carried
photographs of the prime minister and several other members of
parliament 'mambo-ing' in their all-white (political) party uniforms
with enthusiastic party members and friends. *Channel NewsAsia*
reported that the 'PAP has shown that it is not an old fuddy-duddy
party' (de Souza 23 September 2004).

In 2006, the *Today* newspaper reported that Singapore's 'Post-
65 MPs are hip enough to hop, as they'll show at their debut at
next year's Chingay' (Kashinath 4 October 2006: 6). As the PAP
strained under the pressure of trying to connect with the youth, 10
of its younger members of parliament (some looking awkward and
uncomfortable) had been persuaded to rehearse some hip-hop dance
routines in preparation for a major public parade in 2007. The report
was also careful to explain that the MPs would be sticking to their
'wholesome image' as far as dress was concerned. This gimmick could
work if the MPs are able to convince the youth that they are just out
to have some spontaneous fun and are more than happy to make fun
of themselves.

For any government intent on securing political support, the
strategy of connecting with youths – speaking their language, as it
were – is not an easy one to pull off without looking or sounding
painfully contrived. In fact, it is one that can backfire embarrass-
ingly if the government's efforts are viewed as insincere, patronizing,

and thoroughly uncool. This has been demonstrated by unflattering comments that circulate on the internet. For instance, a 21-year old poster on *sgforums.com* observed about the PAP party at Zouk:

> This is the result of having people in power who are fake, shallow and really presumptious [sic], only having the ability to wayang [Malay word that refers to a form of theatre] and yet not have the brains to know that people are laughing at them. They only care about money and power. (LazerLordz 25 September 2004)

But connecting with youths is what the government – indeed the adult world in general – always thinks it needs to do. Failing to connect has been the source of much anxiety and often also resentment that then gets transferred onto a vision of youth as inadequate and therefore a common – even national – source of worry and disappointment. In Singapore, the complaint that youths are apathetic reverberates *ad nauseam*.

The problem with youths ... as imagined by adults

Youths, from many adult-centric points of view, are incomplete versions of adults. They need protection, often in the form of censorship. They are impressionable. And they are not yet fully rational, and may never become fully rational without the tutelage of 'right-thinking adults'. Training for adulthood involves a disciplining process designed to curtail the non-conformist and less predictable tendencies of young people. Through modern social institutions like the school system and military service, young people are expected to internalize the rules, norms, procedures, and reciprocal expectations externally imposed by family, society, and government. This process of internalization 'civilizes' them into workers and citizens. Proper socialization therefore makes young people 'fit for' – or 'fit into' – the adult world.

For this kind of socialization – where parents, teachers, and religious leaders try hard to mould children in their own exact image – the adult world believes it needs to understand, communicate with, and control its young. The challenge of doing this has been the cause of much anxiety in the adult world, where youths – and hormone-driven teenagers in particular – are first and foremost an unfathomable and uncontrollable category of persons. Conservative opinion leaders in

Singapore often articulate a disproportionate yet deeply embedded lack of faith in the next generation's capacity to sustain the achievements of their predecessors. This incapacity, they imagine – or rather, *like* to imagine – will bring about the downfall of the nation, perhaps even humanity itself. No other generation, they would like to think, can ever be as good as their own.

And so, the adult world obsesses about the deficiencies and destructiveness of the younger generation, invoking youth stereotypes and folk devils such as the apathetic, disloyal, and ungrateful youth; the ignorant, materialistic, and superficial student; the pampered, flabby, and effeminate son; and the aimless, vulgar, and sometimes violent *ah beng* (a local Chinese youth subculture). These stereotypes are invoked in ways that help the adult generation to imagine normality – perhaps even to fantasize about normal life where the apathetic, disloyal, ungrateful, ignorant, materialistic, superficial, pampered, flabby, effeminate, aimless, vulgar, and violent youths are punished, converted, or expelled.

In short, the frequent references in the public discourse to youths as a national problem are probably motivated by at least three things. Firstly, they reflect already existing insecurities and anxieties in adults about their own inability to understand, connect with, or control youths, and also reflect the hyperbolic terms that are resorted to in thinking about how youths are unable to meet the responsibilities of securing a future for the nation – even humanity itself! Secondly, deviant youth stereotypes are invoked to help define and police what is conservatively regarded as normal, desirable, and worthy of protection in the face of threats. And thirdly, conjuring up images of deficient and deviant youths provides the adult generation with convenient evidence to support the self-gratifying thesis that 'kids these days' just do not measure up when compared to the 'good ole days'.

Deficient and deviant youths in Singapore

In May 2004, then-Acting Education Minister Tharman Shanmugaratnam described Singaporean youths as 'soft, sheltered, and selfish' (Feedback Unit 2004), suggesting further that they, when compared to earlier generations of Singaporeans and also to youths in other Asian countries, were not hungry enough to succeed, and so presented a much more serious problem for sustaining prosperity, even more serious, he suggested, than the global economic challenges that Singapore faced. His solution: toughen up students by encouraging them to participate in adventurous, outdoor co-curricular activities like sports and uniformed groups, so that presumably they do not all become chess players, computer games addicts, or choir boys. Any sort of overseas component in the learning experience should also, he suggested, take students to developing countries so that they can experience hardship. Presumably, packaging these 'hardship experience tours' for students will make them more grateful about being born Singaporean, turn them into entrepreneurs, and perhaps even make them more civically engaged (Feedback Unit 2004).

In April 2002, parliamentarians huffed and puffed over the provocatively hypothetical question of whether Singapore's youths would stand up and defend their country in times of war. One by one they stood up to speak, comparing with each other to see who had the biggest outrage over the possibility that young Singaporeans might not in fact be willing to kill another human in the name of their nation-state (Chua 5 April 2002).

A couple of months later, in his National Day Rally speech, former Prime Minister Goh (2002) unleashed a passionate public debate by coining the terms 'stayers' and 'quitters', the latter referring derogatorily to an emerging breed of mobile and cosmopolitan Singaporeans who were said to be insufficiently rooted to their homeland and unwilling to make personal sacrifices for the greater good. According to Goh, quitters preferred to stay in Singapore only in good times but readily chose to leave in more difficult times. Morally outraged voices took advantage of this debate to vent in the local media their frustrations on 'other' – mostly younger – Singaporeans who were not as patriotic, or as selfless, or as resilient as they obviously felt they themselves were.

Since the 1980s, the prospects of a declining population in Singapore have brought unwanted national attention on young Singaporeans – especially the more educated, qualified, and affluent ones – who were not getting married or having enough children (Tan 2001). Even in some more recent parliamentary speeches, these young Singaporeans, especially couples with 'dual incomes and no kids', were judged as selfish, irresponsible, unpatriotic, and even un-Confucian for not bearing children for the nation (Tee 10 March 2004).

In 1996, widely-reported results of a survey indicated that young Singaporeans were clueless about the basic facts about Singapore and especially its official history. News reports also highlighted earlier surveys that had shown young Singaporeans to be materialistic and money-minded (*The Straits Times* 5 July 1996). This generation of students, then-Prime Minister Goh lamented, 'have not suffered wars, not lived through political struggles, racial tensions, unemployment and deprivation' (Goh 8 September 1996). A whole generation of youths – the future citizens of Singapore – disconnected from the nation seemed to present a threat to the future of the nation itself. The solution: National Education in the formal and informal curriculum to instil in young Singaporeans a sense of identity, knowledge of history, an appreciation of the nation's challenges, and a set of core values (Lee 17 May 1997). Only then, it was believed, could young Singaporeans be moulded into socially responsible and active citizens who are right for national consultative exercises like Singapore 21 and Remaking Singapore, as Woo Yen Yen and Colin Goh observe in Chapter 6.

In the same year, 1996, Singaporeans read news reports that their low crime rates appeared to be threatened by 'wayward youths', the products of an affluent but alienating society in which the heterosexual family structure seemed to be under threat. Statistical data breathed life into reports about delinquent behaviour that included 'vandalism, theft, drug abuse, glue-sniffing, and extortions, as well as gang fights which could be triggered by something as mundane as groups trying to stare each other down' (Tan 1 November 1996). These accounts of juvenile delinquency provided justification for various proposed drastic measures including sending youth offenders to boot camp and fining parents for offences committed by their children.

Two years earlier, in 1994, Michael Fay and Shiu Chi-Ho, students from the United States and Hong Kong respectively, were both fined, jailed, and caned for vandalizing cars in Singapore (Stewart 23 April 1994; Hubbard 18 June 1994). These foreign youngsters from more liberal societies occupied the public imagination as icons of degenerate youth, contrasted painfully, it would seem, against an orderly and disciplined Singapore that would not hesitate to impose its own brand of harsh punishment to secure this order and discipline. Conservative westerners, and especially Americans, applauded the move and lamented the absence in their own countries of punitive structures that could retrieve the traditional values that they imagined were lost after the counter-cultural movements of the 1960s. Meanwhile, T-shirts and mugs bearing the printed message 'spare the rod and spoil the child' enjoyed brisk sales as business-minded Singaporeans rushed to cash in on the publicity (*Associated Press* 17 June 1994).

The Youth Park at Somerset Road, a gathering place for youths, complete with a café, a free-for-all stage, and a skating park in recent years has been covered by graffiti which, one suspects, is encouraged by the authorities since it helps to simulate authentic youthfulness. Here again is an effort to connect with youths by 'speaking their language'; but it is doubtful whether hardcore graffiti writers would want to have anything to do with a space that has been 'approved' by the authorities who say that 'as long as the drawings are non-offensive in nature – for instance, no vulgarities or religious attacks – we'll take it as healthy creative expression' (Tee 16 January 2002). Much of youth culture is motivated by a rebelliousness that – simply by definition – refuses to be co-opted by the establishment.

To some extent, deviance from the established norms is, to many youths, a desirable thing that helps build up their personal credibility and prestige among their peers. The market is fully aware of this, and capitalizes on deviance as a branding strategy. That money is to be made from amplifying youth deviance is hardly surprising. In 2002, Motorola tried to shed its conservative image by sponsoring raves, street graffiti performances, and other programmes aimed at youths (Hargrave-Silk 11 January 2002). In 2003, SingTel launched an advertising campaign for its new product that was based on the idea of youths losing control of their thumbs in an SMS-crazy world (Tsang 5 September 2003). In 2004, the classified pages of *The Straits Times* and *Lianhe Zaobao* organized a graffiti design contest, requiring contestants to design the tagline 'Buy it. Sell it. Find it' and to 'make it look really hip!' The top prize was a trendy Apple iPod (*The Straits Times* 24 December 2004). While youth culture refuses to be absorbed into the establishment, it often finds the capitalist market irresistible. Or put another way, the market is more skilful at co-opting youth than government leaders and their supporters whose efforts to appear 'cool' often have just the reverse effect.

Youths, moral panic, and capitalism

Other than reflecting insecurity, providing gratification, and enabling normalization, the regular public amplification of youths as a national problem may be serving a larger purpose. It may be a way of transferring attention and blame from the more fundamental problems of globally embedded capitalist societies like Singapore onto recognizable folk devils. This is a form of scapegoating – that is, the reduction of a larger social problem to an identifiable stereotyped category or group of individuals that becomes the object of collective moral outrage and blame. In other words, political leaders, mass media, experts, law enforcers, moral and religious entrepreneurs, and opinion leaders in general converge in the act of inventing the apathetic, disloyal, ungrateful, ignorant, materialistic, superficial, pampered, flabby, effeminate, aimless, vulgar, and violent youths, and according them the blame for the emerging consequences of a much larger crisis inherent in a capitalist society where business cycles seem to be getting shorter, income gaps wider, costs of living higher, and the people's morale lower. Anxieties surrounding Singapore's future performance in the new areas of economic development – the creative sector in particular – need also to be assuaged. Someone needs to be available for blame – enter the young Singaporean!

In this larger crisis, nothing re-enchants the people more than the suggestion of a folk devil. Michael Fay and the righteous indignation of Americans who supported the punishment suggest to Singaporeans that Singapore must not go the way of liberal America; otherwise Singapore youths will turn into vandals and, by association, drug addicts, alcoholics, glue-sniffers, thieves, and gangsters. Statistics presented in ways that suggest a rise in the number of 'wayward youths' in Singapore also motivate efforts to stem the tide of degeneration, and this probably means maintaining, perhaps strengthening, the more repressive aspects of Singapore's system of control and discipline.

The youthful folk devil is also quickly commodified to serve the needs of the crisis-prone market economy, and in particular the mass media as players in the market. Nothing sells quite like a simple story about how an identifiable person or group of persons can be responsible for most of the nation's woes. Gaining a sense of moral superiority, envisioning an enemy, and turning a mundane life into a question of human survival all constitute the pleasure of reading and reacting to such media reports. Capitalist Singapore distracts itself from its inherently systemic crises by blaming youths for its problems, and then commodifying the blame – into media reports and 'deviant' goods – to regenerate the market.

Historical amnesia

Getting all panicky about the deficiency and threat of youths today involves some historical amnesia (Pickering 2001). There is nothing inherent in this generation of Singaporeans that makes it more or less worthy of criticism than the last, or the one before that, and so on. And yet, current problems are exaggerated through a historically insensitive comparison with some imagined previous generation when everything and everyone were better. In 2004, Minister Tharman picked up the story about how young Singaporeans were too soft and comfortable. But in the years following Singapore's independence in 1965, the government was promoting rugged individualism as a national value; and, in spite of resistance from traditional Chinese families, compulsory military service was established to discipline and physically strengthen young male Singaporeans – previously the 'lazy natives' of colonial Singapore – to be manly and focused on the defence of a vulnerable new nation. The recent performance in parliament of outrage at the very idea that Singaporean youths might not be willing to die for their country could just as easily have been performed in a similar way in the years following independence.

In the mid-1990s, Michael Fay became the great signifier of youthful degeneracy and violence, a powerfully negative influence on impressionable Singaporean youths. But in the 1960s and 1970s, the government had cautioned Singaporeans against being influenced by the yellow culture of the so-called 'west'; the sex, dope, and rock festivals of the hippy generation; and the idealistic students who demonstrated against their university administrators and national leaders on civil rights issues and the war in Indochina. At around that time, in the 1970s, the Singapore media generated a public sense that crime was on the rise. Chewing gum – read as a sign of youthful defiance and disrespect – was banned, officially because public money should not be wasted on cleaning up dried gum stuck to walls, floors, and doors in public places. And in 1972, Cliff Richard was turned away at Changi Airport because the popular singer sported long hair. Student demonstrations in Singapore from the 1950s to the 1970s were completely crushed by the government and the idealism that motivated them was redefined as mischief and terrorism in the popular anti-communist folklore.

In 2002, then-Prime Minister Goh raised the question of young Singaporean 'quitters'. But the issue of Singaporean emigration and the 'brain drain' have been a preoccupation since the 1970s. The question of today's apathetic, depthless, and ungrateful Singaporean youths and their lack of loyalty to their country is often explained as the ironic result of national success and affluence. In the late 1970s, the government also lamented that the well-socialized Singaporean workers would only relate to their country – and presumably government too – in terms of a material exchange. But a purely material basis of national and political support was not stable, and so Singaporeans needed to be re-enchanted by talk about national identity, culture, values, and roots. The Goh Keng Swee (1979) report of 1978 – instrumental in establishing mother-tongue policies, religious (and particularly Confucian) studies in the formal curriculum, and the 'Asian values' talk – emerged out of a moral panic about young Singaporeans and the future of Singapore.

Conclusion

Youths escape the comprehension and control of the adult world, a troublesome relationship that provokes disappointment, frustration, anxiety, and indignation often expressed collectively at the national level. Youths become the explanation for most things that go wrong today and most things that will go wrong in the future. They serve as excuses for adult deficiencies and mistakes, which they help to disguise particularly in moments of crisis when everyone needs somebody to blame. Youths are therefore a key element of political legitimation in capitalist societies that constantly must deal with crises inherent in global capitalism.

In Singapore, the public imagination has been dominated by accounts of youth apathy. One particularly pronounced version of this was the claim that today's youths are too comfortable in their material affluence and they have not experienced real hardship or struggle of any kind that could implant the drive to succeed. This account also suggests that Singapore's continued economic success will be jeopardized by today's youths, unless they can be re-programmed or re-activated as a force for good. But this must correspond with the terms set out by the adult world, properly defined by political interests. So, youths who paint graffiti in approved spaces are good. Youths who offer their creative talents to produce (or consume) new economy products are good. Youths who come forward to articulate responsible and correct (read 'predictable') responses to a fixed agenda of abstract questions of national importance are good. And youths who energetically and uncritically heed the nation's call to volunteer their services – often to causes that they barely understand or care for – are good.

Youths who retreat from an alienating adult world or who confront it with foundation-shaking energy and freshness are singled out for blame.

NOTES

1. 1965 was the year that Singapore gained political independence.

REFERENCES

Associated Press (17 June 1994) 'T-shirt cashes in on flogging American youth', *The Associated Press*.
Balakrishnan, V. (4 September 2004) Speech at the Youth Mentoring Convention on 4 September 2004, Singapore.
Chua, L.H. (5 April 2002) 'Lively debate on life and death issue', *The Straits Times* (Singapore).
de Souza, C-M. (23 September 2004) 'PAP celebrates party's 50th anniversary at Zouk', *Channel NewsAsia* (Singapore).
Feedback Unit (2004) 'Are our youths soft, sheltered and selfish?' Discussion list. Online. Available HTTP: <http://app.feedback.gov.sg/asp/dis/dis0003.asp?topicId=1181&catId=622> (accessed 11 September 2004).
Goh, C.T. (8 September 1996) Speech at the Teachers' Day Rally on 8 September 1996, Singapore.
Goh, C.T. (18 August 2002) 'Remaking Singapore – changing mindsets', Speech at the National Day Rally on 18 August 2002, Singapore. Online. Available HTTP: <http://www.gov.sg/nd/ND02.htm> (accessed 22 December 2004).
Goh, K.S. (1979) Report on the Ministry of Education 1978, Singapore: Singapore National Printers.

Hargrave-Silk, A. (11 January 2002) 'Motorola shakes up image to target youth', *Media*.
Hubbard, R. (18 June 1994) 'Singapore cuts caning sentence of Hong Kong youth', *Reuters News*.
Kashinath, M. (4 October 2006) 'Yeah, we can dance if we want to', *Today* (Singapore).
LazerLordz (25 September 2004) 'PAP's political agenda at Zouk disco?', sgforums.com. Online posting. Available HTTP: <http://www.sgforums.com/?action=thread_display&thread_id=95105> (accessed 15 October 2004).
Lee, H.L. (17 May 1997) Speech at the launch of National Education on 17 May 1997, Singapore.
Lee, H.L. (12 August 2004) Swearing-in speech as prime minister of Singapore on 12 August 2004, Singapore Istana.
Lee, H.L. (22 August 2004) Speech at the National Day Rally on 22 August 2004, Singapore.
Ministry of Information and the Arts (2000) *Renaissance City Report: culture and the arts in renaissance Singapore*, Singapore. Online. Available HTTP: <http://www.mita.gov.sg/renaissance/FinalRen.pdf> (accessed 22 December 2004).
Pickering, M. (2001) *Stereotyping: the politics of representation*, Hampshire: Palgrave.
Stewart, I. (23 April 1994) 'Singapore on the defence', *South China Morning Post*.
Tan, A. (1 November 1996) 'Singapore wages battle against wayward youth', *Reuters News*.
Tan, K.P. (2001). '"Civic society" and the "new economy" in patriarchal Singapore: emasculating the political, feminizing the public', *Crossroads: An Interdisciplinary Journal of Southeast Asian Studies*, 15(2): 95–122. Online. Available HTTP: <http://www.niu.edu/cseas/seap/CROSSROADS%20Tan%20Reformat.pdf> (accessed 22 December 2004).
Tee, H.C. (16 January 2002) 'It's not graffiti at Youth Skate Park', *The Straits Times* (Singapore).
Tee, H.C. (10 March 2004) 'It's your "duty" to procreate', *The Straits Times* (Singapore).
The Straits Times (5 July 1996) 'Attitudes in Singapore', *The Straits Times* (Singapore).
The Straits Times (3 October 2002) 'Freedom doesn't come free', *The Straits Times* (Singapore).
The Straits Times (24 December 2004) 'Graffiti artwork contest', *The Straits Times* (Singapore).
Tsang, S.W. (5 September 2003) 'SingTel builds SMS cachet with youth', *Media*.

Refreshing the Young PAP

EDWIN PANG[1]

The need to refresh

The Young PAP or YP is the youth wing of the ruling People's Action Party (PAP). Its main role is to engage younger Singaporeans who are able and willing to contribute to nation building through the PAP. The YP is a key recruitment nexus for the PAP and training ground for future activists and political leaders. Formed in 1987 under the leadership of Lee Hsien Loong, who had been elected to the party's central executive committee the year before, the YP has seen a steady growth in its membership. Today, there are over 6,000 card-carrying members and many more non-member 'friends' who lend support to its activities.

The circumstances that surrounded the establishment of the YP in 1987 were quite different from those that had led to the founding of the PAP in 1954. Lee Kuan Yew and the founding fathers of the PAP led the struggle for independence and fought the communists and communalists (People's Action Party 1991: 33–47). Early party recruits were people who had come forward to join in this fight, and in the process became loyal party members, committed for life. Less dramatic perhaps, but no less serious, have been the more contemporary threats of economic slowdown (Asmani 27 March 2004), terrorism (Ibrahim 21 January 2003), and severe acute respiratory syndrome (SARS) (Lim, H.K. 22 July 2003). These threats have similarly drawn to the YP an increasing number of young citizens with a strong social conscience and sense of mission.

The importance of having a strong and vibrant PAP to ensure the continued well-being of Singapore cannot be overemphasized. As Lee Hsien Loong pointed out to party cadres at the 2003 PAP party convention,

> Singapore has come thus far by responding cohesively and rationally to problems and pursuing strategies which yield long-term results. But the real secret of our success is that we have been able to do this, when other countries have not. Why? Because a strong PAP has looked after the needs of Singaporeans, mobilized support for the government and inducted able and committed MPs and ministers to lead the nation. (Lee 2003)

In an ever-changing world, Singapore is now at a crossroads, faced with vital economic and social challenges. And it is politics that provides the answers to these challenges – gathering ideas, developing consensus, mobilizing people, and generating leadership. With this political master key, Lee said, all other problems can be tackled.

Although the PAP's ideals and goals to build a fair and just society remain constant, the party must nevertheless evolve with the times to reach out to Singaporeans. The YP is an important and effective channel for young Singaporeans to participate in the political process, garnering support from their peers and participating in policy debate and analysis.

More space for ideas

Indeed, with better education and access to information, many Singaporean youths have become more vocal, creative, socially conscious, and politically aware. They want to contribute their ideas for the development of the country in an increasingly competitive economic climate and a political and security environment that is more global and unpredictable. One indication of this has been the active exchange of views in the discussion forum on the YP website (www.youngpap.org.sg). Since its inception on 10 February 2003, YP net has seen an average of 70 postings each day, covering a current total of almost 2,500 topics that range from the building of an integrated resort in Singapore, problems of migration, the performance of individual members of parliament, the war in Iraq, and unemployment. At the more conventional YP 'policy forums' where YP members and non-member 'friends' listen to and engage with ministers on a range of policy issues, attendance figures average around 80 participants per event.

To continue to attract more young Singaporeans into its fold, the YP has embarked on a concerted effort to create more room in the party for the aspirations of youths to be expressed. At the PAP party convention in 2003, the objectives and core values of the party were reaffirmed: the task of building a fair and just society, based on honesty, multiracialism, meritocracy, and self-reliance, is still central to this day. However, these objectives and core values are now presented in a form that can more easily be communicated to a younger generation. Vivian Balakrishnan (2003), then vice-chairman of YP, explained at the 2003 convention that the party 'wanted to ensure that it remains true to the essence of our party values, while using language that the young could identify with'. The attributes that have consistently been manifested by the party were, at this convention, 'refreshed' as

- Compassionate – 'can feel'
- Resilient – 'can last'
- Reliable – 'can trust'
- Pragmatic – 'can work'
- United – 'can stick together'
- Far-sighted – 'can see ahead'
- Decisive – 'can do'

With these values and ideals in mind, the YP expects to reflect the perspectives of young Singaporeans, and to do so may sometimes entail taking a different position from the government's current policy. This will keep the party's thinking fresh, creative, vibrant, and forward looking. Several visible platforms for the contest of ideas, discussion, and articulation of views were introduced. One example of this is the series of policy forums held on 1 November 2003 with then-Acting Education Minister Tharman Shanmugaratnam and on 15 November 2003 with then-Acting Manpower Minister Ng Eng Hen. During these forums, where young Singaporeans were presented with opportunities to engage PAP ministers on matters of policy, controversial issues such as the longstanding practice of channelling students into different educational 'streams', and government support for local entrepreneurs were debated. Forums to discuss the work of other ministries are also being planned.

A second example of how the YP is becoming a bigger platform for discussion and debate is the YP net discussion forum. Hosted on the revamped YP website, the online forum has seen healthy participation by internet-savvy youths who have not hesitated to express a wide variety of opinions on a range of current issues including the punctuality of MPs at constituency events, the cost of education, Singapore's new prime minister, and international relations issues.

Thirdly, 10 YP members were nominated to join the PAP 'policy forum', an initiative arising from the 'refreshing PAP' project in 2003 (Young PAP Executive Committee 16 May 2003). The policy forum provides both an avenue for greater two-way consultation and communication between the party leadership and members, as well as a national platform for party members to express their views on policies and issues of national importance. Launched by then-Prime Minister and PAP Secretary-General Goh Chok Tong on 24 April 2004, the inaugural session saw members airing their views on 'engaging the party leadership' and 'the Singapore dream'.

The combination of diverse perspectives, access to senior government leaders, and participation in party affairs will be a unique opportunity for younger Singaporeans to shape their own future.

Expanding the ranks and building synergy

There are many reasons – and often very personal ones – why people choose to join a particular political party. While a formal recruitment drive may help to search out prospective members, it is the informal social events open to the public that can provide the opportunity for interaction amongst like-minded people. In this way, non-members might subsequently be encouraged to find out more about the party and perhaps to become a friend of the party and eventually a member.

To give the YP a broader appeal, a more relaxed image has been adopted. For instance, the YP's seventeenth anniversary was celebrated at a discotheque, and the 'white and white' dress code at YP functions has been relaxed to include more youthful and casual designs. Several 'young people's action groups' (YPAGs) were formed in 2003 to address specific interests or issues that members feel strongly about, including racial and religious harmony, manpower, education, trade and industry, healthcare, sports and lifestyle, and legal matters. In 2003, YP members and non-member friends of the YP gathered under the banner of 'YPAG fusion' to visit various places of worship to learn more about some of the main religions practised in Singapore, namely Buddhism, Catholicism, Islam, Sikhism, and Hinduism. They also got to know one another better when they participated in several golf and kayaking clinics and nature hikes organized by 'YPAG active lifestyle'. Through these activities, some non-members were encouraged to learn more about the party by visiting the YP branches, and subsequently signed on as members.

In addition, efforts have been made to promote greater synergy between the YP and the PAP women's wing so that the needs and opinions of young Singaporean women could be better addressed. For a start, MP Irene Ng was appointed as a second lady advisor to the YP executive committee (exco), joining MP Penny Low in this capacity. A 'YP Women' (YPW) section was also set up to address the interests and concerns of young women. To engage these young women on 'the opportunities and challenges confronting Singapore' and to provide occasions for them to articulate 'their aspirations and diverse views', the YPW Vision Programme was established. Under this long-term programme, a national essay writing competition was organized on the theme 'Writing our future: Singapore 2020'. The winning essayists were invited to dialogue with prominent leaders and thinkers.

YP members also have more opportunities now to contest for leadership positions in the YP exco. The YP is divided into five district committees, and each district is made up of several constituency branches. The chairmen and vice-chairmen of each district committee, now elected by the delegates of their respective branch committees, can serve on the YP exco. Talented and committed YP members have been encouraged to play more active and prominent roles at party functions. For example, YP members can be found participating in the PAP policy forum, and some of them serve as members of its council. YP members also helped to organize the PAP's fiftieth anniversary celebrations and served as coordinators of the PAP's National Day Parade contingent.

Finally, for 'life after YP', former YP members who 'graduate' on reaching the age of 40 are now encouraged to undertake more active roles at their respective PAP constituency branches, such as assuming leadership for organizing events at branch committee level or accepting positions in their branch executive committees if selected. They may also keep in touch with the YP by joining an informal group of YP alumni.

Conclusion

The YP aims to reflect the perspectives of younger Singaporeans and provide avenues for them to contribute in a meaningful way to Singapore's future. It will recruit, nurture, and develop the future core of the PAP. It will develop its own image and voice, and organize a wider range of activities to appeal to the young. Debate will be strongly encouraged within the party at various PAP and YP forums, dialogues, and party conventions. A 'refreshed' YP will help attract new stalwarts from a younger generation of Singaporeans, keep the party in tune with the people, and enable it to continue to serve Singapore well into the future.

The YP will remain true to the PAP's core values, be 'pro-Singapore' in its approach, and strengthen the unity of purpose among all party members regardless of age. Yet, as it refreshes itself, the YP will evolve and change to draw on the rich diversity of talents, views, and ideas of its members. This will, as then-YP chairman Lim Swee Say (2003) said at the PAP party convention, 'lead to a stronger sense of inclusiveness and openness, so that the party will be strong and united, as well as dynamic and growing'.

NOTES

1. The writer would like to thank the Young PAP executive committee for their input and assistance.

REFERENCES

Asmani, A. (27 March 2004) 'Money woes led to jump in people seeking help of MPs', *The Straits Times* (Singapore), p. 3.

Balakrishnan, V. (2003) 'Coming back full circle (remarks at PAP Party Convention 2003)', *Petir*, November – December, p. 10.

Ibrahim, Y. (21 January 2003) Speech at the parliamentary debate on the White Paper on Jemaah Islamiah arrests and the threat of terrorism on 21 January 2003, Singapore.

Lee, H.L. (2003) 'PAP's style must change (speech at PAP Party Convention 2003)', *Petir*, November – December, p. 2.

Lim, H.K. (22 July 2003) Speech at the SARS commemoration ceremony on 22 July 2003 at the Botanic Gardens, Singapore.

Lim, S.S. (2003) 'Swee Say's sales pitch for YP (speech at PAP Party Convention 2003)', *Petir*, November – December, p. 13.

People's Action Party (1991) *PAP Youth in Action 1986–1991*, Singapore: PAP.

Young PAP Executive Committee (16 May 2003) 'Refreshing YP', concept paper presented to the Refreshing PAP Committee on 16 May 2003, Singapore.

The future of alternative party politics

Growth or extinction?

SYLVIA LIM

Sometime in November 2003, I was invited to address a lunch meeting of the Foreign Correspondents' Association. During question time, one of the foreign journalists asked me why I had chosen to become a member of the Workers' Party (WP) – a 'marginalized' opposition party – instead of joining the People's Action Party (PAP) to try to 'change things from within'.

Change things from within? It seemed to me that one might be able to change things from within only if one were Lee Kuan Yew, Goh Chok Tong, or Lee Hsien Loong, or if one had their ears. The centralization of power within the ruling party is overwhelming.[1]

Marginalized? The journalist was probably reflecting on the WP's one parliamentary seat in the 84-member house, in the context of multi-party legislatures of democracies elsewhere. Nevertheless, to describe the WP as 'marginalized' belies the complexity of the current state of affairs and how Singapore got to this state historically. Such a description also underestimates the potential for political change that is reposed, ultimately, in Singaporeans themselves.

In this chapter, I intend to sketch my perception of party politics in Singapore and my reasons for cautious optimism that Singaporeans will be forthcoming in supporting and participating in parties that offer an alternative to the PAP. My views are those of a practitioner – not a political scientist or historian – and they stated at the dawn of a momentous change in the ruling party leadership from Goh Chok Tong to Lee Hsien Loong, the successor, it would seem, of his and the ministerial cabinet's choice. It remains unclear whether this leadership change will bring a political renaissance in Singapore, but my view is that it is unlikely that the PAP will soften its hard-line stance towards its political opponents. In a much-quoted speech to the Harvard Club of Singapore, Lee expressly encouraged civil society to develop, but to do so with the government leading from the front. However, those who join other political parties were told to expect robust rebuttals and even to be 'demolished', in accordance with the 'rules of the game of politics everywhere' (Lee 6 January 2004).

I should explain why I have deliberately used the term 'alternative party politics' rather than the more familiar 'opposition party politics'. Basically, 'opposition party politics' refers to the actions of parties that happen, at the time, not to be in formal positions of power. With the PAP entrenched in government since 1959, the term 'opposition party' has come to refer, perversely, to parties that oppose the PAP *per se*, and to oppose it on every issue. This is not the aim of the Workers' Party that has on a number of occasions, in fact, supported the ruling party on policies that the WP deemed to be in the national interest. In fact, the WP does not diverge from the PAP on some significant issues, but wants to offer 'non-PAP' options, whether it is at the ballot box or on specific policies. The term 'alternative party politics' captures more accurately the constructive spirit of the WP's political endeavours.

Electoral politics in Singapore

An analysis of data from general elections in 1984, 1988, 1991, 1997, and 2001 (for example, Yeo 2002) would yield a number of observations suggesting that alternative parties are *en route* to demise. And yet, the 2006 general election results seem to buck the trend. Data presented in Table 14-1 reveal some important trends.

TABLE 14-1 Results of general elections in Singapore since 1984

Year	Total no. of seats (No. contested)	% of seats contested	No. of parties contesting (Independents)	Seats won by PAP (%)	Seats won by other parties (%)	% of PAP's popular vote
1984	79 (49)	62	9 (3)	77 (97)	2 (3)	64.8
1988	81 (70)	88	8 (4)	80 (98)	1 (2)	63.2
1991	81 (40)	49	6 (7)	77 (95)	4 (5)	61.0
1997	83 (36)	43	6 (1)	81 (97)	2 (3)	65.0
2001	84 (29)	35	4 (2)	82 (98)	2 (2)	75.3
2006	84 (47)	56	4 (0)	82 (98)	2 (2)	66.6

1. The percentage of contested seats dropped steadily from a high in 1988 when 88 per cent of the seats (or 70 out of 81 seats) were contested to a low of 35 per cent (or 29 out of 84 seats) in 2001. In 2006, however, the trend was reversed, with 56 per cent (or 47 out of 84 seats) contested.
2. The number of alternative parties contesting dropped consistently from nine in 1984 to four in 2001, though the reduced number of parties in 2001 is attributable to the formation of the Singapore Democratic Alliance, a coalition of four alternative political parties standing for election as a single entity.
3. The 2006 general elections were also the first since 1984 not to feature independent candidates, probably a result of statutory changes that complicated the nomination procedure by requiring a candidate's proposer, seconder, and four assentors to appear in person at the nomination centre on nomination day: this requires more planning and coordination.
4. The percentage of the popular vote garnered by the ruling party decreased steadily to 61 per cent in the 1991 general elections, and then increased to 65 per cent in 1997 and shot up sharply to 75.3 per cent in 2001, a level not seen since the 1980 general elections when the PAP won about 77 per cent of the vote and every seat in the house. However, in 2006, it dropped to 66.6 per cent.

Several reasons account for the reduced electoral participation by alternative parties up to the 2001 elections. One significant factor was the introduction of systemic changes to entrench the ruling party and raise the political bar for alternative parties. On 12 January 1988, then-First Deputy Prime Minister Goh Chok Tong moved the Constitution (Amendment) Bill that introduced a new system in order, Singaporeans were told, to ensure minority representation in parliament. The group representation constituencies (GRC) system groups together clusters of electoral wards into multi-member constituencies; in this system, each voter casts his or her vote not for a single member of parliament (MP) to represent his or her ward, but for a team of MPs to represent the entire multi-member constituency that the voter resides in. Through further constitutional amendments over the years, GRCs have increased in size from three-member teams in 1988 to five- or six-member GRCs today. The government's rationale for this increase is that larger GRCs can reap 'economies of scale' in the running of municipal affairs.

What started out as a scheme to ensure minority representation has been whittled down to a device for administrative convenience. Instead of ensuring minority representation, the implementation of the GRC scheme, it has been observed, does the reverse – it disempowers minorities. Lily Zubaidah Rahim (1998) argues that the GRC system, combined with urban resettlement programmes and racial composition quotas for public housing allocation, ensures that the Malay community will always be in the numerical minority in any electoral constituency and that the electoral clout of the Malay community remains diluted. Furthermore, although Goh attempted to argue in parliament that the GRC system *per se* is 'neutral', he had to concede in response to a question from Workers' Party MP Low Thia Khiang that the system favours the party with more resources, namely the PAP (Parliamentary Debates Singapore 28 October 1996).

The re-drawing of electoral boundaries before every election is as certain as it is creative. The shortness of the time interval between the announcement of elections and election day itself is quintessential Singaporean efficiency. At the 2001 general elections, the announcement was made on 17 October and Nomination Day was on 25 October, just eight days later. This puts extreme time pressure on alternative parties to re-group, re-organize, negotiate with one another, and re-orient ground operations.

What is most disturbing about the GRC system is that Singapore's fundamental law, the constitution, went through a series of amendments to implement these changes which, in effect, have taken away the right of the voter to choose his or her own MP. From being able to exercise one vote out of, say, 23,000 votes in an average single-member constituency, the voter now casts one vote out of as many as 150,000 in an average GRC. The force of each vote is thereby weakened. Is the constitution there to safeguard citizens or to entrench the ruling party? Even the very prominent Ngiam Tong Dow (5 October 2003), one of the administration's longest-serving top civil servants, now retired, argued that 'Singapore is larger than the PAP'.

The electorate, to a certain degree, has also been depoliticized. For instance, tertiary students in today's Singapore, unlike their predecessors and their counterparts in many other countries, seem to have eschewed politics in favour of the rat race and finding a spouse on campus! In fact, Singapore undergraduates are regularly exhorted to think about going the family way, since this would help address the low fertility rates. Although Kenneth Paul Tan observes in Chapter 12 of this book that Singapore youths are constantly being singled out for blame by adults who were no better when they were youths, I would argue that increasing levels of competitiveness, pressures to start a family, and a pragmatic and materialistic orientation have effectively depoliticized the majority of young Singaporeans.

It is a myth that the PAP holds the monopoly on political talent. There is no shortage of concerned citizens who are potential alternative party candidates. However, while many acknowledge the importance of providing political competition for the PAP, they themselves are not prepared to risk a good career and a private life to enter the political fray. Some may express alternative views by joining civil society groups like the Association of Women for Action and Research (AWARE) and the (now defunct) Roundtable. While the civil society route is important for fostering an active citizenry, the process nevertheless does not extend to turning causes into election issues and empowering Singaporeans to exercise their right to vote for a change of policy.

The 2006 elections, however, marked a revitalization of party politics and the extent of sacrifices that citizens were prepared to make in order to support not only their candidates but the continuity and growth of alternative parties. Forty-seven candidates were fielded by alternative parties, including 25 first-time candidates. Since a majority of seats were at stake, a majority of Singaporeans now had to vote, which generated much excitement about politics and the elections as people chatted in coffee shops, dining rooms, offices, cyberspace, etc. Many of the first-time candidates fielded by alternative parties were under 40 years of age and, very notably, had university and professional qualifications. The post-65 generation voters saw that their contemporaries were willing to put themselves up to public scrutiny as alternative party candidates. Not surprisingly then, the political rallies in 2006 were able to draw audiences in droves.

The two incumbent opposition candidates – Chiam See Tong (Singapore Democratic Alliance chairman) and Low Thia Khiang (Workers' Party secretary-general) – were re-elected as expected, but with increased margins of victory (55.8 per cent and 62.7 per cent respectively). Even though Senior Minister Goh Chok Tong had directly intervened in the PAP campaign for the opposition-held constituencies, promising to allocate large sums of money for infrastructural 'upgrading', these opposition victories signal clearly that voters placed a premium on their opposition MPs for which they were prepared to pay a 'price' – they were quite willing to reject the almost irresistible upgrading 'carrot'.

What could account for this apparent reversal in the alternative parties' fortunes? Perhaps it is the new generation of Singaporeans who have come to the fore without baggage from the past. Globally-oriented, they expect their country to develop politically, in line with the world's best practices. The ruling party's political hegemony is anathema to those who believe in the value of checks and balances. In these highly globalized times, no government can guarantee economic security. Free market policies have given rise to problems of social justice. In addition, the ruling party's elitist image and policies are beginning to grate on a more diversely talented and confident population.

In spite of these signs of hope for the future of alternative politics, the fact remains that the number of non-PAP elected MPs in the last six elections peaked at four in 1991 and seems to have stabilized at two with Chiam See Tong and Low Thia Khiang securely seated in parliament. Is there a future for alternative politics after Chiam and

Low, or is Singapore returning to the pre-1981 situation when the PAP held all elected seats?

Workers' Party efforts: Promising signs

I am, for a number of good reasons, cautiously optimistic that the WP movement will gain momentum and that there will be some headway made at the next few general elections. Firstly, there are clear signs of renewal in the Workers' Party. A sizeable team of first-time candidates were put through the paces during the 2006 general elections; the tough lessons learnt and experience gained will be invaluable for fighting future elections. Since the WP's commendable performance in 2006, more potential leaders have joined the WP ranks. Many younger leaders have assumed roles in the party's executive council and Youth Wing executive committee. Others have become involved in welfare or policy work.

Secondly, the party has adopted a work ethic that prioritizes constituency 'groundwork' which must begin immediately after each general elections in preparation for the next. The constituencies, after all, are where it matters most. And so, members must work consistently at the constituency level in several strategic areas in addition to the WP constituency of Hougang. The party newspaper, *Hammer*, is published three times a year, and sold by party members themselves all over Singapore. The number of subscriptions to *Hammer* is growing.

Thirdly, the party has made efforts to address public policy matters inside and outside parliament, particularly on issues affecting the lives of Singaporeans such as unemployment, the central provident fund (a comprehensive social security savings plan originally aimed at providing Singaporeans with sufficient funds for retirement and medical expenses), transport, healthcare, and the cost of living. Public and private consultations with interested parties have been organized to enrich communication between the WP and the public on issues of interest.

My own position in the eleventh parliament as a non-constituency member of parliament (NCMP) presents another opportunity for the WP to represent Singaporeans in a public institution. To ensure a minimum number of opposition members in parliament, the constitution provides for the appointment of up to three NCMPs who are usually opposition party candidates who have received the highest number of votes among those who have not been successfully voted into parliament. As such, the NCMP seats have often been regarded as something of an electoral 'consolation prize'. And yet, NCMPs are able to fully participate in debates and to ask cabinet ministers to account for policies or mistakes. Together with Low Thia Khiang (elected WP member for Hougang constituency), I expect that the WP will find yet more opportunities in parliament to broaden its appeal and to demonstrate its constructive contribution to politics in Singapore. Whether this will translate into better prospects at the next polls remains to be seen.

Support for the PAP

Besides the WP's efforts, there have been unprecedented developments that may undermine the people's support for the PAP. Firstly, the PAP may no longer be able to promise 'more good years' – the platform on which many past elections were fought. For example, in a parliamentary debate in 2004, something happened that many years before would have been unimaginable: Mah Bow Tan, the Minister for National Development, acknowledged, in response to a string of MPs who had risen to plead with the minister to build smaller flats as families could not afford to continue living in their larger flats, that there was now a trend towards downgrading of homes (Parliamentary Debates Singapore 13 March 2004). Singaporeans wanted to sell their larger flats and move into smaller three-room flats. In 2003, cash-strapped citizens even turned down a proposal to upgrade their flats at Teban Gardens, a mature public housing estate. It seemed that the PAP's promise of 'asset enhancement', on which it had been riding firmly for electoral support, no longer enjoyed widespread appeal.

Since 1996, the Singapore economy has also been going through what economists call 'boom-bust' cycles – a pattern of alternating periods of high growth and low or even negative growth. Since the economic crisis of 1997, Singapore's GDP growth and export cycles have been volatile (Toh 13 January 2004). The government acknowledged that Singaporeans should no longer expect the high growth of previous decades. It is widely believed that Singapore's economic recovery is highly dependent on the US economy and the government cannot do much to change things (*The Straits Times* 12 August 2002). Structural unemployment in Singapore will not be helped by an intensifying regional competition for job creation. What the PAP has had with the people, up till now, is largely a 'material nexus'. Now, this will need to change. At the opening of the eleventh parliament in November 2006, one important theme in the president's address was that globalization increases income disparity. With the threat of an underclass developing (some MPs' speeches during that debate suggested that it was already present in Singapore), what vision can the ruling party sell? Will Singaporeans be convinced?

A second development that may undermine the support that the PAP now enjoys will have something to do with the unintended negative consequences of PAP policies that are surfacing. The Remaking Singapore committee, set up in 2002, aimed to address new challenges by reviewing social, cultural, and political strategies for twenty-first-century Singapore. The very need to 'remake' Singapore could be interpreted as an unintended outcome of earlier PAP policies. Today, Singapore is losing competitiveness in the region, as Janadas Devan suggests in Chapter 3. Workers, who are being told they are too expensive, do not see this as a result of their own design but a consequence of government policies. Goh Chok Tong (17 August 2003) acknowledged that Singaporean workers are expensive because costs have reached developed country levels and the wage structure remains rigid and seniority-based. Ordinary Singaporeans are also finding out that they will not have sufficient funds for retirement. Home purchases, including public housing, are usually financed through bank loans and withdrawals of significant portions of Singaporeans' central provident fund (CPF) savings, which are meant for retirement. Legislation required a minimum sum of $40,000 to be retained in a Singaporean's CPF account that cannot be withdrawn till he or she reaches the age of 55 years. Goh (17 August 2003) also acknowledged that the minimum sum of $40,000 would not be sufficient for the retirement needs of a Singaporean with an average life span of about 80 years. The minimum sum was increased to $80,000 and will continue to be increased gradually to $120,000 by 2013. The recession of the past several years has not made things any easier, forcing some borrowers to extend their loan repayment period because of retrenchments or smaller pay packets. They could be making repayments to banks well after they reach 55 years of age (Siow 29 March 2004).

Thirdly, as more people face economic hardship and the psychological effects of unemployment, there may be growing resentment of the high incomes earned by senior politicians, particularly the cabinet ministers. In 2003, questions were raised about whether certain persons enlisted for compulsory military service under the Enlistment Act were classified by the Ministry of Defence as 'white horses' and whether these persons with privileged backgrounds were being given preferential treatment (Parliamentary Debates Singapore 11 November 2003). These kinds of questions spring from the perception that there are double standards in so-called 'meritocratic' Singapore and that the higher echelon lead totally different lives from ordinary citizens.

Fourthly, there has been some disillusionment with feedback mechanisms organized by or affiliated to the PAP. Even the PAP itself is aware of this. Minister of State for Trade and Industry Raymond Lim informed the PAP convention in 2003 that there had been cynicism among PAP members at the grassroots level. These members believed that dialogue sessions had been

> initiated by the government on policies that often have already been decided upon. They felt that these sessions were more to inform and persuade them on policies rather than for them to be consulted and give inputs for policy formulation. (Lim 2003)

There has also been some public discussion about the role and purpose of the Feedback Unit organized by the PAP government (and now renamed 'Reach'). Identifying the evolving features of Singapore's political landscape, such as civil society and forum page letters that are increasingly well-written and well-argued, journalist M. Nirmala (2004) argues that the unit needs to 'ask itself what it must do to survive in a changing society that no longer needs it to talk to the Government'.

A fifth development that may undermine the support that the PAP now enjoys is the way that government control over the mass media has been increasingly limited by wider access to cable television and the internet. Although internet postings are often anonymous and unreliable, it is clear that the government takes them seriously and responds to concerns raised in newsgroups. For instance, an official rebuttal of an assertion circulated on the internet that a constitutional amendment would allow the government to squander the country's reserves was actually published in *The Straits Times* (Lim 11 May 2004). Even the mainstream mass media reacts to internet protests of unfair reporting by publishing corrective reports. For instance, in response to an open letter of criticism to *The Sunday Times'* political editor against an article that described the WP's public consultation exercise on 1 November 2003 as a 'griping session' (*The Sunday Times* 2 November 2003), a second report was published describing the outreach and standard of discussion in a more constructive light (Nirmala 5 November 2003). The open letter had been circulated via *The Optical*, an internet newsgroup.

Alternative parties have gained much exposure on the internet, a medium widely used by younger voters. During the 2006 general elections, a photograph taken by an internet-based journalist, Alex Au, showing a massive crowd at a WP rally was re-published in the mainstream media some days later. During the campaign, the internet-based video-sharing service *YouTube* was also loaded with video files by citizens who had recorded speeches at rallies of alternative parties, video files that could be and were rapidly accessed by others and disseminated through the rest of the internet.

Alternative parties and their future role

Sociologist Chua Beng Huat recently commented that, even with the changing of the PAP guard from Goh Chok Tong to Lee Hsien Loong, the PAP has shown that its moves towards liberalization in fields such as the arts and culture as described in the *Renaissance City Report* (Ministry of Information and the Arts 2000) do not concomitantly result in any liberalization in the party political arena. In his view, the political structure will remain unchanged for quite a while longer (Chua 13 January 2004).

The WP is under no illusion that it will win enough seats to form the government in the next 10 years or so, unless there is some drastic change in circumstances. The PAP will continue to govern for the foreseeable future. This is not because there are no able people outside the PAP who can run the country, but there is an insufficient number of such persons joining other parties to form an alternative government. Some have come forward, but more are needed.

What role, then, will the WP play in the meantime? The WP will participate in policy debates and offer alternatives where possible. This is a reasonable expectation of any party, and the WP will do its best within the natural limits of its resources. The party may not be able to prescribe a solution to every problem, but it will do its best to give alternative, workable perspectives.

The WP will keep the PAP responsive to Singaporeans. There is nothing like a little competition to keep politicians on their toes. The PAP has always been concerned about losing seats and even monitors percentages closely. Constituencies at risk are courted heavily. By offering people a choice, the WP can bring pressure on the PAP to perform even better in order to get the people's vote. At the end of the day, it is the people who will be the winners.

The WP will facilitate the people to exercise their voting rights. Since Singaporeans cannot gather freely to protest, voting is about the only means of expressing approval or disapproval of the ruling party. Hence, the presence of other parties is necessary for the people to exercise this right.

I am totally convinced that what the WP is doing is necessary and beneficial for Singapore. Ultimately though, whether alternative parties will grow in a sustainable fashion or diminish will depend entirely on what the people want for Singapore. Contrary to the doomsayers' spin, Singaporeans are still very much empowered to bring about a political renaissance by joining parties such as WP and by voting credible opposition into parliament to provide a check on the ruling party.

NOTES

1. Only four out of the eighteen members elected in 2004 to the central executive committee (CEC) – the highest decision-making body of the PAP – are not members of the ministerial cabinet. Key positions in the council such as secretary-general, assistant secretary-general, and chairman are usually held by the prime minister and deputy prime ministers. In line with the 'refreshing PAP' committee's recommendations (see Edwin Pang's Chapter 12 in this book), the party in February 2004 held its first election of district level representatives who had previously been appointed to their positions by PAP MPs. The refreshing PAP committee must have felt the need to 'open up' the party and move away from its top-down approach. Reportedly, party delegates welcomed this change

(*Petir* 2004). However, exactly how influential an elected district level representative can be in matters of policy-making remains in doubt.

REFERENCES

Chua, B.H. (13 January 2004) 'Changing of the guard: how different will the 3rd generation be?' Paper presented at the Singapore Perspectives Conference organized by the Institute of Policy Studies on 13 January 2004, Singapore.

Goh, C.T. (17 August 2003) 'From the valley to the highlands', Speech at the National Day Rally on 17 August 2003, Singapore. Online. Available HTTP: <http://www.gov.sg/nd/ND03.htm> (accessed 22 December 2004).

Institute of Policy Studies (2002) *The IFER Report: restructuring Singapore economy*, Singapore: Times Academic Press.

Lee, H.L. (6 January 2004) 'Building a civic society', speech by the deputy prime minister at the Harvard Club of Singapore's 35th Anniversary Dinner, 6 January 2004, Singapore. Online. Available HTTP: <http://www.newsintercom.org/index.php?itemid=34> (accessed 22 December 2004).

Lim, L. (11 May 2004) 'No loophole for past reserves to be spent, says Govt', *The Straits Times* (Singapore).

Lim, R. (2003) Speech at the PAP Convention 2003. Online. Available HTTP: <http://www.pap.org.sg> (accessed 29 December 2003).

Ministry of Information and the Arts (2000) *Renaissance City Report: culture and the arts in renaissance Singapore*, Singapore. Online. Available HTTP: <http://www.mica.gov.sg/renaissance/FinalRen.pdf> (accessed 22 December 2004)

Ng, E.H. (17 October 2003) Speech at the signing of a memorandum of understanding for the Distributed Careerlink Network on 17 October 2003. Online. Available HTTP: <http://www.wda.gov.sg> (accessed 23 May 2004).

Ngiam T.D. (5 October 2003) 'Singapore bigger than PAP (interviewed by Susan Long)', *The EDB Society: towards a learning society*. Online. Available HTTP: <http://www.edbsociety.org.sg/content_list.asp?con tentid=35&contenttypeid=2> (accessed 31 June 2004).

Nirmala, M. (5 November 2003) 'WP hopes public will provide "wisdom from the ground"', *The Straits Times* (Singapore).

Nirmala, M. (26 February 2004) 'Hello, is the Feedback link breaking up?', *The Straits Times* (Singapore).

Parliamentary Debates Singapore (28 October 1996), Vol. 66, No. 9, Columns 808–823.

Parliamentary Debates Singapore (11 November 2003), Vol. 76, No. 24, Columns 3443–3444.

Parliamentary Debates Singapore (13 March 2004), Vol. 77, No. 10, Columns
    1609–1702.
Petir (2004) 'District elections a watershed moment', *Petir*, January–February.
    Online. Available HTTP: <http://www.pap.org.sg> (accessed 31 June
    2004).
Rahim, L.Z. (1998) *The Singapore Dilemma: the political and educational
    marginality of the Malay community*, Shah Alam: Oxford University
    Press.
Siow, L.S. (29 March 2004) '55 is danger age for cash-strapped property
    owners', *The Business Times* (Singapore).
The Straits Times (12 August 2002) 'Singapore economy recovering but
    outlook still cloudy, ministry says', *The Straits Times* (Singapore).
The Sunday Times (2 November 2003) 'WP rendezvous', *The Sunday Times*
    (Singapore).
Toh, M.H. (13 January 2004) Paper presented at the Singapore Perspectives
    Conference organized by the Institute of Policy Studies on 13 January
    2004, Singapore.
Yeo, L.H. (2002) 'Electoral politics in Singapore', in A. Croissant et al. (eds.)
    Electoral Politics in Southeast and East Asia, Singapore: Friedrich Ebert
    Stiftung.

Optimists, pessimists, and strategists

KENNETH PAUL TAN

The picture on the cover of this book is part of a series of five entitled *Young Office Worker on a Pilgrimage* by Jason Wee, a Singaporean artist, writer, and community activist who now lives and works in New York and Singapore. Regardless of what the artist might have wanted to convey, when I look at the picture, I see a small section of the monumental Esplanade – Theatres on the Bay, perhaps most emblematic of Singapore's artistic renaissance. In the glass surface is the somewhat distorted reflection of Raffles City – a complex of hotels, shopping malls, and offices, including what was once the tallest building in the world, Singapore's pride. Raffles City, it seems to me, is a microcosm of a global city that thrives on tourism, consumer culture, and commerce. In the picture, Singapore's arts scene refocuses my gaze away from the image of itself and onto the image of what really matters, even if this is somewhat distorted: after all, the arts are rarely prized in Singapore for their intrinsic value, but for the way they can serve the economic interests of this global city. In the picture's focal point, I also see an 'everyman' whose body position mimics the Y-shaped concrete pillars that surround the reflective glass surfaces of the Esplanade building: his expression, like the building's appearance, is lifeless and grim, even if both appear to be brightly accoutred. He holds up a pair of slippers – one green, one red – as if unsure whether the economy, culture, even politics are to move forward or to stop. It is this same kind of ambivalence that characterizes the prospects of liberalization in Singapore over the last couple of decades.

In his first two major speeches as Singapore's third prime minister, Lee Hsien Loong sent strong signals that his government aimed to transform Singapore into 'a more open and inclusive' society. Fourteen years earlier, his predecessor, Goh Chok Tong, had promised to adopt a kinder and gentler style, even to make his government more open and consultative than what Singaporeans had become used to under the more authoritarian Lee Kuan Yew. Singaporeans who desired more liberalization – nearly always projected in the public imagination as a mere minority – chose to be optimistic about Goh's promise. Fourteen years after, they were in fact able to see a kinder, gentler, and much loved (rather than much feared) prime minister in the person of Goh, but they were less convinced that the political system had genuinely become more open and consultative. Goh himself had suggested that the changes would be mostly a question of style, so that the fundamentals of the Singapore system – fundamentals explained as essential to Singapore's continued survival and success – would not be compromised. Liberal Singaporeans acknowledged that the Goh Chok Tong era was different from the Lee Kuan Yew era; but they found the transformation under Goh to be either too slow or simply illusory. Policy U-turns within the larger rhetoric about liberalization fostered a culture of cynicism that the new Lee Hsien Loong administration will find hard to quell.

The Lee administration has contributed to this culture of cynicism – and the disenchantment of the next generation of impressionable youths – through some surprisingly intolerant actions. For instance, in 2005, when a resident displayed cardboard cut-outs of white elephants to symbolize a train station's disuse, the matter was investigated and the resident given a 'stern warning' by the police for putting up a public display without a permit. When the station finally opened a few months later, a group of students decided to raise funds for charity by designing and selling T-shirts printed with the words 'Save the white elephants', a project that drew a warning from the police about breaking the law by raising funds without a permit and wearing the T-shirt 'en masse' (Chua 14 January 2006). A satirical blogger and columnist who calls himself Mr Brown criticized government policies in an article entitled 'S'poreans are fed, up with progress!' (Mr Brown 3 July 2006), and his regular column in the *Today* newspaper was suspended. Mr Brown's podcasts and writings in cyberspace and the print media are particularly popular among young readers. As discussed in Chapter 12, the state has not been very successful at connecting and engaging with youths: it readily adopts superficial youthful gestures but just as easily discourages spontaneous and meaningful youth initiatives.

Tan Chong Kee, in Chapter 9, points out that members of the academic and arts communities were generally unexcited about the prospects that were defined in the *Renaissance City Report* launched at the turn of the millennium. Many of them adopted an 'I'll believe it when I see it' approach. But what would renaissance Singapore look like? In this concluding chapter, I will attempt to present a composite picture based on many of the arguments made in this book. With this picture as a benchmark, I will subsequently discuss how Singaporeans who desire real political changes have approached the recent 'renaissance' rhetoric, categorizing them into three types: the optimists, the pessimists, and the strategists.

Interpreting 'renaissance'

Renaissance Singapore needs a new economy, one that can avoid futile competition against low-cost countries in the region, and pursue global economic possibilities that extend beyond traditional manufacturing and services to knowledge and creative products. In Chapter 3, Janadas Devan argues for the importance of standing out in the region – of Singapore not becoming 'less odd' – because this would, among other things, help to sustain Singapore's attractiveness and relevance to foreign investors who are increasingly eyeing low-cost alternatives in the region. Singapore must offer investors more than its neighbours can, and straightforward efficiency may not be enough. In Chapter 4, Terence Lee discusses the upgrading of the economy in terms of the government's attempts to industrialize creativity and innovation as part of a risky gamble on the new creative economy dominated by biotechnology research and developments in information and communications technology, design, and the arts. In Chapter 2, I observe that the new economy has (at least notionally) fractured the people of Singapore into a more 'cosmopolitan' set made up of the geographically and occupationally mobile high-earners, and the less mobile 'heartlanders' who react to the increased flow of cosmopolitans and foreign talent by becoming more nationalistic and moralistic in their public orientations.

This is, of course, a gross simplification of very complex economic, social, and cultural forces. However, the politics that drives the formation of public discourse has exaggerated this division and the antagonism that characterizes it. The selfish, closed-minded, and anxiety-ridden heartlander, as Woo Yen Yen and Colin Goh argue in Chapter 6, is yet another stereotype encouraged by official policies that censor the creative and identity-forming use of Singlish and render the heartlander voiceless in a committee-dominated public sphere. Similarly, I argue in Chapter 5 that the official caricature of the heartlander-as-majority has become the most effective resource for status quo justifications where the government declares, 'We'd like to change, but our hands are tied'.

It might be argued that a stark division between heartlanders and cosmopolitans is politically and philosophically valuable because it creates a healthy check and balance between unmitigated globalization on the one hand and xenophobic nationalism on the other, so that Singapore's public sphere can properly manage global openness in ways that maximize the mainly economic benefits without destroying a particular sense of place, identity, and values. But for this, the public sphere needs to be more inclusive and dialogically oriented, not colonized – as Woo Yen Yen and Colin Goh argue in Chapter 6 – by official committees made up of the who's who in Singapore. A more inclusive and greatly expanded public sphere – where decisions are made on the force of stronger arguments and where claims are oriented towards factual truth, normative rightness, and honesty (Giddens 1994) – will not be possible in a state deadlocked by materialistic calculations of costs and benefits, and by dogma, mutual ignorance, and self-gratifying prejudices.

The success of a new, more globally savvy economy will therefore need a new society, one with enough confidence to engage with and not condemn too quickly the complex flows of people, ideas, and lifestyles. A new society should be more inclusive of people who do not fit the official mould of Singaporean-ness. The notion of 'Singaporean' itself will have to loosen up and expand beyond simple, essentialist, and exclusionary criteria of geography, blood, values, skills, and eating habits. Kirpal Singh, lamenting Singapore society's poor record of openness, argues in Chapter 7 for a deeper and more active understanding of social and cultural difference, not just simple tolerance.

A new society, compatible with a global and creative economy, would also need to be a strong society, and in particular a strong *organized* society (or civil society). Writers such as Francis Fukuyama (1996) and Robert Putnam (2000) have famously observed that trust and social capital – manifested as networks and norms of reciprocity in civil society – have been directly related to a healthy economy and democratic governance. Conventional wisdom gives an account of weak citizens in Singapore who have become over-reliant on a 'nanny state' that provides and disciplines. Decades of material comfort have led to political apathy. And political apathy and authoritarian government are two sides of the same coin – a priceless coin to many Singaporeans who regard this as the basic unit of their wealth and affluence.

But a more profoundly global economy presents a far riskier environment in which there will not only be clear winners and losers, but winners who can become losers – and vice versa – overnight. For Singaporeans fully to engage with – and not withdraw from – such an environment, a strong society of private, civil, and even political organizations would not only provide a safety net in welfare terms but also act as a 'classroom' for learning the kind of associational, leadership, and administrative skills relevant to the economy. A strong and diverse civil society not only presents citizens with meaningful opportunities for action (that can in turn give them a larger stake in their own country), but also offers a plurality of choices in questions of identity, lifestyles, and ideals, choices that promote imagination and a habit of experimentation so crucial to a creative economy.

What kind of politics, compatible with a new economy and new society, would be expected in renaissance Singapore? Firstly, to help Singaporeans detach themselves from the apron-strings of the nanny state, there should be less government control and intervention particularly in matters that do not need to take on a public character. This should allow the private space to expand; and in the private space, Singaporeans will find the opportunities to develop themselves, experiment, and associate creatively with other Singaporeans. Only in such an un-designed space can meaningful engagement flourish, in ways that could erode the kind of fear-inducing ignorance that, it is widely believed, has come to characterize Singapore society. The government's role would be to ensure the security of this private space, and intervene when individuals or groups threaten the safety of it. Clearly, this is difficult to imagine in paranoid Singapore whose official history has been dominated by an account of vulnerability and fragility – that overnight, an 'oasis can become a desert' (Lee Hsien Loong, quoted in Leifer 2001: 33).

Secondly, the government – justifiably proud of its internationally recognized achievements in terms of efficiency – should nevertheless work towards becoming less bureaucratic, paranoid, and secretive in its relations with citizens and in particular with civil society actors and organizations. A more open and accountable government and civil administration will foster trust that can in turn form the basis of creative and synergetic partnerships among the state, the commercial sector, and civil society.

Thirdly, the government should be more responsive to the people's diverse needs, and not attempt to dictate these needs in such narrowly defined and technical terms. As a repository of information and resources, the government is in a position to facilitate an imaginative society that encourages its constituents to experiment with their lives and ideas. The government should not aim mechanically to perfect its citizens through coercive means and scare tactics, but to provide the space, opportunities, and resources for citizens to work things out for themselves in a self-reflective, critical-thinking, and dialogical mode. Disagreements among citizens, and between citizens and government, are bound to happen; but these are distinct opportunities for learning how to communicate and interact as a mature society. If disagreement is consistently viewed only as personal attack, then the mode of communicating will be defensive and uncompromising. And prickly Singapore will never become a more interesting and fulfilling place in which to live, work, and play.

Fourthly – and probably the most controversial point – is the need for more competitive politics. Lee Kuan Yew argues that Singapore cannot avoid engaging with a plurality of ideas, but asserts that alternative ideas should be debated within the PAP and not among different parties (Lee 2004). As Edwin Pang points out in Chapter 13, the Young PAP too has been trying to provide a platform for a greater diversity of views. Lee's statement is but the latest in a long-standing series of arguments from the PAP that Singapore does not need political opposition of the parliamentary kind, since the PAP has instituted and continues to institute mechanisms and procedures that provide internal checks and balances. Furthermore, the PAP has often implied that Singapore is too small for competitive politics: limited leadership talent should not be dispersed in a political way but should be harnessed in a managerial way. These kinds of arguments, strengthened both by consistent public articulation of PAP-driven material success and by advantageous electoral innovations, have supported the dominant party system in Singapore since the late-1960s. While Sylvia Lim explains in Chapter 14 that 'alternative parties' are in the best position to aggregate and articulate alternative viewpoints in ways that will enable citizens to voice their needs and aspirations through the ballot box, it does not seem as if opposition parties aim – at least in the foreseeable future – to provide the possibility of an alternative government, only alternative voices within a PAP-dominated parliament.

Optimists

Among those who would like to see a Singapore whose creative economy is supported by a more open and inclusive society and politics are the optimists who believe that, even though observed changes are small and often U-turned, society and politics will slowly but surely loosen up over time. Put another way, observed changes are merely fluctuations on a steady and unavoidable trend towards liberalization. Put yet another way, developments in Singapore progress on a 'two steps forward, one step backward' basis – the net effect is still a forward movement. This is because Singaporeans will move up the Maslovian hierarchy of needs – from the physiological and security-related to needs associated with recognition and self-actualization –

as more of them become more affluent, educated, and globally connected. Once a critical mass of Singaporeans is able to look beyond the material and rise above the insecurities and obsessiveness associated with it, there will be increased political (and electoral) pressures for change – pressures that the politically astute PAP government cannot afford to dismiss.

The trend towards liberalization is, the optimists believe, unavoidable also because the global market will force Singapore to open up and accept on the one hand the dominant hegemonic discourse of liberal democracy and on the other hand the disjointed and fragmented diversity of worldviews and lifestyles that flow unpredictably through the complex interconnected networks that characterize globalization. Either way, the authoritarian fixtures in Singapore's political system, legitimized (often spuriously) by an imagined national culture based on Asian values, will crack under pressure.

A third reason for believing that there is an unavoidable trend towards liberalization in Singapore rests on the expectation that the PAP government will not be able to sustain its proven ability to deliver the goods. In Chapter 14, Sylvia Lim questions the resilience of the 'material nexus' that has been the basis of a transactional leadership in which 'the people' have exchanged their political (and electoral) support for the guarantee of economic benefit. At a time when economic crises seem to be more frequent and when Singapore's economy seems to be running headlong into a more complex field with riskier economic games, the common-sensical notion that the PAP government can (or is in the best position to) guarantee national economic victory and well-being will be called into greater doubt as more mistakes are made and injuries sustained with fewer opportunities for soothing the pain.

For these optimists, the underlying reasons for believing that change is inevitable seem to be evidenced by observable developments of a more empirical kind. In Chapter 13, Edwin Pang describes the Young PAP (and indirectly the PAP itself) as undergoing a limited but noticeable process of internal democratization. Though perhaps largely a question of style and form, the changes nevertheless seem to be a response to changing circumstances in Singapore, including the emergence of younger party members who will not be satisfied with the kind of party discipline that compels members to defend the party line as dictated to them from above. Though not an 'optimist' in this sense, Suzaina Kadir nevertheless describes in Chapter 8 how modernization and globalization have transformed the institutionalized and centralized administration of the Malay and Islamic communities under the PAP into more complex sites of contestation, forcing open the neatly compartmentalized vision of 'multiracialism'.

Telling different facets of the same liberalization story, these larger trends may help to explain the way public rhetoric has been shaped in recent years. The government describing itself as 'kinder', 'gentler', 'more open', and 'consultative', and the 'trimming the banyan tree' analogy in the early 1990s; the ideal of 'active citizenship' and the 'renaissance' analogy in the late 1990s; the rhetoric of 'openness', 'inclusiveness', and 'youth engagement' in the early 2000s have all figured strongly in landmark speeches given in the post-Lee Kuan Yew era. This rhetoric, the optimists might point out, has also been accompanied by policy changes. The introduction of Speakers' Corner, the announcement that the government welcomes openly gay civil servants, the issuance of permits for bar table-top dancing, the approval of a facility for reverse bungee jumping, the legal amendment that would allow non-political societies to be automatically registered, the decision to build two casinos in Singapore, and the cultivation of a more youth-friendly image in the PAP government have all been identified as signs that Singapore is in the process of opening up and liberalizing.

Pessimists

Among those who would like to see a more open and inclusive society and politics in Singapore are the pessimists for whom these signs of liberalization do not point to anything 'real' insofar as substantive political changes are concerned. The basic formula is 'liberalize the economy, and to some degree society, but maintain status quo for politics'. For instance, the call for citizenship engagement does not seem to extend to political opposition, not of the parliamentary kind. The less threatening opposition politicians are, however, tolerated in parliament and sometimes praised for being in general agreement with the PAP government, since this – the government believes and wants Singaporeans to believe – is an indication that these opposition politicians are right thinking and loyal to Singapore. Their unthreatening presence in parliament also serves as supporting evidence for the government's democratic credentials, important for Singapore's international image. In other words, these opposition politicians have for the government what Tan Chong Kee in Chapter 9 describes as an advantageous 'canary' value. But 'crow-like' opposition politicians who can – through whatever means – undermine the credibility and integrity of the PAP are regularly portrayed as themselves lacking credibility and integrity, and even as dangerous to Singapore's interests. The advantages of incumbency have severely limited the opposition parties' chances; and even though the PAP government's basis of power has been so well-secured, the ruling party continues to be hypersensitive to criticism, as Sylvia Lim points out in Chapter 14.

Although the government wishes to write a new act in the ongoing 'Singapore Story' that would usher on to the stage many more non-government protagonists (or, more accurately, supporting roles), it nevertheless – and understandably so – refuses to allow itself to be written out of the script and replaced by its antagonists. From the pessimists' point of view, all change is possible as long as it does not threaten the PAP's control of the state, and its extensive powers in this capacity. The dominant mode of activating citizens has therefore been directly to co-opt into the PAP fold the more distinguished members of society or to invite the general populace into PAP-approved spaces of citizenship activity that conspicuously include welfare-related voluntarism and exclude really open political expression and debate that could threaten to oppose the government on questions that it is not ready to talk about. This is the government's campaign for 'civic society', or 'civil society' minus the politics. I argue in Chapter 12 that the government's call to youths to come forward is structured upon this logic; and in this way, the process of state-led political liberalization is analogous to parents who want their children to grow up not on their children's own terms – not even on shared terms – but according to the ultimately rigid, dogmatic, and self-righteous terms of the adult world.

While the first group of pessimists think that the government has not gone – and is unwilling to go – far enough politically, a second group of pessimists focus on the state's management of Singapore's international image as a reason for doubting the prospects of real political change. There have been at least two sets of images associated with Singapore. From the point of view of the international business community, Singapore has been regarded very favourably, and indeed it has been consistently well placed on international rankings. But from the point of view of the international human rights community, Singapore has a long way to go. The difference between Singapore as the most desirable place for expatriates to live in Asia (Radio Singapore International 25 February 2005), and Singapore as number 146 out of 168 countries surveyed for press freedom (Reporters Without Borders 2006) is a stark one. Nevertheless, for the most part, the government has been able to gain economic advantage from the first type of image, without having to care excessively about international criticism of its record on human rights, freedom, and democracy. Though glossy, technocratic, and even one-dimensional, Singapore continues to be a cosmopolitan global city. The question, of course, is whether Singapore can attract the best and most creative talents to work and live in a clean and efficient, but still highly regulated country. With a widening array of location choices available, the mobile creative class may not be attracted to a country once described as a cultural desert where the people and government are equally intolerant of different worldviews and lifestyles not belonging to their bureaucratically constructed and exclusionary 'Asian' identity and value system.

Tan Chong Kee argues in Chapter 9 that the government will tolerate a measure of criticism from Singaporeans because this demonstrates to the international community – and particularly foreign creative talent – that the government is acceptably democratic and, presumably, that Singapore is an economically, socially, and even politically vibrant country in which to work, live, and play. Loosening up – particularly through the vivid but critically vacuous examples of bar table-top dancing and reverse bungee jumping – has therefore been an advertising strategy for luring foreign talent. But as Tan also argues in the same chapter, if political criticism proceeds beyond minor irritation to outright challenge, the government will not hesitate to clamp down on the perpetrators, and make a negative example of them.

A third group of pessimists explain Singapore's limited prospects for liberalization in terms of the nature of bureaucracy in public administration. Broadly speaking, they believe that even though the upper echelon of PAP leaders would really like to open up society and politics, their aims are scuppered by overly anxious middle-level administrators concerned about smooth and accelerated career paths, and front-line staff who are set in their ways and would rather not make their civil service lives any more complicated than they need to be. Anxious public servants often over-react when they try to second-guess their ministers and political leaders: the unnecessarily heavy-handed treatment of well-meaning Singaporeans in the 'white elephant' episode is one example of how over-enthusiastic policing can squander the trust between government and people that has been so difficult to build up. If this 'anxious-bureaucrat' mode is extended into the larger PAP network that includes the grassroots organizations, the military-industrial complex, schools, and even the mass media, then it is hardly surprising that there should be a wide divide between top-level rhetoric and ground-level practice. Some senior bureaucrats recently discussed the need for insurgent and subversive civil servants who would be necessary agents of change. Not surprisingly, while the rhetoric was timely and vivid, it was also met with a large dose of public scepticism (Feedback Unit 2005).

A fourth group of pessimists believe that it is political culture that ultimately puts a substantial limit on what change is possible. Singaporeans are – or, more accurately, are widely believed to be – apathetic and obedient. Singaporeans have been described as parochial, motivated almost exclusively by the goal of personal material comfort and fear of change. Singaporeans have also been described as deferential subjects, obeying authority not only as a reasoned choice, but also because they believe it is consistent with their Asian, or more specifically Confucian, cultural heritage. The construction of Asian values as a national ideology within the nation-building project has limited the possibilities of citizenship performance.

The cautious political approach is to take as true the widespread belief that the majority of Singaporeans are conservative in the ways described above, and so it is not entirely surprising to see the extent to which the PAP government is mindful of the negative consequence of any policy of liberalization. The government will not want to be seen as betraying the trust of the majority of Singaporeans who are thought to be conservative – afraid of difference and afraid of change. Ironically, the conservatism that now prevents the government from fully pursuing 'new economy'-style policies is something of a Frankensteinian creation – the monster that the government created as its own conceit is, in the new economy, regarded as grotesque and it threatens to return to kill its maker. In Chapter 2, I argue that the government has actually continued to cultivate majority conservatism as a politically useful myth, playing off this myth against those who want to liberalize Singapore in ways that the government feels uncomfortable about. In Chapter 5, I explore this idea in the context of censorship policies. Nevertheless, as the widespread conservative resistance to the government's proposals to build casinos in Singapore has shown, the myth of a conservative majority can be a double-edged sword for the government.

A fifth group of pessimists relate the performance of loosening up to the idea of catharsis. According to this view, Singapore politics is little more than political drama in which the government needs occasionally to present liberal Singaporeans with a performance that will have the effect of purging away their politically aggressive inclinations, so that when the show is over, they can leave the theatre feeling refreshed and ready to go on with the business of daily life, purified of their 'un-Singaporean' tendencies to defy authority. The National Agenda in the late-1980s, Singapore 21 and Remaking Singapore at the turn of the millennium, and the open and inclusive society described by Lee Hsien Loong can all be interpreted as cathartic political theatre, or perhaps pre-digested light entertainment, promising the fantasy of active citizenship as an escape from political alienation and helplessness.

These five sets of pessimistic explanations – by no means mutually exclusive – help to account for the 'one step forward, one step backward' or 'one step forward, two steps backward' structure of development, where a period of loosening up is almost predictably followed by a period of tightening up, and where the net movement is at best stationary, at worst backward. Tan Chong Kee, in Chapter 9, argues that the PAP government's continual reversals can lead to a credibility issue that the government will not be able to deal with so easily in time to come.

Strategists

In the last two decades, many conscientious Singaporeans desiring genuine and comprehensive liberalization for their country would have encountered a depressing litany of policy U-turns, empty promises, backlash from a still repressive society, and continual practices of excessive state control – much less explicit perhaps, but certainly no less debilitating. Will the PAP government want to overcome the culture of cynicism that it has managed to foster as one of its unintended legacies? Will Singaporeans be able to rise above this confusing set of messages and take back ownership of culture and society?

The answer to the first must be 'yes', since the basis of the government's political legitimacy in a global city will depend less on the people's fear of its overtly repressive instruments of control and more on the rightfulness of its extended position in and extensive use of power. As argued in Chapter 1, this rightfulness itself will also have to be as much about moral authority as it has been about a transactional relationship between the people (providing electoral support) and the government (providing material well-being). Even in 1994, Catherine Lim's (3 September 1994) article in *The Straits Times* provoked a dramatic response from an angry government: very clearly hitting a raw nerve, the article argued that the government had become so distant from the people that it could no longer be loved by them. But what can the government do to build up its moral authority? Saying that it wants an active citizenry is not the same as being open to one; since being fully open to citizens who engage not just on the government's terms but on their own initiative may undermine the carefully cultivated belief in a talented government with all the best solutions, a government that incontrovertibly deserves the high salaries that its members get. It wants to engage Singaporeans but does not have the courage to go all the way, fearing that this could lead to its own irrelevance. And so, it continues regularly to conjure up 'out-of-bound' (OB) markers by making examples of Singaporeans whom they think – and hope others will also think – have 'gone beyond the pale'.

The answer to the second question must take into account Singaporeans' desire and ability. Will cynical Singaporeans disengage, withdraw, and simply give up? Or will they be motivated by the same cynicism to engage more tactically with what the government says and does? The ability to do this has been learnt gradually and cumulatively: expanding the repertoire of resisting, engaging, and negotiating with the government has been the most significant – and surely least visible – aspect of civil society developments in Singapore. And so, apart from the optimists and the pessimists among Singaporeans who wish for a more open and liberal Singapore, there are also the strategists whose main concern is to work out tactics and strategies for dealing with what are perceived as windows of opportunity created by shifts in the government's rhetoric.

One strategy – a strategy that Tan Chong Kee describes in Chapter 9 as *Sintercom*'s earliest approach in Singapore – is deliberate naiveté. The main idea here is to take the government at its word, directly using the government's own rhetoric to further one's cause. By riding on contradictions in the government's own rhetoric and practice (without causing the government to 'lose face', of course), strategists are able to demonstrate that they are concerned 'insiders' – not critical 'outsiders' – whose proposals for change are conceived completely in the national interest. As concerned insiders, they have a better chance of building trust and synergy with the government that can be the basis of a new, more secure process of opening up. But deliberate naiveté has not always worked – at least not, according to Tan Chong Kee, for *Sintercom*.

A second broad strategy is to establish clearly the conditions of political possibility by encouraging the government to declare where the OB markers lie. Knowing exactly where the ball should not go will help the strategist play with more confidence, purpose, and accuracy. Knowing where the OB markers are, officially, will also help the strategist to identify what needs to be changed – to make the fairways broader and less hazardous – and to make more intelligible and compelling arguments in favour of specific areas of liberalization. Therefore, not only will the strategist be able to play better within the clearly designated OB markers, it would then seem that the markers themselves can more readily come under public scrutiny and debate.

A third set of strategists may in fact prefer to leave the OB markers less defined, as ambiguity may allow for more subtle and sophisticated games to be played in order to push the limits of unnecessary control. The ambiguity, therefore, serves as a new space for creative politics

where innovative modes of communication, interaction, and association present new possibilities for freedom and action. Benefiting from
ambiguity of this kind, Alvin Tan's creative strategy to globalize (or
regionalize) his company's theatre practice has enabled him to find
new political possibilities even after declaring the 'death' of political
theatre in Singapore, as he describes in Chapter 10. Similarly, ambiguity has allowed for the kind of civil society experiments Chng Nai
Rui describes in Chapter 11. The Working Committee (TWC) was a
year-long bottom-up project to build social capital among civil society
activists and organizations. The recently registered Transient Workers
Count Too (TWC2) advocates for the basic rights of foreign domestic
workers in Singapore, when not even 20 years before, a similar initiative led to the arrest of 22 people who were branded Marxists. Many
of the features of Singapore's civil society landscape today may not
look remarkable in comparison with countries like India, Indonesia,
or the Philippines; but they certainly could not have existed in the
same way during the first few decades of Singapore's independence,
when the pervasively technocratic PAP-controlled state sought to
establish and secure its authority by eliminating the competition. In
the process, civil society suffocated and all but died.

Since the mid-1980s, the PAP government has tried to resurrect
civil society – now part of a reborn ('renaissance') Singapore – in
order to decompress the democratic pressures that appeared to be
building up and to harness the 'free' (also in the sense of 'unpaid for')
and 'voluntary' resources and energies of civil society. But the government has also emasculated the resurrected civil society through the
continued use of legal instruments of coercion – the basis of fear and
paranoia – and to feminize it by forcing it to take the role of a junior
partner whose ambit would not extend beyond welfare and community development, and whose voice must retain the tone of respect
and submission that patriarchal societies expect of wives in relation
to their husbands, and of children in relation to their fathers (Tan
2001). The strategists, like some contemporary feminist theorists,
may then be forced to develop subtle and highly creative strategies
of power – such as mimicry, masquerade, and seduction – without
explicitly undermining the public image of government machismo. In
renaissance Singapore – a 'sexier' Singapore (Tan 2003) – seduction
might be the most powerful instrument of civil society.

REFERENCES

Chua, V. (14 January 2006). 'Teens' white elephant T-shirt venture gets police attention', *Today* (Singapore).

Feedback Unit (2005) 'Call for civil service to be innovative – beyond numbers'. Discussion list. Online. Available HTTP: <http://app.feedback.gov.sg/asp/dis/dis0003.asp?pg=2&topicId=1602&CatId=68> (accessed 28 February 2005).

Fukuyama, F. (1996) *Trust: the social virtues and the creation of prosperity*, London: Penguin.

Giddens, A. (1994) 'Jurgen Habermas', in Q. Skinner (ed.) *The Return of Grand Theory in the Human Sciences*, Cambridge: Cambridge University Press, pp. 123–39.

Lee, K.Y. (21 November 2004) Speech by the minister mentor at the 50th anniversary of the inauguration of the PAP, on 21 November 2004, Victoria Concert Hall.

Leifer, M. (2001) *Dictionary of the Modern Politics of South-East Asia*, 3rd edn, London: Routledge.

Lim, C. (3 September 1994) 'The PAP and the people – a great affective divide', *The Straits Times* (Singapore), p. 12.

Mr Brown (3 July 2006) 'S'poreans are fed, up with progress!', *Today* (Singapore).

Putnam, R. (2000) *Bowling Alone: the collapse and revival of American community*, New York: Simon & Schuster.

Radio Singapore International (25 February 2005) 'Singapore comes up tops in survey on Asia's best living location', *Radio Singapore International* website. Online. Available HTTP: <http://www.rsi.com.sg/english/businessideas/view/20050225245415/1/.html> (accessed 28 February 2005).

Reporters Without Borders (2006) 'North Korea, Turkmenistan, Eritrea the worst violators of press freedom', *Reporters Without Borders* website. Online. Available: HTTP <http://www.rsf.org/rubrique.php3?id_rubrique=639> (accessed 1 April, 2007).

Tan, K.P. (2001) ' "Civic society" and the "new economy" in patriarchal Singapore: emasculating the political, feminizing the public', *Crossroads: An Interdisciplinary Journal of Southeast Asian Studies*, 15(2): 95–122. Online. Available HTTP: <http://www.niu.edu/cseas/seap/CROSSRO ADS%20Tan%20Reformat.pdf> (accessed 22 December 2004).

Tan, K.P. (2003) 'Sexing up Singapore', *International Journal of Cultural Studies*, 6(4): 403–23.

Index